FRANÇOIS-XAVIER DU

Holy Spirit of God

an essay in biblical theology

Translated by
Sister Benedict Davies OSU

GEOFFREY CHAPMAN

LONDON

Other books by Fr Durrwell

The Resurrection: a Biblical Study
In the Redeeming Christ
The Mystery of Christ and the Apostolate

A Geoffrey Chapman book published by
Cassell Ltd
1 Vincent Square, London SW1P 2PN

First published in French as *l'Esprit Saint de Dieu*
© Les Éditions du Cerf, 1983

English translation first published 1986
English translation © Geoffrey Chapman, a division of Cassell Ltd 1986

ISBN 0 225 66453 4   Geoffrey Chapman

British Library Cataloguing in Publication Data
Durrwell, François-Xavier
  Holy Spirit of God: an essay in biblical theology.
  1. Holy Spirit — Biblical teaching.
  I. Title.   II. L'Esprit Saint de Dieu
  English
  231'.3   BS680.H56

Typeset in Plantin by Medimedia Ltd, Godalming, Surrey
Printed and bound in Great Britain by Biddles Ltd, Guildford

Contents

Abbreviations

Bib	*Biblica* (Rome)
CCL	*Corpus Christianorum Latinorum* (Turnhout)
DC	*Documentation Catholique* (Paris)
DTC	*Dictionnaire de Théologie Catholique* (Paris)
Dz-Sch	H. Denzinger, revised A. Schönmetzer, *Enchiridion Symbolorum* (Paris/Freiburg)
GCS	*Die griechischen christlichen Schriftsteller* (Leipzig)
JB	Jerusalem Bible
parr.	and parallels in other gospels
PG	J.P. Migne, *Patrologia Graeca*
PL	J.P. Migne, *Patrologia Latina*
RSV	Revised Standard Version
SC	*Sources Chrétiennes* (Paris)
STh	*Summa Theologiae*
TDNT	*Theological Dictionary of the New Testament* (London/Grand Rapids)
TOB	Traduction oecuménique de la Bible

Documents of Vatican II:

DV	Constitution *Divinum Verbum*
LG	Constitution *Lumen Gentium*
PO	Decree *Presbyterorum Ordinis*
SC	Constitution *Sacrosanctum Concilium*

Translator's Note

The work of translation has been done in close collaboration with Father Brian O'Higgins, BA, DD, to whom I am deeply indebted. Our aim has been to reproduce as accurately as possible, for English readers, the thinking of Father Durrwell. I am grateful too to Sister Clare Tanter, OSU (who died in August 1985) for her careful reading of the typescript and for her helpful comments.

Preface

In past centuries books on the Holy Spirit were rare and almost non-existent. The conviction that deep reflection on this mystery was urgently needed became rooted in me when I was preparing my book *The Resurrection*. From that time onwards I was ready to begin this work, but circumstances or – if I may use the language of Acts (cf. 16:6f.) – the 'Spirit of Jesus would not allow me'. I had to content myself with expressing in the preface to the second edition of the above-named book the wish that others would devote themselves to the necessary research, though I did develop the pages about the Holy Spirit in the book itself.

Today there is a proliferation of books on the Holy Spirit. Many of them appear with the signatures of famous names. But none, as far as I know, has chosen Christ's passover as source of inspiration; and yet it is here that the presence and action of the Holy Spirit were manifested. *The mystery of the Father, the Son and the Spirit is revealed where it emerges into the world and thus becomes a reality for us: in Christ whom the Father begets for us in the Spirit, in Christ's passover, where this begetting in our favour is expressed in its fullness.* Apart from this place and this 'Hour', apart from Christ and his passover, the Father is not known in his fatherhood, nor the Son as he truly is, nor the Spirit in whom the Father begets, in whom the Son is begotten. The paschal Christ and the Spirit are inseparable, not only in the mystery of each, but also in the knowledge we are able to have of them. In his passover Jesus is mediator both of the gift and the knowledge of the Spirit.

So once more I have taken up my former project. I should have liked Scripture to be my sole guide, as it was in my study of the resurrection. But recourse to Christian tradition and more carefully developed theological reflection seemed at times essential to explain scriptural data and to provide, or at least to sketch, an answer to problems of our times. Even here I have tried to remain obedient to the Scriptures. Have they not been inspired by the Christian mystery itself, and are they not thus the most faithful conceptual expression of it? My wish was to let myself be wholly guided by them, in the Church's faith and free from all preconceived systems. Whereas theology usually reasons about God according to concepts of essence or nature, a legacy of Greek philosophy, or according to juridical concepts on questions about redemption, the Scriptures have taught us to favour, in all reflection on God and salvation, the mysterious reality of *the person*. Just as faith is an encounter with Someone, theology is research on the part of the intellect into a mystery that is personal.

When I took pen in hand I knew that my book would remain incomplete. Holy Scripture, a vessel beyond compare, enables us to draw abundantly from the fountain. But it is only a vessel, and the fountain, impetuous, inexhaustible, does not cease to flow... About God's Holy Spirit I can offer the reader only a simple essay in theology.

I dedicate this book, humble though it be, to those who collaborated in the publication of *Mélanges La Pâque du Christ, mystère du salut* (*Lectio divina* 112; Paris, Cerf). The honour they showed me was unexpected; it is not deserved. May God grant them the most enviable of rewards: an abundance of the gifts of the Spirit for themselves and for their scholarly activities. My very special gratitude goes to Père Alois Schmid, professor in the University of Fribourg (Switzerland) who, especially on this occasion, gave me proof of an exceptional friendship.

1

Inexpressible yet intimate

After relating these words of Jesus: 'From his breast shall flow fountains of living water', the evangelist explains: 'He was speaking of the Spirit which those who believed in him were to receive' (Jn 7:38).

It is possible to *speak of* the Spirit. Scripture is full of texts about him. But no one will ever be able to understand him as he is in himself and to *express* him, 'neither men, nor angels, nor the Son', not even the Father. The Spirit is inexpressible. He is inexpressible, not only by reason of his boundless perfection, for at least the Father is capable of uttering an infinite word: his Word who embodies divine fullness. 'The Spirit, however, is beyond the Word.'[1] He is the 'unspoken' one, by nature inexpressible, because he is the Spirit.

Infinitely knowable in the Son, God is mystery in the Spirit. In the full light of Christianity, he is the stark reminder of the divine mystery. It is true that the Spirit is the power that urges God to come out of himself, to create, to reveal himself, even to become incarnate: he is the 'mouth', but through the mouth it is the Word who is poured out into the world. The Spirit will never become incarnate: he will never become man or human thought or human word. Although he is at the origin of creation, of revelation, and of the incarnation, he remains hidden, inviolate and inviolable, foundation of that apophatic theology which considers that knowledge of God is best expressed in a silence full of wonder.

The Spirit is divine revelation, the one who inspires the Scriptures, the agent of every manifestation of God, but he is not the One Revealed. To illustrate this difference we might compare the Spirit to the voice that carries the spoken word and makes it audible. When we say of a voice that it is crystal-clear or velvety, that it is deep or warm, we have spoken about it but we have not said it, we have not made it understood. The voice is personal, proper to the person speaking.

Or again we might have recourse to the distinction, favoured by linguistics, which exists between language and word. Like the language we use, the Spirit is inseparable from the Word – the indestructible unity between the Spirit and the Son, Word of God, is stressed throughout Scripture with striking consistency. The word is intended to be understood, it is easy to repeat it; but it is very difficult to grasp and explain the functioning of language.

We might say more simply that the Spirit is the page on which the Word is written: signs we can read are traced on the page, the page itself is not read. 'The Spirit has spoken through the prophets', he has spoken through Christ; he is not the word, he is the one through whom it is transmitted: 'He will not be speaking as from himself...all he tells you will be taken from what is mine' (cf. Jn 16:13f.).[2]

From the very name 'Spirit' we know that we shall never grasp him to make him a household word. As in Hebrew, (*ruah*), so in Greek (*pneuma*) and in Latin (*spiritus*), he is called Breath. His symbol is the wind[3] about which Jesus says: 'The wind blows wherever it pleases; you hear its sound, but you cannot tell where it comes from or where it is going' (Jn 3:8). The Spirit is so mysterious that anyone who lives under his inspiration is himself an enigma (Jn 3:8). The other chief symbols for him are living water and fire. A breath is no longer itself once it ceases, water is no longer living when it stops flowing, fire is extinguished as soon as it is quenched. It is the same with the Spirit, when we think we have captured him, enclosed him in concepts or submitted him to the interplay of analysis. In this sense too we can understand the words: 'Where the Spirit of the Lord is, there is freedom' (2 Cor 3:17). We want to grasp him and already he has eluded us: he who is confined is no longer free. Throughout the Bible and tradition numerous other symbols have been coined; their great multiplicity proves the futility of our efforts to express the Spirit.

Inwardness is one of his characteristics. In the Trinity, he is the mystery within the mystery. To some extent we can represent the Father and Son to ourselves: they have a likeness in the faces of earthly fathers and sons. The Spirit is 'faceless', beyond the image of God appearing in Jesus Christ, or better, he is 'behind' Christ, in order that Christ may thus be the image of God.

Christian faith sees the Spirit as a person. But a human person does not offer more than a faint analogy: the human person exists in himself, whereas the Spirit is a person in two others! A human being is more a person in the measure that he is open to others and gives himself; but the Spirit is essentially openness, gift. How can one imagine a gift that exists in isolation? The analogy with the human person is so distant that most of the symbols of the Spirit are impersonal.

According to the Bible, the Spirit is never the one on whom God's action is focused: he is not begotten or revealed, nor does he become incarnate. The Father's activity has as its issue the Son, in himself and in many beings, in creation and in the Church, where his sonship is reflected. The Spirit is neither cause nor effect, he is dynamism, the one through whom the Father begets, is revealed, becomes incarnate. This is why, in keeping with John 15:26, theology says that he 'proceeds' from the Father: he issues from him like an action. How can one imagine a person who is action? The nature of the Spirit is that of 'event':[4] he is the grace by which God is gracious, the salvation by which God is saviour, he is the power by which God is powerful. However, we must immediately purify the human notion of power, transposing it into a different register: as this power is divine, quite different from that of human beings, it is presented in its manifestations under a different form, that of helplessness (2 Cor 12:9), the extreme helplessness of the death of Christ (cf. 1 Cor 1:23f.). Having recognized omnipotence in the activity of the Spirit we have to add: 'Let anyone who can, understand, with the help of God's grace, this power which is helplessness!' In the theology of the Spirit, the effort to conceptualize is always resolved by paradoxes. Our concepts are limited, true only in the measure in which their contraries oppose them in order to negate their limits. Everything, in the theology of the Spirit, is paradoxical, apparently contradictory.

The purest words about the Spirit were pronounced by St Paul when he presented him as 'the love of God poured into our hearts' (cf. Rom 5:5). But even the transparent clearness of the statement is proof of our inability to express the Spirit. United in love, two beings contemplate one another and they do not bother to define what 'inhabits' them. They tell one another of their love by loving, they explain it by that very love. The Spirit is love, his *raison d'être* is within him and defies all explanation. Our understanding will never grasp the reason for the existence of a God of love.

When the presence of the Spirit makes itself understood in the faithful, it is 'with sighs too deep for words', the meaning of which only God knows (cf. Rom 8:23–26). When he arouses a 'spiritual' language, the faithful speak 'mysteriously', they are incomprehensible unless interpreted by others·whom the Spirit inspires (cf. 1 Cor 14:2-5).

Mystery does not cease to encircle the Spirit. Scripture, above all the New Testament, sees in him the glory of God, that glory which, in the Old Testament, appears as luminous darkness...Why then do we speak about the Spirit? He is love, action; why are we not satisfied with loving, living and acting? Action is proved by acting, life by living and love by loving. Why do we seek knowledge, thus risking the creation of idols which would pride themselves on representing a mystery,[5] when it would be enough to invoke: 'Come, O Name beloved and everywhere repeated, Name whose being we are strictly forbidden to express and whose nature we are forbidden to know'.[6]

* * *

Though inexpressible, the Spirit is not, however, the Un-known God, as he has been called. Although dense, the cloud of glory was not invisible; the darkness which enveloped Sinai and filled the Tent was luminous. If the Spirit is not the Word, he is nevertheless the voice which we cannot echo, but which we can recognize. The wind strikes or caresses the face, shakes the trees, swells the boat's sails: love enkindles the heart. The people of God, without being able to understand him, have experience of the Spirit whose dynamic presence marks the opening (cf. Gen 1:2) and closing (cf. Rev 22:17) words of the Bible and gives rhythm to the different stages of history. Israel benefited from his power and guidance: the Church senses that he dwells within her; St John perceived him as a fountain where one slakes one's thirst, as one who awakens awareness of Christ; Paul and Luke recognize in him the power to disseminate the faith; Paul in particular experienced him as the creative power of the new man. His presence is everywhere (cf. Ps 139:7; Wis 1:7): 'Nowhere can you hide yourself; you who fill all with your glory'.[7]

We cannot express the Spirit but we can speak about him. A reality that cannot be expressed can nevertheless be experienced. A child touches and feels objects which its hand cannot yet grasp. Jesus says that the world does not know the Spirit, 'but *you know him, because he dwells with you, and will be in you*' (Jn 14:17).

We can know him, then – 'you know him' – but in a way other than that of our intellect, which would imprison him in concepts, and reason about these concepts, organizing them into a system. Knowledge of the Spirit comes first and foremost from the experience of the faithful who know by participation: 'You know him because he dwells with you'. This knowledge is intuitive, it perceives with certainty and, at the same time, is aware that the mystery grows greater beyond words the more it is perceived. St Paul makes much of the experience of the Spirit: 'When we brought the Good News to you, it came to you not only as words, but as power and as the Holy Spirit and as utter conviction' (1 Th 1:5; cf. Gal 3:3f.). Thanks to these manifestations of the Spirit (cf. 1 Cor 12:7) theology can draw certain conclusions from the action of the Holy Spirit; through the 'fruits' which his presence brings (cf. Gal 5:22), theology can recognize the tree. It can describe and construct as it were a phenomenology of the Holy Spirit.[8]

With regard to the nature of the Spirit, so paradoxical that concepts cannot grasp it, theology can at least formulate the paradoxes, express contrasting characteristics, while faith recognizes instinctively the harmony, a harmony inherent in all paradoxes of love.

★ ★ ★

The experience of the Spirit is first of all that of a people, acquired in the course of the history of many centuries: the people of the sons of Abraham according to the flesh, and of the other sons of Abraham who, in Christ, have entered into his posterity (cf. Gal 3:16, 29). This experience is recorded in a book, the Bible of the two Testaments, the abundant source of the theology of the Spirit. Not only does it recount the history of a people led by the Spirit, but it has been compiled under the impulse of the Spirit who inspired the prophets and all the sacred writers.

The knowledge drawn from the Bible can be enriched by the more difficult reading of two other works of the Spirit: that of the first book, before the Bible, the creation over which the Spirit hovered from the beginning (cf. Gen 1:2), and that of numberless pages written by grace in the hearts of the faithful: 'You are a letter from Christ, written...with the Spirit of the living God, not on stone tablets but on the tablets of your living hearts' (cf. 2 Cor 3:3).

But creation is vast, its language often ambiguous; there is an abundant history of grace in countless human beings. In contrast, the Bible of the two Testaments is a concise book, its language without major ambiguity; it is a rich source, and one more easily accessible, of the theology of the Spirit.

There are many ways of reading the Bible. Exegesis, as study of the text and of history, tries to discern the significance of the term *Ruah* or *Pneuma* in the thought of earliest times; it follows the variations in different ages, or in the same author, for example, in St Paul. But biblical theology, as *theological* research, is at pains to know not only the idea formed by biblical authors about the Spirit, but *the mystery*. It is careful to put to the best possible use the findings of literary and historical exegesis, but also to forge a method adapted to its purposes: it does not necessarily follow the stages of sacred history, often preferring to come directly to that history at its climax, in order to harvest the benefits of revelation in its maturity. Moreover, the action of the Holy Spirit is fully manifested at one particular time in creation, at one particular moment in history: in Christ and his passover.

The Spirit can be recognized by his fruits (cf. Gal 5:22), above all by his incomparable fruit: the One begotten by the

Father in the Spirit, 'the Son of his love' (cf. Col 1:13). Moreover, this divine sonship of Jesus is revealed in its fullness, Jesus accepts himself entirely from God, even in his bodily existence, when the Father raises him from the dead in the Spirit (cf. Rom 8:11), as is said in Psalm 2: 'You are my Son, today I have begotten you' (cf. Acts 13:33).

The resurrection of Jesus is the *total* outpouring of the Spirit in the world, the flowing into creation of the immense flood which pours out from the Father in the Son. In the Christ of glory the Spirit is present to the world just as he is in God himself. There, in the full measure in which he can be known, he is found.

The other divine interventions in the world and in the history of salvation radiate from the rounded work of creation and salvation. God begets the Son solely in the Spirit, and this Son in the world is the Christ. This unique begetting is at the beginning and end of God's activities in creation: 'He (Christ in glory) is the first-born of all creation...all things were created through him and for him. He is before all things and in him all things hold together' (cf. Col 1:15-17). All the manifestations of the Spirit have their significance in their assimilation into the mystery of the Son, the Christ whom God raises to life in the fullness of the Spirit. The theology of the Holy Spirit is worked out in the light of Christ's passover. More than once our attention will be turned, according to their appropriateness or the attraction of the moment, to other manifestations of the Spirit in the world and its history, or to biblical texts which do not appear to concern the mystery of Christ, but we shall never be entirely deflected from this central activity of the Spirit.

2

The Spirit of God

The Easter cry of the early Church: 'Jesus is risen!' was a cry of astonishment at God's power which broke out in Jesus 'crucified through weakness but living through the power of God'. Through the resurrection 'Jesus was established Son of God in all his power', he became the Lord, to whom 'all power was given' (cf. 2 Cor 13:4; Rom 1:4; 10:9; Mt 28:18). To describe the glorification of Jesus, the letter to the Ephesians calls on various kinds of terminology expressing the idea of power: 'May...the Father of glory...enlighten the eyes of your mind, so that you can see... how infinitely *great is the power* that he has exercised for us believers. You can tell this from the *strength of his power at work* in Christ, which he used to raise him from the dead' (1:17–20).

The inexpressible vigour of God is wholly vested in this unique action; it cannot accomplish a work of greater excellence. The resurrection is the eternal action of the Father operating within the world: the fact that he raised Jesus from the dead is expressed in Psalm 2: 'You are my Son; today I have begotten you' (cf. Acts 13:33).

Spirit of power

The Holy Spirit is, in person, the action of God which raises Christ from the dead: 'If the Spirit of him who raised Jesus from the dead is living in you, then he who raised Jesus from the dead will give life to your mortal bodies through his Spirit living in you' (Rom 8:11). 'God is the one who raises Jesus from the dead' (cf. Rom 4:17; 8:11; 2 Cor 1:9); this is how he is characterized as God and as Father of Jesus. Similarly, it is characteristic of the Spirit of God to be the 'Spirit of him who raised Jesus from the dead' (Rom 8:11), the Spirit of the resurrection in which the infinite power of the Father is deployed. While Paul writes: '(Christ) was crucified through weakness, and still he lives now through the *power* of God' (2 Cor 13:4), Peter's interpretation is: 'In the body he was put to death, in the Spirit he was raised to life' (1 Pet 3:18). The Spirit is the impulse of God in his omnipotence.

The two words, Spirit and power, used together with unfailing fidelity, recur throughout the Bible. The strength of the Spirit is familiar, as is the weakness of the flesh, 'flesh' designating the creature in its enclosed self-centred autonomy, deprived of energy from on high. 'The Egyptian is a man, not a god, his horses are flesh, not spirit' (Is 31:3).

The strength of the Spirit is the strength of God; it comes down on man from above, seizes hold of him (cf. 1 Sam 16:13) and clothes him with itself (cf. Jg 6:34): 'The Spirit of God will seize on you (Saul)...and you will be changed into another man' (1 Sam 10:6).[1] The Spirit of 'counsel and power' will rest on the new David (Is 11:2), who thenceforward will have as his name 'Wonder-Counsellor, *Mighty-God*' (Is 9:5).

The New Testament inherits these titles, above all in Luke's writings. The Holy Spirit comes upon the young woman, Mary, the power of the Most High covers her with its shadow (cf. Lk 1:35): Spirit and power are two names for a single reality. Omnipotence – the Spirit – *comes down* from on high, makes Mary *capable* of being the mother of a child, the Son of God, and proves that nothing is impossible to God (cf Lk 1:37).

The ministry of Jesus, inaugurated 'with the power of the Spirit' (cf. Lk 4:14), is developed under the action of this power which rests upon him (cf. Lk 4:16). 'Anointed with the Holy Spirit and with power' (Acts 10:38), Jesus performs mighty works (Lk 4:18).[2] He shatters the power of devils by the finger of God, that is, by his power, a characteristic of the Kingdom of God (cf. Mk 9:1). 'If it is through the finger of God that I cast out devils, then know that the Kingdom of God has overtaken you' (Lk 11:20). This power of the Kingdom is interpreted by Mt 12:28: 'If it is through the Spirit of God that

I cast out devils...'.[3] After the resurrection Jesus promises: 'And now I am sending down *to you* what the Father has promised. Stay in the city, then, until you are *clothed with the power* from on high' [Fr.: 'the power of the Most High'] (Lk 24:49; Acts 1:8).

Throughout the story of the Church the union of the two notions of Spirit and power is invariably maintained. The Gospel is spread 'as power and as the Holy Spirit' (1 Th 1:5); preaching is a 'demonstration of the power of the Spirit' (1 Cor 2:4): people submit to the 'obedience of faith' by the power of 'signs and wonders', by the power of the Holy Spirit (cf. Rom 15:19; 2 Cor 12:12; Gal 3:2–5). The apostles 'boldly' bear witness to Jesus, filled with the power of the Spirit (cf. Acts 4:31 and *passim*). Among them, Stephen is 'filled with grace and power...filled with the Holy Spirit' (cf. Acts 6:8; 7:55). The faithful are 'powerfully strengthened by the Spirit' (cf. Eph 3:16) who gives them 'power' to confess the Lord Jesus (cf. 1 Cor 12:3) and to observe God's law (cf. Rom 8:2f.). 'The power of the Holy Spirit will remove from them all bounds to hope' (Rom 15:13), a hope which will be fulfilled when they rise in power...in a spiritual body (cf. 1 Cor 15:43f.) through the Spirit living in them (cf. Rom 8:11).

This is a lengthy list of testimony to the power of the Spirit, but it is not exhaustive. We can draw from it a firm, fundamental conclusion: *the Spirit is the omnipotence of God.* Furthermore, 'Power' is even the name of God: 'You will see the Son of Man seated at the right hand of the Power' (Mt 26:64). The Spirit is God in his characteristic attribute, God himself in his infinite action. For Christian faith the Spirit is a person; it can therefore be said that he is the personification of action, that he is the 'working' member or person in the Trinity.[4]

Whenever, then, God is active, when he creates, intervenes in history, enters through the incarnation into creation, raises Christ from the dead, establishes a covenant between himself and a people, even when, in his trinitarian action, he begets an eternal Son, it is in the Spirit that all this is brought about, for the Spirit is the power and action of God.

But this power differs from that exercised by human beings. In the work accomplished in Jesus, the truest form of omnipotence is wholly grace, infinite love, mingled with the absolute weakness of Christ's death: 'We preach a crucified Christ...the power...of God' (cf. 1 Cor 1:24f.). In order to avoid error as to the nature of the Spirit, we must, after recognizing omnipotence in him, immediately recall a double manifestation of the Spirit: at the beginning of the Gospel account he is associated with the humble handmaid of the Lord (cf. Lk 1:35) and at the end he appears under the symbol of the water that flows from the open side of Jesus: omnipotence humble, immolated.

As an artist mixes his colours, theology should endeavour to create, through admixture, a new language, one where opposites form but a single entity. Omnipotence, in its final revelation in Jesus Christ, is part of the newness which, according to Rom 7:6, is proper to the Spirit: new wine bursting our ways of thinking.

Spirit of glory[5]

In the resurrection of Jesus, power and glory are two very closely related realities which even mingle to become identified with the unique Spirit of God.

Glory is a very concrete reality.[6] It takes on the appearance of a fire encircling the top of Mount Sinai, or a dense cloud luminous and mysterious (cf. e.g. Ex 16:10; 24:15–17; Num 9:15; Dt 5:22–24); it is the sign of the sovereign presence of the Almighty (cf. Ex 40:34; Num 10:34; 1 Kgs 8:11; Ezek 10:4; 43:2–5; 44:4 and *passim*), 'the flashing radiance of the divine being',[7] the mystery of God in the majesty of his manifestation. It breaks forth in spectacular works: 'In the morning you will see the glory of God' (cf. Ex 19:16; Dt 5:22). John's gospel re-echoes these words: 'If you believe, you will see the glory of God' (11:40), that glory which assumes the form of 'signs and portents' (2:11; 4:48). In the New Testament, glory and power interpenetrate one another, to the extent that one can speak equally of the 'glory of his power' and the 'power of his glory' (cf. Eph 3:16; Col 1:11; 2 Th 1:9), of the coming of the Kingdom in glory and of its coming in power (cf. Mk 8:38; 9:1; 13:26).

Was it this affinity between glory and power that led to the cloud of glory being replaced by the Spirit of God who also is omnipotence? The cloud had 'rested heavily' on the mountain (cf. Ex 24:15–17), but it is the Spirit who rests on the messianic king (cf. Is 11:2). The cloud had guided the exodus of the Hebrews, but, according to Is 63:10–14, it is the Spirit 'who led them to rest'. Luke's narrative is inspired by this change: the luminous cloud which had covered the tent of God and which is to appear as a dais above the messianic hill (Is 4:5f.) is called the Holy Spirit when it comes down on Mary and covers her with its shadow; at the same time God's omnipotent energy is at work in Mary (cf. Lk 1:35–37). In his resurrection Christ is the Lord, possessed of power, he is the Lord of glory (cf. 1 Cor 2:8) and the Lord of the Spirit.[8]

The whole of the eschatological promise is accomplished in the resurrection of Jesus: the full outpouring of the Spirit, the triumph of power, the dazzling light of glory. Christ was raised from the dead through the Spirit (Rom 8:11), 'he lives through the power of God' (2 Cor 13:4), he was 'raised…by… glory' (cf. Rom 6:4). The resurrection is simultaneously the glorification of Jesus, his becoming Lord and life-giving spirit (cf. 1 Cor 15:45). Power, glory and Spirit produce this unique effect because they constitute a unique cause: Christ was raised through the Spirit of power and glory and transformed in him.

In the radiation of Christ's glory, the faithful, too, are transfigured into a spiritual body: 'Where the Spirit of the Lord is, there is freedom. And we, with our unveiled faces reflecting like mirrors the brightness of the Lord, all grow brighter and brighter as we are turned into the image that we reflect; this is the work of the Lord who is Spirit' (or 'the Lord of the Spirit') (2 Cor 3:17f.).

This impregnation by the Spirit and the transformation into glory proceed at the same pace. The believer possesses the first fruits of the Spirit (cf. Rom 8:23), his pledge (cf. 2 Cor 1:22; 5:5), a foretaste of the final gift of the Spirit (cf. Rom 8:11); he also experiences an incipient glory by which he is justified (cf. Rom 3:23f.) and gradually transfigured (cf. 2 Cor 3:18; 4:6), a glory which will one day make him like Christ in glory 'by the power of his resurrection' (cf. Ph 3:10, 21). This transform-ation is at the same time the work of the Spirit, the power and the glory: 'Out of his infinite *glory* may he give you *the power through his Spirit for your hidden self to grow strong*' (Eph 3:16). On the day of the final encounter with the risen Christ, the faithful will appear with glorified bodies, bodies full of strength, spiritual bodies (cf. 1 Cor 15:43f.). The last-named attribute is the explanation of the others: the faithful will live in glory, in strength, because they will rise again in the Spirit.

The identity of the Spirit and glory is as certain as that of the Spirit and power.[9] The first letter of Peter (4:14) created this formula: 'The Spirit of glory, the Spirit of God'.[10] The mysterious luminous cloud which was called the glory of God, the symbol of a sovereign Presence, is also the symbol of the Spirit. Moreover, glory is God himself in the radiance of his being, in the magnificence of his strength, infinite mystery in its manifestation, Without renouncing his transcendence in the exercise of his omnipotence, God comes out of himself by his action, creating, revealing, communicating himself, glorifying himself. There exists in God a trust, a power of outpouring, by means of which the mystery becomes at the same time revelation, a breath by which God breathes: this is the Spirit. Active, irradiating power, *he is God himself in his ecstasy*. God is carried outside himself by the one who is his inwardness, he makes himself known, though he cannot be expressed, he establishes contact, in virtue of his transcendence, that is, in virtue of his holiness.

Spirit of holiness

It is fairly late in the Bible that holiness is attributed to the divine 'Breath';[11] it begins to appear in the book of Wisdom (cf. 1:5; 7:22; 9:17) and becomes current at Qumran and in rabbinical literature. The idea was always latent, for the notions of glory, power and holiness are very closely connected: '*Holy, holy, holy* is Yahweh Sabaoth (the *Almighty*): his *glory* fills the whole earth' (Is 6:3).

Holiness is the attribute of God in his infinite grandeur, in his impenetrable light; God is called the Holy One because of his transcendence: 'I am God, not man; I am the Holy One in your midst' (cf. Hos 11:9; Ps 71:22; Is 5:24; Hab 3:3).

The Spirit too is transcendence. When contrasted with the

flesh, with man in his mortal weakness, he is the Spirit of God, God's indefectible power, He is from above, 'strength from on high' (cf. Acts 1:8). With marked consistency biblical images express the heavenly character of the Spirit. He comes down, he comes upon someone (cf. Num 11:17, 25; Jg 3:10; Is 11:2, 60:1 and *passim*). He descends upon Jesus like the flight of a dove (Mk 1:10).[12] He is given by the heavenly Father (cf. Lk 11:13), is 'sent from heaven' (Jn 14:26; 1 Pet 1:12). He comes down on the disciples (Acts 8:16; 10:44) like a wind 'from heaven' (cf. Acts 2:2). The man who is born of him is born from above (cf. Jn 3:3, 5).

The 'Holy One of God' is among the most ancient titles given to Jesus in recognition of his divine character (Mk 1:24; Jn 6:69; Acts 3:14; 4:27, 30). Moreover, it is through the presence of the Spirit that he is consecrated to God. 'God had anointed him with the Holy Spirit and with power' during his earthly life (Acts 10:38). Later 'he was proclaimed Son of God in power, according to the spirit of holiness, through the resurrection of the dead' (Rom 1:4).[13] Raised through the Spirit (cf. Rom 8:11), 'raised on high' by God (cf. Ph 2:9), 'having been made perfect' (Heb 5:9), with that perfection which, according to the letter to the Hebrews, is transcendence and glory. Jesus is the heavenly man (cf. 1 Cor 15:47–49) who can send the Spirit from on high (cf. Jn 16:7). It was said of the risen Christ, living, even in his body, through the fullness of the Spirit: 'in his body lives the fulness of divinity' (Col 2:9). This holiness, like a seed, was present in Jesus from the very beginning: 'The Holy Spirit will come upon you' (Lk 1:35).

Because the Spirit is the reality from on high, omnipotence, glory, he is rightly called the *Holy* Spirit.[14] In trinitarian language he may be said to be holiness in person. For an understanding of his mystery it is of great importance to know this. Holiness is God in his transcendence, in the fullness of his being: *the Spirit is holiness, he is the transcendent totality of being,* the depths of the inexpressible mystery, he is *the* reality. Apart from him, all is only mere shadow, all is destined to die, all is *void of meaning*. Flesh, which is his opposite (cf. Gal 5:17), is a flesh of sin and death. If the observance of the Law is not animated by the Spirit, the Law is a lifeless document bringing death (cf. 2 Cor 3:6). But Christ, in whom the Spirit dwells, is the profound reality of history, he is 'the spirit' (2 Cor 3:17) that gives meaning to everything.

The biblical notion of holiness, even in the Hebrew word which expresses it, suggests the idea of separation (cf. Lev 20:24–26). Wholly other, God is apart. But identified with the Spirit who is God in his glory, in his outpouring, holiness has a paradoxical aspect; far from being separated, the Holy One who is wholly other is reunited with, and intimately bound to, the creature. Heavenly, and remaining heavenly, the Spirit 'comes down', 'overflows', 'is given'; divine, he divinizes; holy, he sanctifies: in God, he communicates himself. Divine transcendence is also God in his intimacy with creation! God becomes incarnate through the power of the Holy Spirit (cf. Lk 1:35). Christ risen in the Spirit is sent into the world by the very power that exalts him in God (see below, p. 47). Formulas such as 'sanctification by the Spirit' (cf. 2 Th 2:13; 1 Pet 1:2), 'made holy by the (Holy) Spirit' (cf. Rom 15:16), 'sanctified and justified through the Spirit' (cf. 1 Cor 6:11) are proof of the paradoxical character of holiness. Far from signifying separation, holiness, as made concrete in the Spirit, is a denial of all that is enclosed in itself: the flesh (cf. Gal 5:17) and sin (cf. Rom 8:2). Transcendence is openness and nearness. God communicates himself to us through the holiness that makes him unique.[15]

Spirit of love

Communion is a key word. By pronouncing it we come to the climax of the discourse about the Spirit, to the root of the explanation. The Spirit of power, glory and holiness is presented in his truest, most mysterious light when he appears as the fullness of communion, transcendent charity.

A single text proclaims the identity of the Spirit and love, just as the definition that God is love is found only in the first letter of John (4:8, 16). Perhaps there is a certain reticence about speaking of love because there is divine discretion with reference to revelation of the depths of its mystery. This unique statement is itself expressed in an indirect and veiled manner: 'This hope is not deceptive, because the love of God has been poured into our hearts by the Holy Spirit which has been given us' (Rom 5:5) In the gift of the Spirit it is divine charity that is spread in the hearts of the faithful.

Although it is expressed only once, the identity of the Spirit with love is suggested everywhere. There is a whole series of synonyms in the Pauline formulas 'in the Spirit' and 'in charity'; 'walk in the Spirit and in charity' (cf. Rom 8:4; Eph 5:2); in both we are sanctified (Rom 15:16; Eph 1:4); the body of Christ is fitted and joined together by both (cf. Eph 2:22; 4:16; Col 2:2). Final salvation is guaranteed by 'love poured into our hearts' (cf. 2 Cor 1:22), by the seal of the Spirit, the pledge of our eternal salvation (cf. Eph 1:13f.; Rom 8:23).

The Spirit is a powerful movement active in the hearts of the faithful (cf. Rom 5:5; 2 Cor 1:22), in that deep centre of man where love is born. It is opposed to the flesh (Gal 5:17), to which it deals a death blow (cf. Rom 8:13): the fruits of the flesh are 'feuds and wrangling, jealousy, bad temper and quarrels' (Gal 5:19f.) Happiness is the first fruit brought by the Spirit, together with 'Joy, peace, patience, kindness and goodness' (Gal 5:22); this happiness is the 'love of the Spirit' (cf. Rom 15:30). In the letter to the Colossians, the Spirit is named only once, but in this form: 'your love in the Spirit' (1:8). Charity is the eschatological virtue, one that is lasting (cf. 1 Cor 13:13), the virtue of fullness and synthesis (cf. Rom 13:10; Col 3:14); the Spirit, too, is the eschatological gift, the symbol of every messianic blessing (cf. Gal 3:14).

The Spirit does not only produce fruits of charity, he is himself the fruit which God's sacrificial love bestows on man. It ripens on the tree of the cross: 'He gave up the spirit (Spirit)', 'fountains of living water flow from his pierced side' (cf. Jn 19:30, 34; 7:37–39). (See below, p. 51.) He is 'given' (cf. e.g. Acts 5:32; 15:8; 18:18; Rom 5:5: 2 Cor 1:22; 1 Jn 3:24; 4:13), he is 'received' (cf. e.g. Jn 7:39; 20:22; Acts 1:8; 8:15; 17:19), he is 'the gift' (cf. Acts 2:38; 8:20; 10:45; 11:17) in which God's love is made concrete. In the Church's liturgy and in theology he is called 'gift of the Most High'.[16]

The 'fellowship of the Holy Spirit' (2 Cor 13:13; Ph 2:1) is a formula that Paul doubtless did not coin himself;[17] it was known before his time that the Spirit is oneness and creator of communion. Paul calls Christ, in his resurrection, a 'life-giving spirit' (1 Cor 15:45), a being whose gift of self is life-giving communion. The abundant outpouring of the Spirit is the foundation of the New Covenant (cf. Jer 31:31; Ezek 36:26f.), in communion with Christ (cf. 1 Cor 10:16; 11:25). The Spirit is the strength which makes of many one single being: 'In the one Spirit you have all been baptised and made one body' (cf. 1 Cor 12:13; Eph 4:4). Likewise, in human language, the power that unites husband and wife in one body (cf. Eph 5:31f.) is called love. Because the Spirit is love, his yearning is associated with that of the Bride of the Lamb saying 'Come!' (Rev 22:17).

Because the Spirit is love, all his attributes are pure paradox. *Power*, a reality often cruel when human beings cling to it, is found transposed into an innocent, helpless strength, unstained by the blood of any victim except the blood of the one who is triumphant. The Lamb that was sacrificed 'is given power' (Rev 5:12). The divine character of power is thus shown to be totally different: 'power is at its best in weakness' (2 Cor 12:9), far exceeding the human concept of power.

Love without bounds, *holiness*, is not imprisoned in what is inaccessible; it transcends what is infinite, involves God in creation, even urges him to become incarnate. In the eyes of the last prophet of the Old Testament, John the Baptist (cf. Mt 11:13; Lk 16:16), the fire of the Spirit is the symbol of a devouring holiness, consuming the impure and the impurities of the nation (Mt 3:11f.); but the Church, strengthened by the experience of a sacrificial Messiah, makes of the fire of the Spirit the image of a burning love, She begs the Spirit to 'fill the hearts of your faithful, and kindle in them the fire of your love'.[18]

The *glory* of God, which is power in its majesty and holiness in its brightness, is first and foremost love outpoured. In humility God is glorious through his love. The dense cloud of light, a very concrete reality in the Old Testament, is still more concrete in the New, where, more than once, it is expressed by the Son begotten in the Spirit and given for mankind in the Spirit. The theological axiom 'God acts always for his own glory' means that, since 'the glory of God is man truly alive',[19] everything God does for his creature is an act of self-giving.

Spirit of life

The power used by human beings often promises death, but love makes life. Omnipotent, it is creative, it destroys death. When, at Easter, God invests Christ with the fullness of the Spirit, he awakens to life without end, in an eternal birth (cf. Acts 13:33). By begetting his Son in the outpouring of the Spirit, God 'calls into being what does not exist' (cf. Rom 4:17, 25). In this way he creates the worlds, in this 'first-born of all creation, for in him were created all things...all things were created through him and for him' (Col 1:15-17).[20] The begetting of the Son in this world, in the full power of the Spirit, is the synthesis of the work of creation from the beginning to the final resurrection of the dead: 'In the spirit of holiness that was in him, (he) was proclaimed Son of God in all his power through the resurrection *of the dead*' (Rom 1:4).[21] In this culminating action in Christ and in his passover, the Spirit is the universal source of being and of life. He is 'the Spirit of life' (Rom 8:1).

From its first appearance in the biblical narrative, *Ruah* is creation and life. It moves over the waters rather like a bird hovering over its nest, setting in order the primordial trackless waste and emptiness (*tohu-bohu*) (cf. Gen 1:2) and bringing life. The word of God, it is true, is creative too: 'God said "Let there be light..." and there was light' (Gen 1:3). At the beginning, as at the climax of the passover, the Word of God and the Spirit act together, just as, in man, a word is inseparable from the breath producing it: 'By the word of God the heavens were made, their whole array (the stars) by the breath of his mouth' (Ps 33:6; Job 34:14f.).

The world, created in the Spirit, is not without a soul. Breath is the symbol of life; the world, called into existence by divine Breath, has life in it. According to Rom 4:17-25, creating is synonymous with raising the dead to life. God breathed into Adam's nostrils a breath of life, and thus man 'became a living being' (Gen 2:7).[22]

This Breath of life passes over the face of the whole earth: 'If you give breath, fresh life begins, you keep renewing the world' (Ps 104:30). In the eyes of biblical man, creation has life, the stars sing, the mountains rejoice, the rivers clap their hands, inanimate objects have a soul.[23] St Paul, with his deep perception of the world, understands the breathing of the material creation, its aspiration to share the life of the children of God (cf. Rom 8:19-22). *The act of creation is already a Pentecost, a first and permanent outpouring of the Spirit of life.*

Because the Spirit is creation and life, his promise forms part of the messianic hope. At the time of the exile, the people of Israel seemed like a valley filled with bones, but the Spirit, rising from the four winds, came down upon them. They will rise again, for God promises: 'I am now going to make the Breath enter you, and you will live' (Ezek 37:1-14).

The messianic resurrection constitutes the horizon of the 'hope of Israel' (cf. Acts 28:30; 23:6; 15:26f.) and that of Christians. It is the Good News announced by the Apostle, the promise made to our ancestors (cf. Acts 13:32f.). The creation of the world through the Holy Spirit is already a salvific action. It calls into being what does not exist, God lays the first stone of the work of salvation which will be completed in the resurrection (cf. Rom 4:17), through the same power of the Spirit.

* * *

From the time of the exile onwards the Bible offers us an image of the Spirit not previously used. In countries burnt by the sun, where people are tormented by thirst, water is the divine gift *par excellence*, the symbol of life. When God gathers his people together after the dispersion, the miracle of the rock will be repeated: 'He made water spring for them from the rock, he split the rock and water flowed' (Is 48:21). When they arrive back in their native land, the rains will fall, the springs will gush forth (cf. Is 41:18; 43:19f.; 49:10; 58:11; Joel 4:18; Zech 13:1).

Through the abundance of water promised, the gift of the Spirit is proclaimed: 'I shall pour clean water over you...and put a new spirit in you' (Ezek 36:25-27). Because the Spirit is divine water, the prophets coined the formula 'the spirit will be poured on us'. 'I will pour out water on the thirsty soil...I will pour my spirit on your descendants' (cf. Is 32:15; 44:3; Joel 3:1f.; Zech 12:10). These running waters will issue from Jerusalem (the city of God) (cf. Zech 14:8), a stream comes out from under the Temple (cf. Ezek 47:1), for it is from within God that the Spirit is poured on the people.

He is compared not to the waters of the sea, which are an object of fear, but to a spring, which is gentle, and to rain, which is refreshing. Such water is strength, strength for life. Revealed in this form, the Spirit is a power free from threat, he is the grace of God in his crowning generosity at the moment of salvation.

Water makes the earth fruitful by penetrating it. Whereas in his earlier manifestations, the Spirit 'fell upon', 'came upon', 'clothed' man, as it were from outside himself, henceforth the Spirit will impregnate man: 'I will put my spirit in you' (cf. Ezek 36:27). The New Testament takes up once more the image of life-giving water, Johannine literature makes it the favoured image of the Spirit. A believer is born of water and of the Spirit for whom water is the sacrament (Jn 3:5). He is given to drink by the Spirit: 'One Spirit was given to all to drink' (cf. 1 Cor 12:13; 10:4) The 'outpouring' of the Spirit in the hearts of men is the characteristic of the New Testament inaugurated by God by his raising Christ from the dead through the Spirit.

Divine inwardness in the outpouring of the Spirit

When God promises 'I will pour out my spirit' (Ezek 36:27) he is expressing himself in terms apparently contradictory. The Spirit is the inwardness of God, yet he will be poured out!

All the attributes of God are found personified in the Spirit who is as it were the synthesis of the divine mystery. *Power* is the first divine attribute: God is called the Lord, the sovereign Master; he is the 'Almighty who does great things' (cf. Lk 1:49). To avoid using the sacred name of Yahweh, the Jews used to say 'Power'; according to Mt 26:64, Jesus himself speaks in the same way: 'You will see the Son of Man seated at the right hand of the Power'. And the Spirit is omnipotence, the sovereign action of the Creator. God is the *Holy One*, the wholly Other; the Spirit too is divine transcendence, he is the Holy Spirit. The *glory* of God is God himself in the radiance of his power and holiness; moreover, the Spirit, divine power and holiness, is also the glory of God. God is the *Living One* (cf. Dt 32:40) and the Spirit is life. John's gospel pronounces the definition: God is *'spirit'* (4:24),[24] and that is what the Spirit is. Finally God is *love*, and the Spirit is love. *All the attributes of God are personified in the Spirit*, who is God himself in the depths of his being.[25]

Moreover, God overflows in the depths of his being. The one who is intimate mystery is also the tendency to come out of himself; the Inexpressible One urges God to utter himself through his Word in Christ and in creation. The Spirit is both divine inwardness and its outpouring, its diffusion; power is creative, holiness is sanctifying, life is vivifying, love gives itself.

This is why the Spirit is identified with glory; he is the radiation of God, the key which opens, the thrust which causes a 'coming out'. God is not imprisoned in his transcendence: without being at variance with it, without giving up his inwardness – for the Spirit himself is this – he 'comes out' through his Spirit, creating, revealing himself and intervening in history. The Spirit, who is infinite reality, forms the link between God and finite beings. Through him holiness penetrates right into our world, and even becomes incarnate there (cf. Lk 1:35); through him God lives in man as in a temple (cf. 1 Cor 3:16; 6:19). The heavenly Spirit is the intimacy of God with the earth, the hand of God touching this world: 'If it is through the finger of God...' (Jesus says, according to Lk 11:20), 'if it is through the Spirit of God' (Jesus says, according to Mt 12:28) 'that I cast out devils...'. The Spirit is the divine secret, but in disclosure, the mystery of God, but of a God who reveals himself, a God in his transcendence which exceeds itself.

Man has some experience of this inwardness which overflows in its very depths: he is capable of love. Love in the heart of a man is this man in his innermost being and is profoundly outgoing: he comes out of himself in virtue of his innermost being and, in leaving himself, he becomes more himself. In condescending to be united with man, God appears to renounce himself, but it is the depths of his being that he manifests.

Although he is a key, openness, ecstasy, the Spirit is, and remains, the depths of God (cf. 1 Cor 2:10f.). God comes out of himself without leaving himself and thereby he attracts to himself. The divine fullness is creative, it gives birth to beings outside God, but through appealing and attracting towards this fullness. God's exodus attracts towards God. *The Spirit is a simultaneous movement of ebb and flow.*

This movement reaches its supreme intensity in Christ and his passover, where God comes completely out of himself through the power of the Holy Spirit; there is a total assumption of humanity even to death; in this very death he brings Christ wholly back into himself, glorifying him in the Spirit so that 'in his body lives the fulness of divinity' (Col 2:9). God leaves himself in Jesus Christ through the power of the Spirit, when, through the same power, he takes this human nature into himself.

The whole history of salvation is developed according to this unique movement of breathing out and breathing in, proper to the Breath of God.

Agent of history

Israel probably recognized in the Spirit the agent of its history before seeing in him the creative power of God. The revelation of God as saviour, as founder of the covenant, preceded faith in God the creator.[26] The Spirit was seen to fall on people, making them heroes, prophets, without as yet any knowledge that he had hovered over the primordial waters. According to older documents it was into *man's* nostrils that God breathed 'a breath of life' (Gen 2:7).[27]

As creator, the Spirit does not raise up a static universe, he involves it in an evolution. He himself is movement, action: every reality that he creates tends to become event. He is by nature creator of history.[28] By coming out of himself through the Spirit, God unites his action with that of human beings. He asserts himself as master of the destiny of a people with whom he enters into a covenant; there he manifests his presence through many interventions of the Spirit indicated in the 'historical books' of the Bible. Like a shepherd he leads Israel to rest through his Spirit (cf. Is 63:14); 'but they rebelled, they grieved his Holy Spirit' (Is 63:10). Then God announced another covenant by which, through his Spirit, he imposed his law (cf. Jer 31:31; Ezek 36:27). He prepared this covenant by raising up again, through the breath of his Spirit, the people scattered by the exile (Ezek 37:1-14). The decisive hero of this historical work of God, the Messiah, will be, like so many men, chosen by God, but filled infinitely more than them with the Breath of Yahweh (cf. Is 11:2).[29]

The gospels, especially that of Luke, pick up the thread of sacred history again at this point. They present the life of Jesus as theological history, a life unfolded under the movement of the Spirit. The Precursor is 'filled with the Holy Spirit' (Lk 1:15); Jesus is 'raised' in the Spirit and through his power (cf. Lk 1:35), he who, one day, will be fully 'raised' (raised from the dead) through the Spirit.[30] By the Spirit he is anointed Messiah (cf. Lk 3:22; 4:18; Acts 10:38), he is 'driven' by the Spirit into the desert for the first struggle; then he undertakes his ministry 'with the power of the Spirit in him' (cf. Lk 4:14). In the person of Jesus and the strength of the Spirit, sacred history arrives at its full term which is the Kingdom of God: 'If it is through the finger of God – through the Spirit of God – that I cast out devils, then know that the Kingdom of God has overtaken you' (Mt 12:28; Lk 11:20).

The Spirit is the friend of man, the history over which he presides is salvific. Having been anointed, Jesus proclaims that the Good News of the salvation of the poor becomes a reality now. Because the Spirit rests on him, 'he will not break the crushed reed, nor put out the smouldering wick' (Mt 12:18, 20). In his interventions, the Spirit testifies that God is love.

* * *

In the making of history, the Spirit is revealed, as always, both as the emergence of God, his intimacy in the world, and as the inwardness of God, making a rapport with the world. On the one side he is the hand of God, contact with the world, on the other he is transcendence, so that what he touches becomes the place where God's Kingdom is established. The Spirit is the agent of history for the transformation of creation into the Kingdom of God.

God does not begin by coming out of himself through creating, so that he may subsequently attract and lead to himself. The movement is a single one: God creates in the measure that he 'weaves' the world into himself. He gives it increasingly the power *to be*, through attraction towards his divine being. He comes out in creation and creates sacred history by drawing men towards himself like a magnet. History progresses from its first imperfection, though even then the Spirit is not absent, towards the final fulfilment when God is all in all in a fullness of the Holy Spirit.

Christ in his Easter glory is the culminating point of sacred history; the Apostle assures us that everything is created 'for him' (cf. Col 1:16). *Every action of the Holy Spirit has as its purpose the bringing about of the mystery of sonship and its accomplishment in the world.* The Christian looking into the Old Testament perceives the rising dawn of the One New-Born; the faithful of the New Testament know they are called to union with the Son 'on that Day' (cf. 1 Cor 1:9); the whole of creation is marked with the seal of the Son; worked on by the Spirit, creation aspires to participate in the glory of the Son (cf. Rom 8:18–30). The intimate relationship between the activity of the Spirit and the mystery of the Son, in view of its accomplishment in the world, is intrinsic to theology as a fact of paramount importance.

History over which the Spirit presides is not, therefore, inevitable; contrary to appearances, people are not confined to a cycle of birth and death. Since he is the openness of God, the Spirit does not create a closed world: history over which he presides is open to the infinite, its final goal is Christ whom the Spirit raises in the very moment of death. Moreover, where death itself is a birth, there is no end.

Christ begotten through the Spirit is not only the summit of fulfilment. God creates from the place towards which he attracts, he makes the world exist by participation in his fulfilment. Everything has its origin in the Son, and in his being begotten in this world, which is created by being called and impelled towards its future fulfilment. The Christ of glory is the initial work of God through the Spirit as well as its completion; he is the 'first-born of all creation, for all things were created in him' (cf. Col 1:15f.). Creation and sacred history begin where all is accomplished: in the Son whom the Father begets through his Spirit in the world. *The Spirit is the agent of history in that he is the Spirit of the Father who begets his Son in the world.*

At the beginning and at the climax

It is a remarkable fact that at the beginning and at the end of everything we find the Holy Spirit present. He is at work in the first chapters of Genesis (cf. 1:2; 2:7), and his voice is heard in the last verses of Revelation (22:17). The Breath of God stirs the first man to life and awakens the dead on the last day (cf. Rom 8:11). The Spirit is at the beginning of the life of Jesus (cf. Lk 1:35) and his ministry – having declared: 'The Spirit of God has been given to me', Jesus *began* to say... (cf. Lk 4:18, 21) – and it is in the Spirit of the resurrection that his life and mission find their culmination. The believer is born of water and the Spirit (cf. Jn 3:5) and comes to the fullness of his birth as son through resurrection in the Spirit; the Spirit is present at the departure and the arrival, and the intervening space is also filled by him.

This fact is very significant. The Spirit is neither the beginning nor the end: it is the Father who is the beginning and all is accomplished in the Son. But the Spirit is the fullness where everything has its origin, where everything is enriched and completed. The movement of sacred history is the repercussion in the world of the eternal mystery, in which the Spirit is at the beginning and at the end and forms the link between the two. For the Father begets through the Spirit the one who, in the Spirit, is the Son, and the two are united in the Spirit (cf. p. 141 below).

★ ★ ★

Instead of beginning and end, we can speak of a depth where everything reaches its climax. A relationship exists between the Spirit and the profound being of man: 'I shall put my spirit *in* you' (cf. Ezek 36:26f.; 37:14; 1 Th 4:8). 'Deep within them I will plant my law' (Jer 31:33); 'God has sent the Spirit of his Son into our hearts' (Gal 4:6); 'it is God himself who gives the pledge, the Spirit that we carry in our hearts' (cf. 2 Cor 1:22); 'the love of God has been poured into our hearts by the Holy Spirit' (Rom 5:5). It is also in our hearts that the Spirit comes to our help in prayer (cf. Rom 8:26). According to John 14:17 Jesus says: '(The Spirit) is *in* you'. It is there, in our hearts, in the intimate depths of the believer, that the Spirit chooses his dwelling. In God himself he reaches the 'depths' (cf. 1 Cor 2:10). He is, as it were, the heart of God.

The heart is man's centre, the core of his person, where he is himself and becomes more and more himself. 'Person' is a word unknown in the Bible, but its meaning is often expressed by various symbols, among which the heart is the principal one.[31] In Pauline language the word 'spirit' is frequently close to the notion of 'person' (cf. Rom 1:9; 8:10, 16; 1 Cor 2:11; Gal 6:8; Eph 4:23). Furthermore, there is a close relationship between the spirit and the Spirit,[32] so close that at times one is uncertain whether to write the word with a small or a capital letter.[33] The Spirit is present and works in the innermost part of the person at the highest point he reaches, and this is also the source of his choices and activities. For someone who wishes to approach the eternal mystery of the Spirit, it is not a matter of indifference to know that the Spirit comes to dwell in man at this innermost part, where depths, climax and starting-point meet. The Spirit thus manifests that he himself is the mystery of God in its eternal depths.

The eschatological gift

In a very different kind of language, but one in which a similar truth is expressed, it is said of the Holy Spirit that he is the eschatological gift.

Prophecy foretold his rich outpouring for the last days, those of the New Covenant characterized by the presence of the Spirit in our hearts. Judaism of the time of Jesus was aware of the eschatological role of the Spirit. Since Malachi there had been a lack of prophecy, making people feel the absence of the Spirit.[34] This caused John to say in his gospel that, before the glorification of Jesus 'there was no Spirit as yet' (Jn 7:39).

However, the Precursor proclaims that baptism in the Spirit and in fire is imminent and that eschatological judgement will then be accomplished. Over Jesus the heavens open, the Spirit descends, God's voice is heard;[35] all this means for the synoptic evangelists that the final era is inaugurated, that

Jesus is the more powerful one 'who will baptise with the Spirit'. The driving out of devils in the power of the Spirit is proof that 'the kingdom of God has overtaken you' (Mt 12:28). The coming of the kingdom is accompanied by a display of power (cf. Mk 9:1) and of glory (cf. Mk 8:38); but the Spirit is both power and glory. At the last supper, what Jesus had habitually called the Kingdom, he called the Covenant or the New Covenant; furthermore, according to prophecy this Covenant was sealed in the outpouring of the Spirit (cf. Jer 31:31; Ezek 37:14). It is 'communion in the Holy Spirit'. The last days are those of the uncontested triumph of God's law (cf. Jer 31:33); the spirit of life is God's law in person (cf. Rom 8:2); it is expressed in that charity which is the fulfilling of the law (cf. Rom 13:10). The last days are the days of the Spirit.

The resurrection of Jesus himself is already 'the resurrection from the dead' (Rom 1:4), the eschatological event destined to be spread among men. It is also the full outpouring of the Spirit. God thus brings sacred history to its accomplishment, to which nothing can be added, towards which the world was created in order to participate in it: 'In him (Christ in glory) lives the fullness of divinity, and in him too you find your own fulfilment' (cf. Col 2:9f.). The resurrection of Jesus is the final mystery, for the Spirit is the total outpouring, the divine fulfilment.[36] It is thus 'the Good News, the promise made to our ancestors', as it is accomplished (Acts 13:32f.). The Spirit, for his part, is 'the promise of the Father' in its realization (Lk 24:49; Acts 1:4f.; 2:33), he is the 'Spirit of the promise' (Gal 3:14; Eph 1:13).[37] Under the form of the gift of the Spirit God imparts the blessing promised to Abraham (cf. Acts 3:25f.; Gal 3:14). At Pentecost Peter states that 'the last times have arrived' (cf. Acts 2:17): according to Paul the fullness of time has come now that, in the Spirit of the Son, man can say to God: 'Abba! Father!' (Gal 4:4, 6).

For an understanding of the resurrection of Jesus, the meaning of salvation history and the mystery of the Holy Spirit, it is very important to know that the outpouring of the Spirit is the eschatological gift, the coming of the Kingdom of God. Beyond this gift there is no other: the Spirit given in Christ is the supreme grace; with regard to the world 'in process of becoming' it is the heavenly reality in its fullness.

That is why the Christ of glory, too, is *the* reality, but present in creation; he is the fulfilment of the world (Eph 4:10), simultaneously its depths and its whole future where everything finds its source, meaning and foundation, where all is completed. For God has filled it with the Spirit, to the point of transforming it into 'a life-giving spirit' (cf. 1 Cor 15:45), of making it 'the spirit', the meaning of the world (cf. 2 Cor 3:17).

3

The Spirit of Christ

There is in the world and in its history a very special moment and place: Christ and his passover when the Spirit breaks into this world just as he is in himself; when he acts according to his eternal mystery. In this place and at this moment holiness shines out in all its brightness, power is exercised, glory is manifested, love is declared, life is triumphant. Here the sum-total of the divine attributes is displayed (cf. Ph 2:9–11), those attributes which describe the mystery of the Spirit. Paul describes the Christ of glory by the name proper to the Spirit: 'The Lord (Jesus) is the Spirit' (2 Cor 3:17),[1] he 'has become a life-giving spirit' (1 Cor 15:45).

This deliberate confusion of expression, giving Christ the same name as the Spirit, reveals an essential aspect of the mystery of Christ and that of the Spirit. Their nature unites them. It is impossible to understand Christ without recognizing in him the man of the Holy Spirit, or to know the Spirit without seeing in him the Spirit of Christ, the Son of God. If it is possible to define God by calling him the Father of Jesus Christ, the one 'who raised Jesus from the dead' (Rom 8:11), the Spirit can similarly be characterized as the Spirit of the Son, the one through whom God raised Jesus Christ from the dead.

The Spirit is not revealed directly in Christ. He is the one through whom Jesus is the Son, is sent and manifested.[2] However, he cannot remain hidden, he himself becomes manifest in Christ, just like a light shining in the objects it reveals.

Jesus, man of the Spirit

The Old Testament had an intuition that the Messiah would be invested with the Spirit. The Holy Spirit had been withdrawn from King Saul and had passed from him to come down upon David; but he would rest on the branch from the stock of Jesse: his presence was to be definitive (cf. Is 11:2).

Jesus is the one whom 'God had anointed with the Holy Spirit and with power' (cf. Acts 10:38). He is born of the Spirit (cf. Lk 1:35); on him the Spirit descended visibly;[3] the fourth gospel is precise: he came down on him and rested on him (cf. 1:31). This presence is permanent, a distinctive attribute and sign, inseparable from Jesus.[4] It is total: 'God gives him the Spirit without reserve' (Jn 3:34).

The Spirit came down on the charismatics of the Old Testament and stimulated them to prompt action: power came from without. In Jesus the Spirit rests, without brilliance or disturbance, in the calm of an interior fullness. Once only is Jesus seen to exult in the Spirit (cf. Lk 10:21), though the presence of the Spirit in him is constant: he speaks with authority, acts with power, and casts out devils through this power (cf. Lk 11:21) which is the Holy Spirit (cf. Mt 12:28). He has the lasting use of this power and disposes of it with assurance. Between him and the Spirit there is always collaboration and a shared nature.[5]

According to John's gospel, Jesus promises the simultaneous coming of the Spirit and himself: 'The Father will give you another Advocate to be with you for ever...I will not leave you orphans; I will come back to you' (cf. 14:16–18). The Spirit will not replace Jesus, he will not be a substitute for his absence: his coming will effect the presence of Jesus, the bond between them is indissoluble.[6] In his death Jesus gives up his spirit and at the same time sends the Spirit (19:30) (see below, p. 54); but the water, symbol of the Spirit, and the blood of Jesus flow jointly from his open side (19:34). Although intimate and inseparable, Jesus and the Spirit are not however one and the same: like Jesus, the Spirit is an Advocate, but 'another' one (14:16). However, the bond is so close that before the glorification of Jesus and apart from him, who is the fount, 'there is no Spirit' (cf. 7:39).

In St Paul the Holy Spirit is called, as in the Old Testament, Spirit of God. But sometimes – this is a very significant fact – he is called the Spirit of the Son (cf. Gal 4:6), the Spirit of the Lord (cf. 2 Cor 3:17), the Spirit of Christ: '...since the Spirit of God has made his home in you;...unless you possessed the Spirit of Christ...' (Rom 8:9; Ph 1:19).[7]

Christ and the Spirit together engage in the same activity: the faithful are 'justified through the name of the Lord Jesus Christ and through the Spirit' (1 Cor 6:11). The frequent formulas 'in the Spirit' and 'in Christ', which describe the sanctifying activity of the one and of the other, cover, without confusion, wide areas of the same meaning. In Pauline writings, as in St John (7:37–39), the faithful rejoice in the Spirit through communion with Christ: 'in him' they are 'stamped with the seal of the Holy Spirit of the promise' (Eph 1:13); the body of Christ, they are the temple of the Spirit (cf. 1 Cor 6:15, 17); with the Spirit dwelling in them, they belong to Christ (cf. Rom 8:8); between the Spirit and Christ such intimacy, reciprocity and dynamic unity prevail that the Apostle can speak of Christ become spirit (cf. 1 Cor 15:45; 2 Cor 3:17).

This is a most remarkable fact. The New Testament speaks instinctively and in various forms of this unity because it sees in Jesus the very mystery of God in the world. Unless one believes in the incarnation, the formula 'Spirit of Jesus', 'Spirit of Christ' is unexpected, unacceptable, contradictory. To say that this man has the Spirit and his power at his service, that he can send him, that the Spirit rises in his own body (Jn 7:37–39) would be absurd if Jesus had not, also in his body, been raised to the level of God. For the Spirit is the divine mystery. To speak of the Spirit of Christ is to profess that 'Jesus is Lord' (1 Cor 12:3; Ph 2:11), that 'in his body lives the fulness of divinity' (Col 2:9).[8]

A Christology is inconceivable without being complemented by a theology of the Spirit. Christ is misunderstood, there is no inkling of the depths of his being, if he is detached from the Spirit through whom he is conceived, through whom he acts, through whom he rises from the dead and who is at his service. The one who knows that the Spirit of God is the Spirit of Christ is more than man.[9]

Conversely, since the eternal Spirit is revealed as the Spirit of Christ, could one construct a theology of the Spirit independently of that of Christ? There exists a relationship between the Spirit and Christ, just as one exists between the Spirit and God, a relationship which affects Jesus, but also the Spirit.

Christ and Son in the Spirit

The presence of the Spirit confers on Jesus a function: that of consecration as Messiah. At a deeper level, this function characterizes the person of Jesus: it is the mark of his divine sonship.

The anointing by the Spirit and title of Messiah reciprocally require each other; 'God had anointed him with the Holy Spirit and with power' (Acts 10:38), says Peter, recognizing in Jesus the Messiah, the one whose name means God's Anointed One. The outpouring at Pentecost is the proof that God has enthroned Jesus in his function as Messiah-King: 'The whole house of Israel can be certain that God has made this Jesus whom you crucified both Lord and Christ(messiah)' (Acts 2:36).

This is the meaning of the account of the annunciation: God will give the throne of David to the one who will be born of the Holy Spirit (cf. Lk 1:32, 35). The coming down of the Spirit at the Jordan is the manifestation of the messiahship. Jesus is introduced as God's Anointed One, that is, as the Messiah, when he claims for himself the words of Isaiah 61:1: 'The spirit of the Lord has been given to me, for he has anointed me' (Lk 4:18). Risen again in the Spirit, Jesus entered upon the full exercise of his function (cf. Acts 2:36). In the eyes of his disciples, the presence of the Spirit is the expression of the messiahship of Jesus.[10]

The Spirit thus brings sacred history to its final end, his presence is the messianic consecration of Jesus which inaugurates the Kingdom of God.

* * *

In early Christian thought the messiahship of Jesus and his sonship are inseparable (cf. e.g. Mk 1:1: 'The beginning of the

Good News about *Jesus Christ, the Son of God*'). The messianic anointing is also the seal of sonship, messiahship is itself filial, function is rooted in the mystery of the person.

By his Breath God created Adam in his image and likeness: he thus made for himself a son in the world.[11] Through his Spirit, God raises Jesus from the dead and makes him his perfect image (cf. 2 Cor 3:18; 4:4; Col 1:15) by saying over him the words: 'You are my son: today I have begotten you' (cf. Acts 13:33).

The resurrection is the final great work that God accomplishes in the Spirit, 'the promise made to our fathers, the Good News' (cf. Acts 13:32). It is the eternal mystery brought further into creation, the definitive begetting of the Son as man, through which God causes the fullness of divinity to live in his body (cf. Col 2:9).

The disciples' faith in the divine sonship of Jesus has its origin in the resurrection and in their experience of the glorified Christ. When Paul encounters the Risen Christ, he recognizes that God is the father of this man: 'Then God...chose to reveal *his Son* to me' (cf. Gal 1:16).[12] For Paul the title of Son, like that of *Kyrios*, Lord, is given to Christ in his paschal and eschatological glory;[13] the faithful 'are now waiting for Jesus, his Son, whom he raised from the dead' (1 Th 1:10), they are called to communion with his Son, our *Kyrios* (cf. 1 Cor 1:9). The infinite glory of the resurrection is the dazzling light of sonship: 'We saw his glory, the glory that is his as the only Son of the Father' (Jn 1:14). There is no divine sonship other than the glorious sonship in the image of the Father.[14] *Moreover, it is the Spirit who is the glory of the risen Christ: Jesus is the Son of God in the Holy Spirit.*

God was already the Father of Christ before the final glorification. Jesus came into the world in the 'shadow' of the cloud of glory, through the power of the Spirit; the child thus born is holy, Son of God (cf. Lk 1:35). The Spirit hovers over Jesus at the Jordan and God says: 'You are my Son, the Beloved' (Mk 1:11). At the sight of the Spirit resting on Jesus, the Precursor testifies according to John 1:34: 'He is the Chosen One of God'. 'On the holy mountain' a cloud appeared, 'the sublime glory of God' (2 Pet 1:17f.), enveloping Jesus with 'its shadow', and from the depths of glory a voice sounded: 'This is my son, the Beloved' (Mk 9:7). Was the cloud the symbol of the Spirit? Spiritual exegesis – inspired by the Spirit – gives a trinitarian interpretation of the transfiguration, certain that the cloud, God's glory, is the symbol of the Spirit.[15]

*   *   *

Word of God is a title synonymous with Son; Christ is the unique, eternal Word expressed in the world. The relationship between Spirit and divine sonship, revealed in the New Testament, was already announced in the Old Testament; it appears in the passage which unites the Spirit of God and the word of God: 'By the word of Yahweh the heavens were made, their whole array (the stars) by the breath of his mouth' (cf. Ps 33:6; Jdt 16:14). God creates by breath (cf. Gen 1:2: 2:7), he creates by word (Gen 1:36). The word of a person is conveyed by the breath of that person, and it is the same with the word of God. By his breath and by his word God comes out of himself and acts in the world. The word of the prophets is inspired, conveyed by the one who is the Breath, the spiration, of God: 'He (the Spirit) has spoken through the prophets' (Nicene Creed). In the New Testament the message of the apostles, which is that of God (cf. 1 Th 2:13), is conveyed by the Spirit: 'when we brought the Good News to you, it came to you not only as words but as power and as the Holy Spirit' (1 Th 1:5). The union of the Word and the Spirit is such that, by being open to the former, it is the Spirit that the believer receives (cf. Gal 3:2). Every work by God is accomplished by the concerted action of the Spirit and the Word.

Moreover, Word of God is another name for Christ in his filial relationship. When God invests himself wholly with the Word addressed to human beings, it is in the fullness of the Spirit that he speaks; St John Damascene expresses this admirably: 'The Spirit is the breath from the mouth of God, the one who announces the Word'.[16] By reason of the Spirit who lives in him, our God is a God who speaks. He comes out of himself and enters into an intimate relationship with mankind.   *   *   *

When the fullness of time came – and in order that it might come – God sent both his Son and his Spirit: 'When the appointed time came, God sent his Son...God sent the Spirit of his Son into our hearts' (Gal 4:4, 6). It was the fullness of time because in Christ the fullness of God entered time. Without laying aside his transcendence, God filled history with his presence in his Son and through his Spirit.

The sending of the Son is different from that of the Spirit. The action of the Father as he sends is turned towards the Son. He 'came from God...and has come into the world' (Jn 8:42; 16:28). But the Spirit is the one *through whom* this is effected, this coming out, this begetting of the Son in the world. It is *through him* that Jesus is born Son of God, in a glory at first veiled, then manifested in the resurrection. The Spirit is like the divine womb from which Jesus is born Son of God in the world.

In the light of Easter, the eye of faith is granted access to the mystery of the Trinity. The Spirit here appears as the action of God in his fatherhood, an action thanks to which Christ is Son; he is the omnipotence of God, his infinite life; these attributes are expressed and completely realized in the divine begetting of which the resurrection is the full revelation. The mystery of the Spirit is here in its full entirety: involved in God's fatherhood, in Christ's sonship and in their mutual relationship: *he is the Spirit of the Father as father, of the Son as son.*

Saviour in the Spirit

The Spirit plays an important part in the work of redemption, since salvation is achieved in Christ's passover, the filial mystery in which the Spirit reigns.

There is a so-called juridical theology of the redemption, formerly very widespread, and common even today, in which the Spirit plays no part. This theology interprets Christ's merit according to the idea of merit held in human relationships, where an action, a price paid, gives the right to some sort of exchange. When the Apostle writes: 'You have been bought at a high price' (cf. 1 Cor 6:20; 7:23), it is explained thus: Jesus made superabundant reparation for the infringement of God's justice; by the price of his death he acquired for mankind the right to pardon and grace.

This theology considers redemptive death as outside the personal relationship of Jesus with his Father, contrary to a personalistic anthropology. Death is understood as a price paid, a reality exterior to the person. However, nothing is as personal to a man as his death; the death of a man is his final achievement in his relationship with God. In death 'Jesus was made perfect' (cf. Heb 5:9) in his being as man, as man the Son of God.

The God of this theology is, for his part, impersonal, identified with the divine attribute of justice.[17] Yet the God of salvation is a Father, he acts as a Father, welcoming the Son, glorifying him through himself (cf. Jn 17:5), giving him life in the Spirit (cf. Rom 8:11). The relationship between God and Jesus is wholly personal, fatherly on one side, filial on the other.

The image of the price paid is biblical, the understanding and use of it in this theology are not. No ransom was paid to the Father in order to reconcile him; God paid the high price of salvation by giving his Son for the life of the world (cf. Jn 3:16; Rom 8:32), by making him the redemption of the world and by reconciling mankind with himself (cf. Rom 5:10; 2 Cor 5:18–20; Eph 2:6; Col 1:22).[18]

For Christ did not only acquire for mankind the right to salvation, through his Father and in the Spirit, he *became* in person the mystery of salvation: 'You (the human race) God has made members of Christ Jesus and by God's doing he has *become*' wisdom (the realization of the plan of wisdom), virtue, holiness and redemption (cf. 1 Cor 1:30). Salvation was accomplished in the filial mystery of Christ, with which we were called to enter into communion (cf. 1 Cor 1:30; Rom 3:24). The letter to the Hebrews is explicit: 'Although he was Son, he learnt to obey through suffering; but having been made perfect, he became for all who obey him the source of eternal salvation' (5:8f.). In St John two theologies, apparently contradictory, appear: sometimes the incarnation, sometimes the passover of Jesus is given as the mystery of salvation. Yet John's thought is coherent: in the passover of Jesus it is mystery of the incarnation, that of sonship, that is firmly established.

In Jesus the messianic, redemptive function is identical with the mystery of sonship, the Spirit living in him is the consecration of redemptive messiahship and at the same time the seal of sonship. *As the Spirit of sonship, his role is essential in the mystery of salvation, which is none other than the mystery of sonship in its accomplishment.*

★ ★ ★

On earth every human being is in process of becoming; he has to become a human being according to his potentialities in his physical, psychological being and above all in his personal integrity which matures slowly through free choices. A Christian, too, has to become Christian. Having clothed himself with Christ in baptism (cf. Gal 3:27), he must ceaselessly 'clothe himself' with him (cf. Rom 13:14); pure unleavened bread, he must ever purify himself of the old leaven (cf. 1 Cor 5:7); brought back to God, he must look for the things that are above (cf. Col 3:1–3) until death, when the seal will be set on the identifying communion with Christ in his passover (cf. Rom 6:3 and 2 Tim 2:11).

Jesus shared our earthly condition, and by this very fact he was subject to the law of history. Although Son of God in the Spirit from his human beginning, he yet had to become what he was, to consent freely to the mystery of his sonship, always accepting his identity from his Father, and receiving power from him (cf. Jn 5:36; 10:25), uttering his Father's words (cf. Jn 14:24; 17:14) and living on the daily bread of his will (cf. Jn 4:34), finally accepting, in death, no longer to exist except through the Father who begets him.

The Spirit is the agent of sacred history above all in Christ. By means of his human freedom, Jesus becomes through the power of the Spirit what, in the Spirit, he is from the beginning: the Son of God in the world.[19]

Jesus had the heart of a son. Where did he get this from? After his conversion St Paul experienced a sensation which astonished him, it was that of a divine intimacy with God which made him cry out: 'Abba! Father!' (Gal 4:6). It was doubtless thus that he discovered within himself the presence, hitherto unknown, of the 'Spirit of the Son'. Jesus says little about the Spirit, we do not learn from him that the Spirit lived in his heart and made him a son. He was Son by birth and had never known God in any other way than as his Father; for him a filial attitude was entirely natural.[20] To him belonged this expression of tenderness, this word of childlike intimacy, a word unknown until then to Jewish piety, 'Abba'.[21] This invocation rose instinctively to his lips as a cry from the heart. As Christians we know that this cry is that of the Spirit poured into our hearts. The Apostle assures us that the cry 'Abba!', which thenceforth rises from the heart of the faithful, is the cry of the Spirit, that this Spirit is that of the child of God *par excellence*, the Spirit of divine sonship. It is in communion with Christ that, in the Spirit, we say 'Father!'

Jesus is son above all in his death. It is in the mystery of death that a person arrives at an achievement which is eternal. Nothing that precedes is perfect; a good act performed today, intended to be definitive, has to be repeated tomorrow; save in death, no human decision is truly decisive. And Jesus is man. It is in his death that his being as man, son of God, finds its crowning triumph. The letter to the Hebrews says several times that Jesus was 'made perfect' in death (cf. 2:10; 5:9; 7:28).

The death of Jesus is the climax of sonship. Jesus is the Word who 'was with God', 'the only Son who is nearest to the Father's heart' (Jn 1:1, 18), he became so in the fullness of truth when *his* Hour came, the one that characterizes him, the 'filial hour' when he passes from this world to the Father (cf. Jn 13:1). In this passage he is pre-eminently the Son who is with the Father; the mystery of salvation is that of Jesus in his 'accomplished' sonship. The letter to the Hebrews represents the redemptive act as the entry of Jesus through the veil of flesh (cf. 10:20) into the heavenly Holy of Holies, that is, into intimate divine communion, through winning an eternal redemption (cf. 9:11).[22]

Moreover, it is 'through the eternal Spirit' that Christ was thus offered (cf. Heb 9:14) by entering into divine communion. Would he have been able to ascend to the Father without that strength from on high which is the Spirit? As an earthly man whose existence according to the flesh was limited, would he have been able to accept the fullness of God without the Spirit who is contrary to the flesh, who is infinite openness? In his death is fullness of the Spirit.

It is there that the total submission of Jesus to his Father is realized. Just as a Christian arrives through his trials at a deep acceptance, a consenting to what God sends him, that he has not previously experienced, so Christ 'learnt to obey through suffering' (Heb 5:8), complete obedience even unto death (Ph 2:8), and was thus 'made perfect' (Heb 5:9). According to St John, obedience is a manifestation of Jesus' divine sonship (cf. e.g. Jn 4:34; 10:17f.; 14:31). Moreover, the spirit of filial submission is the fruit of the presence of the one who is the Spirit of the Son.

To return to God, Jesus had to rise to the total gift of himself. On earth everything is in process of becoming, all is fragmentary; apart from dying for love of another, there is no absolute gift of self (cf. Jn 15:13). Jesus says: 'That the world may know that I love the Father...' to signify that his death is out of love (cf. Jn 14:31). St John writes: 'This has taught us love – that he gave up his life for us' (1 Jn 3:16). In death Jesus is identified in his whole being with love, returning to God who is love. Furthermore, it is the Spirit who is the love of God poured into our hearts. When, in death, Jesus became love, he also 'became spirit' (cf. 1 Cor 15:45).

Jesus had to become open to God's universality, beyond the limits imposed on him by time, space and membership of a nation (cf. Mt 15:24), in order to include all mankind in the salvation brought about in his person (cf. Gal 3:28). Whereas flesh is enclosed in itself, the Spirit is infinite openness, limitless communion.

Jesus put all his faith in the Father and committed himself into the hands (cf. Lk 23:46) that save from death. However, no one can believe except through 'the Spirit of faith' (cf. 2 Cor 4:13). The Spirit of sonship is, as such, the Spirit of faith. He gives the faithful strength to believe (cf. 1 Cor 12:3) and was the source of perfect faith first of all for Jesus, who, in his death, became for all mankind the precursor (cf. Heb 6:20) of the faith in God which saves from death.

The first Christians noted the time when Jesus died: 'It was the ninth hour', Israel's official hour for prayer. This coincidence was significant for them: their Master died at the time for prayer! When Luke shows Jesus as a great man of prayer, his intention is theological: this man lived in intimacy with God, he is 'holy, son of God'. The word 'Father' is contained in the first words of Jesus reported by Luke (cf. 2:49) and in the last words (cf. 23:46): the first protest his communion with the Father, the last manifest his entry into total communion. In this final prayer expression is given to the movement of the spirit of Jesus, the meaning therefore of his death. Jesus worships in such a way that the sacrificial rites are replaced by a heart at prayer: 'You took no pleasure in holocausts or sacrifices for sin; then I said..."God, here I am! I am coming to do your will" ' (Heb 10:6f.). Death and resurrection are portrayed in Hebrews 5:7–9 in the form of a prayer of entreaty that is heard: 'During his life on earth he offered up prayer and entreaty...to the one who had the power to save him out of death and he submitted so humbly that his prayer was heard. Having been made perfect he became...the source of salvation'.

Prayer is the 'raising of the mind to God'.[23] Jesus was often thus raised in prayer to the Father, his prayer expressed the filial mystery which is being with the Father. When the hour comes for him to pass from this world to the Father (cf. Jn 13:1), he is raised in prayer to God with his whole being, *he becomes prayer*, the Son who is wholly with God.[24] The passover of death and resurrection is the mystery of Jesus become prayer. Moreover, it is the Holy Spirit who releases the movement of prayer, making it filial: his presence in the heart is a prayer (cf. Rom 8:23–27), just as it is love (cf. Rom 5:5). In his death Jesus became both prayer and 'spirit' (cf. 1 Cor 15:45) and it is thus that he is the Son in all truth.

Such is the work accomplished for the salvation of the world: through his human freedom and in the strength of the Spirit, Jesus consents fully to the Father's gift which, in this same Spirit, begets him and makes him the universal source of salvation (cf. Heb 5:9).

*　　*　　*

Any theology which ignores the role of the Spirit in the work of salvation ignores the salvific meaning of the resurrection. Such a theology is turned towards the past: a religion of sin and its expiation long since completed. A theology of death alone does not know the real meaning of this death, does not know that it is filial fulfilment, filled with the Holy Spirit and creative power, and that it constitutes a single mystery with the resurrection.[25]

The work of redemption is first and foremost God's affair: the initiative for it is his right as Father, since it is carried out through the begetting of the Son in this world through the power of the Spirit. Christ did not have to take the first step, to pay a price which would reconcile God with man. His role was to consent, through his human freedom, to the God and Father who begot him. This he did through the Spirit of his divine sonship.

Furthermore, the redemption is not limited to the expiation of sin. Redemption is God giving birth and bringing creation to fulfilment and it is the resurrection from the dead through the use of the power of the Spirit. Although this redemption is rooted in history, at the time of Pontius Pilate, it constitutes the eschatological mystery, the coming fulfilment in which human beings are called to participate (cf. 1 Cor 1:9; Col 2:9f.). Christianity is a religion of hope.

As for sin, it is abolished, not in virtue of a price paid that God may be reconciled: it is removed in the sanctity of the heavenly Lamb.[26] God forgives sin, neither by effacing it, as if it were a stain, nor by forgetting it. In all his action God is father and creator through the Holy Spirit. *He destroys sin by begetting his Son in our world in the sanctity of the Spirit*, by calling mankind to communion with this Son, by thus creating a world of sanctity. Whoever eats the Lamb of God is purified from all sin, in the sanctity of the Spirit who consumes this Lamb (cf. Jn 1:29, 33).

Salvation consists in communion. The eschatological covenant formerly announced is now concluded and sealed for ever. It is engraved in the mystery of God. For a man, Jesus, is integrated into the mystery of the Trinity for the sake of mankind. In the midst of human beings and for them, Jesus was begotten by the Father in the Spirit. It is for them, henceforth, to enter into this covenant by allowing themselves to be drawn to 'communion with the Son' (cf. 1 Cor 1:9).

★   ★   ★

In the work of redemption the Spirit plays the role that is proper to him in the mystery of the Trinity: he is the Spirit of sonship in whom the Father begets. His action throughout sacred history and in the death of Christ is at the service of the Father who begets and at the service of Christ, so that the divine sonship may be accomplished through him, and from him spread abroad.

In the Trinity the Spirit is the person who provides a personal character for living beings. The Father begets through the Spirit and thus constitutes himself as a person; the Son is begotten through the Spirit and is similarly constituted as a person. In the world too the action of the Spirit establishes a personal character. Thanks to him creation is raised to that summit which is the human person. Adam vivified by the Breath appears as a person among other living beings. *In the Spirit, the man Jesus receives divine personality*, is assumed into the person of the Word: 'The Holy Spirit will come upon you...and so the child will be holy and will be called Son of God' (Lk 1:35). When Jesus rises from the dead in the fullness of the Spirit, this granting of a divine personality is confirmed in him as immutable reality. The Spirit is the agent of salvation in Jesus Christ in the same way as he is the intimate movement of God by which the Father begets *his Son* through the sanctity of the Spirit.

The salvific mystery is identical with the personal mystery of Jesus. It is the mystery of a man who, in his life and in his death, is begotten through the Holy Spirit and receives divine personality through this Spirit.[27]

Christ–Spirit

In death and in glory, the intimacy of Christ and the Spirit is such that they seem henceforth to form a whole: Christ 'has become...spirit' (1 Cor 15:45). The work of salvation was accomplished in a process of complete spiritualization in which the attributes of the Spirit – holiness, power, infinite life, gift of self – became, in their very transcendence, proper to Christ.[28]

The risen Jesus is an unfathomable mystery. The paradox of the incarnation, that of a man who is God, reaches its climax:

Jesus is the heavenly man (cf. 1 Cor 15:48f.), the Trinity is his habitat.

He entered into the Trinity through birth: God raises him from the dead by saying: 'You are my Son, today I have begotten you' (cf. Acts 13:33; Heb 1:5). The whole of his human being is woven, by the Spirit, into his eternal filial origin; his earthly life-history comes to its completion in the beginning, there where the Son is: the climax of his life is also his birth. Henceforth he does not grow older; he will never go beyond this moment. For the Spirit who animates him is life as it is outpoured in his boundless triumph over death. Jesus is for ever newborn in the Spirit. To the eternal begetting in the Spirit there corresponds, again in the Spirit, the eternal cry of love and gratitude: 'Abba! Father!'. When men enter into affiliation with him, the outdated Adam is abolished in them; they too become new, filial creatures and their voice becomes one with that of the Son as they invoke the Father.

Transformed in the Spirit, *Jesus is gift of self, sharing and communion*; he rises again in person, in the form of community, a single grain of wheat, but one whose fruit is manifold, in the power of the Spirit who is *one* person in many. Henceforth these words are confirmed: 'I am in my Father and you in me and I in you' (Jn 14:20; 17:21).

The Spirit raises Jesus *without denying his death*. It is here that he makes him fully a person by wholly divinizing him.[29] He is the movement that brings about the ascent of Jesus to the Father, he does not do this without yielding him to death. Himself essentially self-giving, he brings Jesus to the supreme gift of love in death. Himself communion, he glorifies Jesus by the encounter with the Father in death. The Spirit does not give the lie to the death of Jesus, a death which is full of him. Jesus offered himself in an eternal Spirit (cf. Heb 9:14); the offering, like the Spirit, is eternal, in a liturgy celebrated 'once and for all' (Heb 9:12). Death is the mystery of the incarnation in its greatest depths, there the earthly life-history of Jesus culminates in a heavenly fulfilment: never again does Jesus leave these heights. Death and glory are aspects of a single mystery in which the standing Lamb is immolated (cf. Rev 5:6), in a glory which does not follow death but consecrates it. The Spirit glorified Jesus in granting him a death divinely filial; it is here that Jesus is reunited for ever, in love, with his Father who is love.

Jesus is henceforth identified with his mission of salvation; 'become spirit' (cf. 1 Cor 15:45), he has 'become redemption' (cf. 1 Cor 1:30). The Spirit, who is action, makes of him the very event of salvation, 'Christ our passover' (1 Cor 5:7). Jesus is eternal in the gift of himself, in the consent he gives to his Father, in redemptive merit.

It is hard for us to imagine such an existence: a person who is both immolated and glorious, and at the same time an event. – All revelation is made in the Holy Spirit; when he takes possession of Jesus and glorifies him, he reveals him to the world, but by making him a mystery. For he himself is the unfathomable mystery of God...

This immolated Lamb is, as such, the lion of Judah (cf. Rev 5:5f.). God has given him the Name which belongs to him, that of *Lord*, before whom every knee bends; he has set him up as 'Son of God in power', 'Lord of glory' (cf. Ph 2:11; Rom 1:4; 10:9; 1 Cor 2:8). For the Spirit in whom God raises him from the dead is the infinite power of God.

Previously, although Son, he had been subject to the condition of a slave (cf. Ph 2:7) by belonging to a race, by obedience to the Mosaic law (cf. Gal 4:4) and by subjection to the numerous laws of the human condition. His life and activity were restricted by the limits of time and space. Now he is *free*, with the freedom of God: 'Where the Spirit of the Lord is, there is freedom' (2 Cor 3:17). The Spirit comes and goes mysteriously, defying all restraint, establishing freedom by his presence (cf. Rom 8:2). All barriers are removed in the risen Christ, all helplessness is withdrawn and the Law is abolished. Even in his existence according to the flesh Jesus was a free man, in the measure in which, even then, his life was borne along by the Spirit; in the fullness of the Spirit he *is* freedom and deliverance.

Whereas the flesh is selfish and enclosed in itself, the Spirit is love; by raising Christ from the dead, he imposes on him his law. While on earth Jesus existed for others; glorified, he lives in death for each individual, *he exists to give himself*; he is not only kind, but has become kindness itself. In the Spirit, who is the outpouring of God, he has 'become life-giving spirit' (1

Cor 15:45), boundless friendship, gift of self and communion. His symbol is the bread eaten and the cup offered.

In those who are in Christ, *every difference which separates is abolished*: 'there are no more distinctions between Jew and Greek...all of you are one in Christ Jesus' (Gal 3:28). The spirit is a power for love, intent on the times running their course to the end and on 'bringing everything together under Christ as head' (cf. Eph 1:10). In the realms of the Spirit of unity, there can be no distinctions that separate; the only possible difference is that of greater or lesser unity.

Because the Spirit is the eternal fulfilment, the risen Christ, who is, as it were, 'the body of the Spirit',[30] has also become *the heavenly fulfilment* (cf. Col 2:9), but this fulfilment is henceforth within the world. He is 'the spirit' who gives meaning to everything (cf. 2 Cor 3:17). Easter is the central and final day in sacred history, when all is accomplished, towards which all is created, the day of rest for God, that is, from his activity now come to its peaceful climax, that rest to which human beings are called (cf. Heb 4:2–11). The Easter Christ is the supreme triumph of the works of the Spirit, the Kingdom of God, the paradise God creates for himself, where he walks in the world (cf. Gen 3:8), coming out of himself without leaving himself, the paradise too for human beings where the first companion of Christ's passover, the good thief, enters (cf. Lk 23:43), where all the faithful enter: 'he brought us to life with Christ...and gave us a place with him in heaven, in Christ Jesus' (Eph 2:6). Raised to life in the Spirit, Jesus is not only the spiritual, heavenly man, he is the spirit (cf. 2 Cor 3:17) and constitutes heaven. Final reality belongs to him alone. The creative work of the Spirit is achieved when the Son is fully begotten in the world, just as within the Trinity the Son is the goal of the activity of the Father in the Holy Spirit.

Christ is also the beginning of creation: 'He is the image of the unseen God and the first-born of all creation, for in him were created all things...through him and for him. Before anything was created, he existed, and he holds all things in unity' (cf. Col 1:15–17; 1 Cor 8:6; Rev 3:14). Doubtless, the coming of Christ is the last age in history; his glorification introduces the final conclusion of creation whose fulfilment is yet to come.

Indeed, Christian faith has recognized in him the beginning of creation, the first-born of every creature. *For all begins with the begetting of the Son in the world*; there the whole action of the Spirit is concentrated and thence it is deployed; from this fullness flows everything. It is not easy to imagine that the future of the world is also its starting-point; but if Christ lives in the fullness of the Spirit and thus holds in his possession creative being and life and power in their totality, nothing is created, except in relationship with this totality. He is the source within the world where all begins and is completed: 'I am the Alpha and the Omega, the Beginning and the End' (Rev 21:6).

This cosmic role of Christ is implicitly recognized in the title 'Lord' bestowed on him in his glory (cf. Ph 2:9–11). This name belongs to God in virtue of his creative presence which fills the world. Glorified in the fullness of the Spirit, Christ shares with the Father indivisible omnipotence which extends to the deepest origins of the world. That is why the Apostle can write: 'There is one Lord, Jesus Christ, through whom all things come' (1 Cor 8:6).

The world bears in its heart and at its roots this mystery of fulfilment, and therefore of eternity: the begetting of the Son within a creation. Creation has a beginning, *but its beginning is steeped in eternity*. This beginning is the first-born of every creature begotten by the Father in the fullness of the Spirit, in the eternal today.[31]

Thus the fact is verified once more that the Spirit is at the beginning and the end, in everything. Christ is the Alpha and Omega of creation, but in the Spirit. The fact is also once more verified that the action of the Spirit in the world is at the service of the begetting of the Son through whom God creates everything.

The lordship of Christ is salvific: the power of the Spirit is given to him in death for the many. He is creator of the world in that he is given for the life of the world: *his cosmic lordship is identical with his redemptive power*. Every human being is created in Christ and through a call, 'unto him', and therefore exists within the mystery of salvation, is commissioned through creation for communion with Christ on his Day, and in some fashion already shares in it (cf. Vatican II, *LG* 16).

The Spirit is love in his creative activity, he is the love of the Father who begets his Son in the world and who, in this begetting, creates the world. The *redemptive* sonship of Christ is the initial mystery where creation is anchored, towards which all is created...A vast field is open here for Christian meditation, for hope and gratitude.[32]

Sent in the Spirit[33]

The Spirit is simultaneously the intimacy of God and his transcendence – glorified in him, Christ is at the same time exalted to the heights of God – 'I am going away', he says – and having been sent into the world: 'I will come back to you' (Jn 14:18, 28). Easter is the climax of the mystery of the incarnation which John defines as Christ consecrated to God and sent into the world (cf. 10:36).[34]

If in his passover Christ had not been sent into the world, neither his glorious death nor his birth would be 'for us', both would remain without impact on the world. For the death of one person is not that of another, it is this individual man in his death, inseparable from him. It is the same with birth. It is impossible to share with another one's own dying and birth. But the death of Christ is full of the Holy Spirit who is openness, gift of self, communication of self; by this fact Christ is, in his very death, divinely glorified, sent and given in communion. It is thus that he 'died and was raised to life for us' (2 Cor 5:15), *becoming ours in his death and resurrection.*

The 'sending' proper to the paschal mystery is expressed in many ways. The glorification is a sending by God: 'It was for you in the first place that God raised up his Servant and sent him to bless you' (Acts 3:26). The glorification is a coming: 'I will come back to you' (Jn 14:28). It is an appearance: 'You will see me' (Jn 16:16). It is a presence in the Church: 'I am with you' (Mt 28:20). The glorification is also a gift to the Church: (God) 'made him, as the ruler of everything, the head of the Church' (Eph 1:22). Jesus 'rose higher than all the heavens to fill all things' (Eph 4:10).

In a language less full of images, Scripture expresses the same reality when it says of Christ: (he) 'has become a life-

giving spirit' (1 Cor 15:45). Raised in the Spirit, he thenceforth exists to give himself, to communicate himself, the very
personification of communion. The Spirit exercises on him the
personalizing action proper to him – first of all in the Trinity
(see below, pp. 146–147) – making him subsist in himself and
at the same time wholly in reference to others.

In other words, we can say that Christ has made himself the
Good News. He did not only preach the Good News, he
became the content of the Good News; in the Holy Spirit who
is the fullness of the gift of God, he is the Good News in its
reality and in its diffusion.

★   ★   ★

The early Christians had an extraordinary intuition about the
sending of Christ to those who had died before him: 'In the
body he was put to death, in the spirit he was raised to life,
and in the spirit he went to preach to the spirits in prison' (1
Pet 3:18f.); 'the dead had to be told the Good News as well, so
that though...they had been through the judgement that
comes to all humanity, they might come to God's life in the
spirit' (1 Pet 4:6).[35]

No one can enter the Kingdom except through Christ, who
is the door.[36] We go through this door thanks to faith, which
enables us to accept Christ and adhere to him. But how can we
accept and adhere to him if we have not encountered him? The
just of the Old Testament, who had not encountered him
during their life on earth, could not accept him; 'they did not
receive what was promised...they were not to reach perfection
except with us'. They had to wait and enter into communion
with Christ together with Christians (cf. Heb 11:39f.). Behind
the images in which early Christian literature describes the
descent of Jesus into hell, the meaning is that *in his glorifying
death* – 'brought to life in the Spirit' – *Christ met in their death
the people who died before him and in this encounter enabled them
to share in his saving passover.*

In our times, too, the majority of people are 'pre-Christian':
they do not arrive, during their earthly life, at the 'now' of
salvation, of which St Paul often speaks and which is found in
the meeting in faith with Christ in his passover. They have not
been moved by the gospel and are not as yet aware of the end

of time (cf. 1 Cor 10:11). It would seem that, in their death, they too benefit from the descent of Christ to hell which was intended for human beings before Jesus Christ, that is, they benefit from a unifying meeting with him in his glorifying death.

While on earth, the faithful themselves are to some extent 'before' the Easter Christ who is the future of the world. While living in him – 'you are in Christ' (cf. 1 Cor 1:30) – 'they are called to him' (cf. 1 Cor 1:9). In their death they achieve an encounter with him in order to die and be brought to life together with him (2 Tim 2:11).

For all men, Christ in his passover is the mediator of a good death, otherwise he would not be the universal saviour. The Holy Spirit makes him the meeting-point for all at the end of their lives, the eschatological crossroads where the scattered children of God are assembled (cf. Jn 11:52). Christ saves them by joining them in their death; he changes it by reversing it, and makes it like his own death in the Holy Spirit: a passage, an adoptive birth. The text of 1 Thessalonians 4:14, literally translated, is very beautiful: 'Those who have been put to sleep *through* Jesus...'. We die through him; he is, in person, a good death, the passover for mankind. In him we rest far from the world, near God, in order to rise in him.[37]

The sending of Christ into this world will have its full impact on the Day of the Lord. The second coming is not a return after a long absence, it is the resurrection of Christ in the full strength of his impact in the world, his paschal coming in splendour, when men will know Christ in all 'the power of *his* resurrection' (Ph 3:10).

The end of sacred history is to be found where it begins: in the strength of the Spirit in whom the Father begets his Son in this world.

Source of the Spirit

Sent in the power of the Spirit, Christ brings to the world the gift of the Spirit. He does not rise again in the Spirit for himself alone, the outpouring of Easter is intended for the many: 'For us he died and was raised to life' (cf. 2 Cor 5:15). In the superabundance of the Spirit, he is the source of the Spirit.

Paul writes: 'The first man, Adam, became a living soul', an imperfect creature endowed with no more than earthly life, but 'the last Adam has become a life-giving spirit' (cf. 1 Cor 15:45). To signify that the risen Christ is a being open to others through the gift of himself and the radiancy of his life, it would have sufficed to say: 'He has become a spirit'. The Apostle reinforces the statement to bring out the evidence: 'he has become a *life-giving* spirit', a spirit living by radiating life, a source of being, like the Spirit through whom he is transformed.

Christ radiates the Spirit by communicating himself. Unlike the first Adam, he does establish living cells outside himself. Between Jesus and the Spirit the unity is indestructible; the Spirit is spread abroad when Jesus shares himself, when the faithful are taken up into him, in one body, submissive to the power of the Spirit who raises up Christ.[38] Scripture knows nothing of the language of the 'distribution of graces', where these graces are offered as realities in themselves, exterior to Christ; Scripture knows only the language of communion. Christ does not give the Spirit like a fruit plucked from a tree; he gives him in the gift of himself.[39]

For God is a source of the Spirit only in his Son and in favour of him: the Spirit flows from him in the begetting of the Son. When God makes men his sons he does not beget again, he does not infinitely repeat his action of raising from the dead: he raises his only Son in the Spirit and he begets and raises men 'together with him' in communion with the Spirit. Just as God has nothing to say apart from his Word, nothing to add, so he grants no grace apart from the total gift of the Spirit who raises the Son (cf. Col 2:9f.). The Spirit is not given apart from the Son; the Son is the future towards which the world is called.

★ ★ ★

St John says: 'On the last day and greatest day of the festival (of Tents), Jesus stood in the Temple and cried out:
   "If any man is thirsty, let him come to me!
   Let the man come and drink who believes in me!"
According to the words of Scripture: "from his breast will flow fountains of living water" '. The evangelist explains: 'He

was speaking of the Spirit which those who believed in him were to receive; for there was no Spirit as yet because Jesus had not yet been glorified' (7:37–39).

Among the Jewish festivals that of Tents was the most spectacular, 'the greatest and the most holy'.[40] It recalled the spring of water flowing from the rock and anticipated the days of the Messiah when God would cause the same spring to well up (cf. Is 43:20), when water would flow from under the Temple (cf. Ezek 47:1), when the Spirit would be poured out on the whole nation (cf. Ezek 36:25–27). Now here comes someone who proclaims that the hour has come when from his own side will flow the rivers of water of the Spirit.

This gift will be a new one. First of all because of its abundance: the waters will flow like rivers. It will be new by its very nature, so different that the evangelist can say that before this there had been no Spirit. No one had ever known in Israel a Spirit of the kind now given.

He will be given by Christ in glory; the departure of Jesus is the condition for him to be given: 'Unless I go, the Advocate will not come to you; but if I do go, I will send him to you' (Jn 16:7). We know the meaning of this departure: the ascension into heaven of which John speaks is not spatial; it is an exaltation within the divine mystery, a passage from this world to the Father, a divinizing transformation in death. Being heavenly, the Spirit is sent only from heaven: 'I shall send to you, from the Father, the Spirit of truth who issues from the Father' (Jn 15:26); 'it is (therefore) for your good that I am going' (Jn 16:7). The sending of the Spirit forms part of the paschal mystery: dead for the salvation of the world, Jesus died to give the Holy Spirit.

The place whence he flows is the body of Jesus: a tempestuous fountain will pour out from his side once Christ wholly inhabits his Father. The heavenly waters of which God alone is the source are born in this world in a man: this statement is revolutionary, it presupposes a man assumed into God even in his body.

The words he cried out on the feast of Tents were prophetic; Moses had to strike the rock, the side of Christ had first to be pierced. Ezekiel had seen water flow from under the threshold of the right side of the Temple; according to

Zechariah 12:9 – 13:1, a fountain 'will be opened from the house of David and the children of Jerusalem...a spirit of goodwill and supplication' will be poured out on them when the one sent by God has been pierced. On Calvary 'one of the soldiers pierced his side with a lance; and immediately there came out blood and water' (Jn 19:34).

The episode is so important that the evangelist feels he must confirm his testimony with an oath: 'This is the evidence of one who saw it...and he[41] knows he speaks the truth' (19:35). Here the whole of John's gospel, 'recorded so that you may believe' (20:31), reaches its climax. The whole of the mystery of faith is revealed in this event.

Blood and water have the value of symbols. In the Bible, blood often designates man as a victim of violence. The blood of Christ which purifies us today (cf. 1 Jn 1:7) and is for evermore at the service of the faithful (cf. Rev 7:14), with which they are sprinkled (cf. Heb 12:24; 1 Pet 1:2) in baptism and during the course of their life, this blood which the faithful drink from the chalice at the Eucharist and which forms part of an eternal liturgy, is not only blood shed in the past: it points to Christ himself in his immolation. The blood which flows from his open side is the symbol of Christ in his immolation.

In the symbolism of the fourth gospel, water is a heavenly principle.[42] Sometimes it is understood in a metaphorical sense and suggests the gift of eternal life (cf. 4:14), which is really the Spirit whose source is Christ (cf. 7:37). Sometimes it is real water used as a symbol: that of baptism (cf. 3:5), or again the water through which the man born blind is healed, recalling baptism.[43] Furthermore, baptism brings about birth in water and the Spirit (cf. 3:5), the Spirit whose symbol is water.

Therefore blood and water symbolize the pierced Christ and the Spirit who flows from his side. Blood is named first, for, before the fountain, we have the earth whence it flows, we have the wound from which the water pours out; before the gift of the Spirit, we have Christ who mediates him. Until the end of time (cf. Rev 1:7), men will be able to contemplate the image as seen by the eyes of the evangelist: 'they will look on him whom they have pierced' (Jn 19:37). In faith they will come (cf. 7:37) and drink of the rivers of the Spirit.[44]

Jesus had announced that rivers would flow 'from his side'; today we should say 'from his heart'. The fountain springs up from the depths of the mystery and flows from his open side. These two things are worthy of note. The Spirit is the inwardness of God, he rises forcefully from the depths, a powerful rapture and at the same time a mystery. He flows from Christ's side, from his human body, revealing a paradoxical closeness to material realities. The Spirit of God is present to mankind in the body of a human being!

Still more astonishing: the focal point of this welling up is in this body as it is immolated. The rock was struck, the body was pierced 'and *immediately* there came out blood and water' (Jn 19:34). The relationship between the blood and the water, between death and the Spirit, is unbroken. The Spirit of infinite life, whose power is boundless, who is unafraid of death, at the same time utterly transforms death, without abolishing it, into life and power. This convergence of death and the Spirit would seem already to be ratified by John when he writes: 'and bowing his head, he gave up the spirit' (Jn 19:30). Doubtless we must understand that at the same time as Jesus gave up the spirit, he sent forth the Holy Spirit.[45] At this moment 'all is accomplished', the work is finished (cf. 19:30). The mystery of this death is indeed immense, and this Spirit too is full of mystery in his association with death!

Whence comes this convergence of death and the Spirit? Is it not because the death of the Son is the coming into this world of God in all his trinitarian holiness, the coming into history of the God of love? In order that the Spirit may be dispersed through the world as he lives in God, infinite love, it was necessary that, in the death of Jesus, God should enter the world as infinite love. The mystery of the glorious cross is the mystery of the Trinity aligning itself with the world.

The Father was entirely involved in creation when 'he did not spare his own Son' (Jn 3:16; Rom 8:32), when in his Son he did not spare himself. All his fatherly love is therefore expressed as love of mankind. In the paschal mystery, God reveals himself as father of Jesus for man's benefit, *he begets him by giving him up for men*. But it is the Spirit who is the love of the Father, it is through him that he begets his Son, it is he who, in the death of Jesus, comes into the world.

As regards Jesus, he in his turn accepts death, no longer to exist except through his Father, he consents without reserve to be the Son. Then his Father brings it about that 'in his body dwells the fulness of divinity' (Col 2:9), the fullness which is the Spirit. The death of Jesus is a passover, the powerful passage from this world to the Father, in which Jesus becomes, with the whole of his humanity, the Son who is 'with the Father'. Moreover, the Spirit is in person the mighty movement which bears the Son to the Father. It is he who gives the death of Jesus its paschal meaning, it is through him that Jesus, 'offered...through the eternal Spirit' (Heb 9:14), dies and leaves this world to go to the Father. *The death of Jesus is the fullness of the Holy Spirit, now within creation.*

The Spirit who flows out in the death of Jesus is therefore truly the Spirit of the Father in his fatherhood, the Spirit of the Son in his sonship. Nowhere, except in the glorious death of Jesus, is the Spirit thus present in the world; never before had he been given as he flows out in this glorious death: 'There was no Spirit as yet because Jesus had not yet been glorified' (Jn 7:37).

We can understand too that the fountain flows from *his wounded body*. For it is through this body that Christ is in touch with human beings: in order to become in his body the source of the Spirit it was necessary for Jesus to be born of his Father even in his body – which previously was earthly and fashioned in the likeness of sinful flesh (cf. Rom 8:3). It is from his open heart that the waters flow, for the Spirit has his source in the heart, where Christ is most fully himself, that is, in the depths of his person, in his relationship with his Father. From then onwards we can say that the heart of Christ has become the heart of the world and here it is that the Spirit of God flows, in whom the world lives and breathes.

We do not lack light to clarify the strange convergence of death and the spring of water. Yet the contemplation of the one who was pierced will always give rise in the faithful to admiration full of astonishment, and simultaneously to joy and thanksgiving.

When Jesus appeared at Easter, he showed the wound in his side (cf. Jn 20:20f.). The reader will then recall the amazing occurrence of the blood and water, the announcement made previously and now achieved: 'Rivers of living water will flow from his side'.[46] In all ages the Church contemplates this Christ and takes up the testimony of the gospel by singing in her liturgy: '*Vidi aquam*...I saw water flowing from the Temple, on the right side, and all those who were touched by this water were saved'.

According to John and Paul, the Spirit is given in encounter with Christ. The faithful approach and drink at the very same fountain from his open heart (cf. 7:37). When Christ is offered to them in the form of the bread of God (6:33), who is 'flesh (given) for the life of the world', they eat and their thirst is assuaged: 'I am the bread of life. He who comes to me will never be hungry; he who believes in me will never thirst' (6:35). This bread appeases thirst too, for the eternal fountain flows for the believer in communion with the body of Christ.[47]

Other texts, outside Pauline and Johannine literature, bear witness that Christ in his glory gives us the Holy Spirit. On the day of Pentecost Peter says: 'Now raised to the heights by God's right hand, he has received from the Father the Holy Spirit who was promised, and what you see and hear is the outpouring of that Spirit' (Acts 2:33). In his glorification Jesus receives the Spirit and radiates him. The first letter of Peter speaks of the 'news they brought you of all the things which have now been announced to you, by those who preached to you the Good News through the Holy Spirit sent from heaven' (1:12). The Spirit who inspires the apostles is sent from heaven, for he is divine transcendence. By whom is he sent? The preceding verse calls him 'the Spirit of Christ', he is therefore sent by Christ. According to Luke: 'Now *I* am sending down to you what the Father has promised' (Lk 24:49).[48]

Here the sovereign greatness to which Christ has been raised is manifested: the Spirit of God is in very truth his Spirit, the Spirit who is at his service. A man has become 'Lord of the Spirit'! But he has become this through the Spirit himself in whom he was raised to life: the one who is gift makes of Christ the giver. The Spirit is at the root of the lordship of the Christ Lord of the Spirit, at the beginning of the life of the one who has become source of life. In Christ, as elsewhere, the Spirit is at the beginning and at the end; he inaugurates the work of salvation and is the gift of salvation.

Because Christ is the image of the invisible God, the manifestation of the eternal mystery, we can conclude that in God the Spirit too is at the beginning and at the end, divine activity begins and is completed in him, the Father begets the Son in the Spirit – who, however, proceeds from the mystery of the Father and the Son. He is *at* the beginning of the trinitarian movement of which the Father is the principle, he is also the final seal of divine perfection.

The Spirit, witness to Jesus

St John introduces an original insight into the theology of the Spirit; for him the Spirit plays the part of witness to Jesus: 'When the Advocate[49] comes, whom I shall send to you from the Father, the Spirit of truth who issues from the Father, he will be my witness' (Jn 15:26).

John the Baptist was the first to bear witness, 'he came as a witness' (1:6). Then it was the Father (cf. 8:18), by means of the works he gave Jesus to carry out (cf. 5:36; 10:25). From Easter onwards the Holy Spirit assumes this role. The testimony was given first by a man, then by divine works; now God in person speaks through his Spirit. From now on the mystery of the Trinity is within the world.

All the political and religious powers of the world, and apparently even God's law, were drawn up against Jesus (cf. 19:7). Jesus found no human advocate and, after the crucifixion which was the compelling proof of his imposture, no one could any longer raise a voice in his favour. The one witness therefore was the Spirit who refuted the world by educating its conscience. As advocate and defender of Jesus, he proved that sin and lies belong to the world, that Jesus is raised to the Father and that the Prince of this world is judged (cf. Jn 16:8–11).[50] When, during the trial, there seemed to be no appeal against his condemnation, a witness emerged capable of confounding all the authorities of the world: 'Jesus is the Son of God...with the Spirit...as witness' (1 Jn 5:5f.).

In the strength of the Spirit God raises Christ to life,

reversing the significance of his death, not only in Jesus but also in human thought: condemnation is changed into glorification; the world of darkness which had triumphed sees itself condemned in its turn (cf. Jn 12:31).

The Spirit bears witness in various ways. He proclaims the resurrection through the mouth of the apostles (cf. Lk 24:48; Acts 1:8, 22; Rev 11:3); this testimony of the Spirit is intended for the whole world. As John understands it, at first the testimony of the Spirit is not intended for the world 'which neither sees nor knows him' (cf. Jn 14:17). The tribunal before which the Spirit makes his voice heard is a nobler one: his testimony is interior; he speaks in the hearts of the faithful, through the faith he enkindles in them.[51] This testimony is convincing: the Spirit speaks by his presence, influencing the heart with his 'interior anointing' (cf. 1 Jn 2:20, 27). The knowledge that he gives is of the heart; the heart has reasons against which no argument of the world or the mind can prevail. The experience the evangelist had of it was so new that he could say: 'There was no Spirit as yet, because Jesus had not been glorified' (cf. 7:39).

The testimony of the apostles, intended for all, proclaims the salvific lordship of Jesus (cf. Acts 2:36); the interior testimony of the Spirit, intended for the community of the faithful, 'will lead them to the complete truth' (Jn 16:13), to the intimate mystery of Jesus, *to his divine sonship* (cf. 1 Jn 5:5f.).[52]

The Paraclete testifies in favour of Jesus because he is the 'Spirit of truth' (cf. 1 Jn 5:6; 4:6; Jn 16:13). This formula is astonishing. For the Spirit is power, the principle of action, love; he represents in God the aspect of will, whereas light and truth are ordinarily attributes of Jesus: 'I am...the Truth' (Jn 14:6).

However, there is a close link between the Spirit and truth, just as there is between the Spirit and Christ who is truth. In the Old Testament the Spirit of wisdom fills the leaders given by God to his people (cf. Num 27:15f.; Dt 34:9); he gives 'knowledge for every kind of craft' (cf. Ex 31:3; 35:31); he rests, as the Spirit of wisdom, on the messianic king (cf. Is 11:2). The book of Wisdom simply identifies the Spirit and God's Wisdom.[53] The New Testament can distinguish them:

however, it attributes to the Spirit a role connected with knowledge. At a tribunal 'the Spirit will teach you what you must say' (Lk 12:12); he will instruct the hearts of the disciples (cf. Jn 14:26). Jesus had said everything (cf. Jn 15:15), and yet he still had many things to say (cf. Jn 16:12), for his mystery, even when revealed, remains unfathomable. The role of the Spirit would be to recall everything (cf. 14:26) and to interpret Jesus, to 'lead to the complete truth' (Jn 16:13).

The attributes of power and love proper to the Spirit are not hereby contradicted. The text, which very forcibly underlines the illuminating action of the Spirit – 'he will lead to the complete truth' – does not present the Spirit as light, it recognizes in him the role of discovering the truth, of leading to it. The Spirit is action, he is revelation; without being the light, he enables us to perceive it. In short, 'the Spirit is the truth (1 Jn 5:6) because it is he who communicates it'.[54]

He enables us to know the mystery because he enables us to be united with it; he teaches according to his nature, which is to be charity, relationship, divine inwardness communicating itself. Christian knowledge comes from the heart, it comes from encounter. We see with the eyes of the heart (cf. Eph 1:18) which are opened through the influence of the interior mystery, just as a bud blossoms through the thrust of the sap. We know each other by possessing each other: Jesus knows *his* sheep and *his* sheep know him; they are his and belong to him through the gift of his life (cf. Jn 10:14f.). It is thus that the Father and the Son know one another. Without being light in person, the Spirit enlightens the faithful; he causes them to see the light by uniting them with it.

The light is Christ, but it remains invisible without this witness. No one knows Jesus as Son of God except by being united with him in his sonship, in a co-birth where the Spirit enables us to share the life of sonship: 'You will see me because I live and you will live' (Jn 14:19). We have access to the Son by being united with his life, that of the Spirit. The Son and the Spirit are inseparable.

4

The Spirit in the Church

According to Matthew 26:64, Jesus says: 'From this time onward you will see the Son of Man seated at the right hand of the Power and coming on the clouds of heaven.' In the prophecy of Daniel, the Son of man who comes on the clouds of heaven is the symbol of the kingdom that God will entrust to his people (cf. Dan 7:13f.; 18:27). Before the Sanhedrin, Jesus announces not only his own glorification, but also the coming to fruition of his message concerning the coming of the Kingdom. When he rises from the dead, his body is built into the temple of the New Testament (cf. Jn 2:19); the grain of wheat revives and yields a rich harvest (cf. Jn 12:24); the Church is born in the passover of Jesus.

The Christian community was not created *after* the resurrection of Jesus; the wheat does not come *after* the revival of the grain, it *is* the 'resurrection' of the grain itself; Jesus is glorified in person and in the fruit born of his death.[1] According to Ephesians 1:18–22, the Church is the body of Christ in glory; she is not an addition, since she is his body, 'brought to life with Christ' (cf. Eph 2:5f.). Jesus himself rises again and he rises too in the form of community: the Easter event is the coming of the Church.

Furthermore, it is in the Spirit that the Father raises Christ to life.

The Spirit at the beginning of the Church

The birth of the Church, accomplished in the mystery of Christ's passover, is concretely manifested in important gestures and in words: 'The evening of the same day, the first day of the week...Jesus came...and said to them: "Peace be with you. As the Father sent me, so am I sending you"...After saying this he breathed on them and said: "Receive the Holy Spirit. For those whose sins you forgive, they are forgiven" ' (Jn 20:21–23).

Very sensitive to biblical symbolism, John notes that the event dates from the first day of the week. According to the biblical account, creation began at the beginning of a week. The Breath of God hovered over the water; through the action of the Breath, Adam awakened to life. On this other first day of the week, Jesus breathes on the disciples. The gesture is creative, the Church is created in the Spirit of the risen Jesus.

Luke is a story-teller. In the Acts he tells of the birth of the Church disclosed as an historical reality. In this account the heavenly exaltation of Jesus, although inherent in the resurrection, appears only forty days later (cf. Acts 1:9). It is only on the fiftieth day that the outpouring of the Spirit is revealed in all its splendour, although Luke knows that it is part of the Easter glory: 'God raised Jesus to life...Now raised to the heights by God's right hand, he has received from the Father the Holy Spirit...and what you see and hear is the outpouring of that Spirit' (Acts 2:32f.).[2]

According to Acts 1:5, Jesus announced: 'Not many days from now, you will be baptised with the Holy Spirit'. He was speaking to the disciples who were once more to become, by the election of Matthias, the group of the Twelve, symbol of the new Israel. Others join them. When indicating their number, the account seems to stress the meaning: 'There were about a hundred and twenty persons in the congregation' (Acts 1:15). The congregation is marked by the ecclesial number of twelve, multiplied by ten, when the Spirit comes down on the disciples and baptizes them. Such is Luke's way of telling of the mystery of the birth of the Church.[3]

Born in Jerusalem among the Jews, breathed on by the Spirit, the Church grows from this moment, ceaselessly being born in the breath of the same Spirit. It is born among the Jewish heretics in Samaria and among the pagans in Caesarea when the Spirit comes down upon them (cf. Acts 8:14–17; 10:44–48). For the communities already established, it is a continuous beginning: 'In the one Spirit we were all baptised' (1 Cor 12:13). Each community begins in the sacrament of water and the Spirit. In this world where all are born pagans and have yet to become Christians, the Church is always being 'founded'. Even in her baptized members, the Church finds herself involved in a phase of being built into a house where God lives in the Spirit (cf. Eph 2:22).

A place and a date can be assigned to the permanent beginning of the Church: the person of Christ at the hour of his passover when the Spirit is outpoured. She is born of the glorious death 'when all is accomplished', in the living water which flows eternally from the pierced side of Christ, at the moment when Christ is the well-beloved Son, begotten in the Spirit even in his body. *This body is also the Church.*

It is here too that God creates the world, in 'the first-born of all creation', in whom and for whom all was created (cf. Col 1:15–17). But the Church was created in the immediate proximity of Christ, and, more than the rest of the world, she is the body of Christ. She is the first-born in the first-born (Son), the one most deeply rooted in the Son, preceding in divine causality the rest of creation. That is why the letter to the Ephesians shows the origins of the Church as going back into the heavens before the beginning of the world: 'He has blessed us with all the spiritual blessings of heaven in Christ. Before the world was made, he chose us, chose us in Christ' (1:3f.).[4] Christ in glory is the absolute beginning, the first work pronounced by the Father in the Spirit: 'You are my Son; today I have begotten you' (cf. Acts 13:33). Nothing, in divine causality, precedes the 'divine today' which is the begetting of the Son in the world; everything, but in the first place the Church, depends on this.

A Spirit of incorporation

The Spirit acts in Christ as a power both of resurrection and incorporation in Christ; through his action Jesus himself rises again and he rises in the form of community. The same power glorifies Christ and the faithful, by incorporating them into him: 'You have been *raised up with him*...in Christ Jesus' (Col 2:12; cf. Eph 2:5f.).

Thanks to the Spirit, the faithful are constituted as the body of Christ: 'In one Spirit we were all baptised' in a single body which is the body of Christ (cf. 1 Cor 12:13, 27). The frequent formulas 'in one body' and 'in one Spirit' should be thought of together, just as they are found together in Ephesians 4:4: 'one Body, one Spirit'. The presence of the Spirit brings about adherence to Christ: 'Unless you possessed the Spirit of Christ you would not belong to him' (Rom 8:9f.): 'we know that he lives in us by the Spirit that he has given us' (1 Jn 3:24; 4:13).

It is thus that Christ was effectively raised to life *for us* (cf. 2 Cor 5:15); through 'the power of *his* resurrection' (Ph 3:10) man was incorporated in him and 'raised with him'. The Spirit of sonship is a Spirit of incarnation: by integrating the world into the Son, *he gives a body to the Son in the world*. He acts according to his habitual dynamism, like a centrifugal force leading the Son to the deepest point of human existence, and like a power of attraction calling men to the most intimate 'union with his Son' (cf. 1 Cor 1:9).

Within the Church, this power of incorporation is still exercised, even in material realities as well. In her, the body of Christ – the essential symbol – the Spirit creates a sacramental world, the highest point of which is the Eucharist where bread and wine are also incorporated into Christ and become Christ's body. Beyond the confines of the Church, every human being is caught up in this attraction and becomes in some way [5] the body of Christ, a symbol of sonship. The whole of creation is destined to be drawn up one day 'into the glorious freedom of the children of God' (Rom 8:21). This destiny belongs to man in virtue of his creation, for God created the world in and for Christ (cf. Col 1:16) in the power of the Spirit.

This incorporation into Christ is very real. When the Apostle declares: 'In the one Spirit we were all baptised' (in one body) (1 Cor 12:13), this body is more than the union of several in one and the same community of faith and life. The body to which the faithful are joined, in which they are clothed (cf. Gal 3:27), which they become, this body precedes the community (cf. 1 Cor 12:27): it is the body of Christ raised to life by God in the Spirit. It is in him that they become 'one in Christ Jesus' (Gal 3:28). The Church has a sacrament which manifests her mysterious character and the realism of union with the body of Christ: 'The fact that there is only one loaf means that...we form a single body because we all have a share in this one loaf ' (1 Cor 10:17).

All the activity of the Spirit in the Church is concentrated in the Son, in his presence in the world; it enables him to be embodied in the faithful, by incorporating them into himself. When this influence is brought to bear on them at the last day, it will take them up wholly into Christ, rather as it takes up the bread to make it into the very body of Christ in that celebration of the Eucharist which proclaims the resurrection from the dead.

The Spirit of the resurrection of Christ acts differently upon the Church and upon creation in general. In his creative action, omnipotence issues a command: 'He spoke, and it was created' (Ps 33:9). In the Church, omnipotence is infinite love; it attracts, it invites, it woos the heart. The Spirit grants Christ the power to *subdue* everything under his lordship (cf. Ph 3:21); but, in order that he may be her Lord, he makes the Church *his bride*. He is the Lord of the faithful, but our own Lord, to whom the faithful belong because he belongs to them: *our* Lord Jesus Christ.

In Christ and in the Spirit

St Paul created two formulas to characterize the mystery of the Church: he says that the faithful exist and live 'in Christ' and 'in the Spirit'.

These formulas are so close to one another in meaning that some people think of them as synonymous.[6] The faithful are justified, sanctified in Christ and in the Spirit (cf. 1 Cor 1:2, 30; 2 Cor 5:21; Rom 14:17; 15:16); they possess joy and peace in both (cf. Ph 3:1; 4:7; Rom 14:17); the love of God is obtained for them in Christ (cf. Rom 8:39) and in the Spirit (cf. Col 1:8). St Paul states: 'Christ is in you' (Rom 8:10) and 'the Spirit of God has made his home in you' (Rom 8:9); in both the faithful are sons of God (cf. Gal 4:1–7). They are simultaneously christianized and spiritualized. This shows once more the indestructible unity of the Spirit and Christ; the Spirit of God, power, holiness, glory, divine action, is also the Spirit of Christ.

In the harmony of these formulas, an attentive ear can perceive two melodies. Collaboration is perfect, but each one plays his own part. The Spirit is the guest, he inhabits the believer of whom he makes a temple of God: 'You are God's temple and the Spirit of God is living among you' (cf. 1 Cor 3:16), 'your body is the temple of the Holy Spirit' (1 Cor 6:19). The Apostle never says that the Christian is the temple of Christ.[7] Christ does not inhabit the house, he is the foundation (cf. 1 Cor 3:11; Eph 2:20) and the entire building, of which the faithful form part; similarly, he is the head and the whole body, of which the faithful are the members. The difference is that of indwelling and incorporation; the believer is incorporated into Christ and inhabited by the Spirit.

This difference is expressed in many different ways: 'God has sent the Spirit of his Son into our hearts' (Rom 5:5), '(the Spirit) that we carry in our hearts' (2 Cor 1:22), he is 'given', 'received'. He is the gift, the grace, whereas Christ is the mediator of divine gifts (cf. Eph 4:7–13). The faithful are the temple where the Spirit dwells, but they are the body of Christ where the Spirit reigns. The Apostle's formulas are carefully thought out: the faithful 'possess' the Spirit and thus 'belong' to Christ (cf. Rom 8:9). The first fruits of the Spirit in the present time foreshadow the gift of fulfilment, our present belonging to Christ is destined to become full union (cf. 1 Cor 1:9). The Church is the body of Christ through identifying union with him; she is not the body of the Spirit, she is not identified with him.

For the Spirit does not appropriate the faithful to himself; his action is at the service of the Son and of his being begotten in the world. In raising Christ to life, through dwelling in him and sanctifying him, he incorporates men into him, so that through him they may rise again and be sanctified.[8]

In this work Christ is not passive, he is not just a platform on which the Spirit is to build the Church. He has at his service the power of the Spirit (cf. Tit 3:6) and, through it, he unites men to his body. How does he do this? Power is love: by giving himself to men, he unites them to himself. The Eucharist is the manifestation of this; here he incorporates the congregation into himself, nourishing it with his body.

The Church mysterious yet visible

The Church is a mystery, she is an assembly 'in God and in the Lord' (cf. 1 Th 1:1), but she lives in this world and in it she presents the image of a visible, organized society. The unity of the two aspects may be compared with that of the Eucharist which 'is constituted of two things, the one earthly, the other heavenly',[9] comparable first with Christ on earth, whom all could see, but whose real truth remained unknown to most people.

This duality is not analogous with the origin of the Church, which is both of Christ and the Spirit. No one has ever thought that the institutional, sociological aspect of the Church is derived from the incarnation, with the mysterious aspect deriving from the presence of the Spirit. The Church depends in every respect on her double, indivisible origin: through the Spirit and through Christ she is simultaneously an institution and a mystery.

For the Spirit himself is the agent of the incarnation. During the earthly life of Jesus, one could touch with one's hand the Word (cf. 1 Jn 1:1) who was made of flesh through the power of the same Spirit. Now Christ is, through this Spirit, both glorified in God and risen in the midst of this world in the sacramentality of a *visible* Church. The Spirit is the fullness of all that is real: he confers on the Church, which is the body of Christ in this earthly world, a real, earthly existence.

According to what the Apostle says, the Church is the new Covenant (cf. Gal 4:24, 26), the one announced by Jeremiah (31:31) in which the heart of man is full of the Holy Spirit (cf. Ezek 36:27).[10] It finds its expression in the celebration of the Eucharist of which it is said: 'This cup is the new covenant in my blood' (Lk 22:20; 1 Cor 11:25). Moreover, the bread, the wine, the congregation, the Eucharistic meal are ambivalent realities, earthly and eschatological. The congregation gathers at a definite place in the world, at a definite time; but also in a mystical 'place', Christ, and at a mystical 'time', the Hour of the passover. Christ presides invisibly and all the faithful celebrate with him the paschal mystery; yet the priest, a man belonging to this earth, presides visibly, ministers in a central position and it is with him and in his celebration that everyone celebrates. The Eucharistic community is therefore structured. Furthermore, the Eucharist is wholly the work of the Spirit and of Christ. The Church, visible and yet mysterious, is entirely subject to the power of the Spirit and of Christ.

That is why the covenant transmits grace. Baptism is the source of life in that it is a 'washing with water' (cf. Eph 5:26), and the Eucharist is the anticipation of the banquet in the Kingdom, in that it is a meal taken in this world. The Spirit assembles the earthly community and it is this community that diffuses him. The Spirit consecrates ministers and it is they who disseminate him. Grace is conveyed by the institution which itself is stirred to action by the grace of the Spirit.

Rooted in the Spirit, who is communion, the ecclesial institution is at the service of communion. The Eucharist, its constitutive symbol, testifies that communion is the fundamental requirement, for 'the bread that we break is a communion with the body of Christ' (1 Cor 10:16), that is, communion with this body and communion of all the members of this body.[11] The Eucharistic model is indicative of the general thrust; canon law must be inspired by it. If, in the structures of the Church, there are distinctions, they are not intended to separate, but to unite. Thus, the difference which characterizes the priest does not separate him from the faithful, they do not confront each other, nor is he above them; he is drawn into the community, making his ministry a central one.[12] The bishop of Rome is not raised above the episcopate, he is at the heart of collegiality. The Spirit of communion is the first source of Church law; he constitutes true power in the Church, the essential canon law, just as he 'is in person the (moral) law of the New Testament'.[13]

The Spirit of communion tends to make everything personal; he imprints a personal stamp on the ecclesial covenant. The Church is not just a group of individuals, her members are bound to one another by personal bonds; the institution is a network of personal relationships. The activities of the Church – the ministries – are administered by persons, not by bureaucrats and 'hirelings'. The sacraments are not part of an impersonal structure, but lived by those who administer them as by those who receive them. The institutional aspect, inevitable in the Church on earth, must ceaselessly be converted from bureaucracy to personal relationships. The personalization goes so far that the whole Church can be found, in reduced form, in the person of each believer: 'the whole Church is in each one'.[14] The ecclesial institution is faithful to the Spirit who creates it, in the measure in which it brings about a communion of persons, in which the ministries are creators of community.

One, yet made up of many parts

The Church is one, for Christ, with whom she forms one body, is not divided. Unity thus looked at may seem to be uniformity, since in Christ 'there are no more distinctions between Jew and Greek...male and female' (Gal 3:28), and all are one in him. But it is in the Spirit that the Church is baptized into one Christ (cf. 1 Cor 12:13); by this fact the Apostle finds her one, yet made up of many parts, one in an abundant diversity (cf. 1 Cor 12:4–30).

It is the Spirit's role to unite while diversifying, while making the identity of each one manifest. He acts, in that he is love, by creating beings who form relationships, where the union of persons does not abolish but accentuates the identity of each, in the interplay of relationships. The Spirit unifies the Church according to the role he plays in the eternal mystery where the Father is a distinct person because he begets the Son in the Spirit, and the Son is a distinct person because he is begotten through the Spirit; where, however, the Father and the Son are one in the same Spirit, in whom they are diversified. In the Church there is unity in diversity, just as God is one in the Trinity.

The Spirit is paradoxical also in this respect: unique, yet unifying – 'in the one Spirit' (1 Cor 12:13) – he is lavish. The faithful constitute a single body in the diversity of the members; great is the variety of ministries and the gifts of the Spirit which are all exercised in the body of Christ in view of its unity (cf. 1 Cor 12:4–30).

We might think, then, that a Church which tended to uniformity might risk atrophy or turmoil, for it might stifle the Spirit who brings about unity in diversity. This diversity is however the sign of the presence of the Spirit only in integration into unity.

The Spirit given to the Church

The two principles that hold the Church together, Christ and the Spirit, are also those that sanctify her. She is holy in Christ Jesus (cf. 1 Cor 1:2; Ph 1:1) and in the Spirit of our God (cf. 1 Cor 6:11). She is united by the Spirit in a holy place: the body of Christ; and at the moment of all sanctification, when Christ enters into full communion with his Father in the unity of the Spirit. The Church is born in the paschal mystery, at the moment of contact of the Son with the Father, at the point where the Spirit is poured out.

Holiness is a divine attribute: God alone is holy. Creatures are sanctified by being consecrated. This word is a sacrificial one; Jesus says that he is consecrated by his Father (cf. Jn 10:36), like a victim consumed by the fire of a holocaust. Before his death Jesus asks to be glorified (cf. Jn 17:1–3) with the glory which is the Spirit. This is how these words become a reality: 'I consecrate myself ' (Jn 17:19), for 'in an eternal Spirit' Jesus 'becomes a perfect sacrifice to God' (Heb 9:14). United to Christ in his passover the Church in her turn is 'an offering made holy by the Holy Spirit' (Rom 15:16; cf. 2 Th 2:13), holy in Christ's consecration.

Because holiness is best expressed in liturgical terms, the Apostle considers the Church and each believer as a temple in which the Holy Spirit makes his home (cf. 1 Cor 3:16; 6:19; Eph 2:20, 22). But this image, static in nature, needs to be completed by that of sacrifice. The Church is a sacrificial offering as well as a temple, she is the body of Christ in union with his death and resurrection. Being and event are joined together, as in Christ who has become the event of our salvation, 'Christ our passover' (1 Cor 5:7). The Spirit transforms Christ and the Church into his own mode of being: he is an act of love, a flame existing of itself, he makes of those whom he animates a living holocaust.

* * *

What does the image of the temple comprise? It reminds us of the idea of a space that is lived in, but the Spirit transcends space, he cannot be contained by it. Local presence is not the only one known to man; there is another, personal, where the 'I' of the one and that of the other come close to each other, and, to a certain degree, are joined together and penetrate each other. This presence is the effect of a love which makes a reciprocal inwardness possible: 'The one who loves comes out of himself and is transferred into the beloved'.[15] This is the way in which the Father and the Son are present to each other: 'I am in the Father and the Father is in me' (Jn 14:10). A similar union takes place between Christ and the believer: 'You will understand that I am in my Father and you in me and I in you' (Jn 14:20). The presence of Christ in the believer is accompanied by that of the Father (cf. Jn 14:23).

However, the indwelling of the Spirit is different. It would not seem that the Spirit establishes between himself and the believer the reciprocal inwardness of two people united in friendship. He *is* love; he provokes the union, but he does not bring it about for his own benefit: he is at work for the Father and the Son. He is present in virtue of the union between people, an anointing which impregnates the 'I' and makes it capable of relationship. His presence is creative of relationships; it enables Christ and Paul to be united to the point where Paul can say: it is 'Christ who lives in me' (Gal 2:20).

His presence is therefore basic, it establishes reciprocity. The Spirit is the bond of union, the love which 'causes one to be in love'. Through the presence of the Spirit, the believer belongs to Christ (cf. Rom 8:9) and enters into the relationship of the Son with the Father. The Spirit is the intimacy between God and his creature, the divine touch which brings about union, the love at the root of Christian love (cf. Rom 5:5). He *divinizes* the believer and introduces him into the trinitarian movement.

It is understandable that the Apostle envisages this presence as in the heart of the faithful (cf. Rom 5:5; Gal 4:6; 2 Cor 1:22), at the deepest point penetrated by the Spirit, where the believer becomes more and more a person in union with Christ who himself is united with the Father. It is doubtless thus that St Paul was conscious of the presence within him of a divine guest, a Spirit of sonship; through a completely new experience of personal intimacy with God in Jesus Christ, through an irresistible impulse of confidence, hitherto unknown, which made him say: 'Abba! Father!'

This activly corresponds to characteristics of the Spirit already known to us. He is creative power and love; he creates by making personal, by setting up relationships. He is not present to a person as an object of love, he is Love, he is union. His presence is related to the Christ in whom he incorporates the faithful, to the Father to whom offspring are thus born; he is always at the service of the begetting of the Son in this world. The Spirit is the ecstasy of God and the power of indwelling attraction to God: by his presence the Trinity is rooted in the creature and the creature is integrated into God. The Spirit is at the beginning: he enables the believer to open himself to communion; he is at the end, he is the seal which consecrates union.

Henceforth God and man are intimates: 'We can know that we are living in him and he is living in us because he lets us share in his Spirit' (1 Jn 4:13). The new and eternal covenant is concluded in the Spirit (cf. Jer 31:31–33; Ezek 36:26f.), it bears the same name as the eternal trinitarian union; 'oneness in the Holy Spirit'. Through the Spirit who is sovereign freedom, God attaches himself to the creature, never again able to be separated from him; divine freedom consists in loving infinitely and being bound to each other in love.

★   ★   ★

The Spirit who lives in the believer is not therefore inactive. He is power and action and is manifested as a presence and as *a call* towards the future. The first Christian communities had a very clear perception of the grace at work in them. To express what it means to be a Christian, they managed to create original formulas, the precision of which has never been surpassed. They defined Christian identity by the three theological virtues; another stroke of inspiration was to define the grace of the Spirit as a call.

For the faithful, God is 'the-one-who-calls-them' (cf. 1 Th 5:24; Gal 1:6; 5:8), just as much as he is the 'God-who-has-raised-Jesus-from-the-dead' (cf. Rom 4:24; 2 Cor 1:9; Gal 1:1;

1 Pet 1:21). God who raises Jesus in the Spirit calls the faithful in the Spirit. They themselves say that they are 'called' (cf. 1 Cor 1:24; Rev 17:14; Jude 1), 'you...by his call belong to Jesus Christ' (Rom 1:6). They bear this name, just as they bear the name of Christians, for their existence as Christians is vocational, identical with the vocation to which they have been called (cf. 1 Cor 1:26; Eph 1:18; 4:1; 2 Tim 1:9). All the action of the Spirit in the faithful is in the form of a call: 'You were called into one and the same hope' (cf. Eph 4:4), to freedom (cf. Gal 5:13), to peace (cf. 1 Cor 7:15; Col 3:15); by this call they are journeying towards the Kingdom and glory (cf. 1 Th 2:12). St Paul combines the two notions of call and grace: (The one) 'who called me through his grace' (Gal 1:6, 15). The familiar antithesis: 'not by your works but by grace' becomes in Romans 9:12: 'it depends on the one who calls, not on human merit'.

In the image of a call, theology finds rich insight into the nature of grace. The presence of the Spirit is active like a call; God transforms the earthly man by call, by attraction towards fullness of being. Christ was the first to be called in this way, to be raised to life by the God who 'brings the dead to life and calls into being what does not exist' (Rom 4:17).

Vocation is creative. God calls 'what does not exist', people without a name, without virtue, and makes them 'members of Christ Jesus' (cf. 1 Cor 1:26–30). The call does not presuppose any merit, he raises them from nothing at all. It is he who sanctifies, who creates 'saints by calling' (cf. Rom 1:7; 1 Cor 1:2; 1 Th 4:7); this is the call which makes a persecutor into an apostle (cf. Gal 1:15f.), 'an apostle by calling' (Rom 1:1; 1 Cor 1:1).[16] The grace of the Spirit is creative, it creates by attraction.

The purpose of this call is Christ. God creates a new man by attracting him towards his Son, so that man may have a share in his sonship: 'God by calling you has joined you to his Son' (1 Cor 1:9); 'God...is calling you to share the glory of his Kingdom' (1 Th 2:12); moreover, glory and the Kingdom are contained in the Son he loves (cf. Col 1:13).

Grace is not simply a quality that enhances man. It is energy calling and creating by attraction. It attracts by opening a person to union with the Son (cf. 1 Cor 1:9) who is the goal of all the activity of the Spirit.

A Church of sonship in the Spirit

The presence of the Spirit makes the Church one of sonship: 'The Spirit you received...is the spirit of sonship, and it makes us cry out: "Abba! Father!" ' (Rom 8:15); 'the proof that you are sons is that God has sent the Spirit of his Son into your hearts: the Spirit that cries "Abba! Father!" ', and it is this that makes you a son, you are no longer a slave; and if God has made you a son, then he has made you an heir' (cf. Gal 4:6f.).

This sonship is not the effect of mere adoption. The Spirit is creative, the believer is a son by birth and not by juridical act. He is born of water and the Spirit (cf. Jn 3:5): of water as from his mother's womb, of the Spirit symbolized by this water. Scripture speaks of a divine seed (cf. 1 Pet 1:23), of a share in the divine nature (cf. 2 Pet 1:4). Adam became 'son of God' by creation (cf. Gen 5:1–3; Lk 3:38), a Christian is 'created in Christ Jesus' (Eph 2:10), son of God, by nature, like Adam, but in an inexpressible way.[17]

The first man was created by the Breath of God and in the Christ to come, 'all things were created through him and for him' (Col 1:16). His creation was the distant proclamation of those sons whose father is God, simultaneously in Christ and in the Spirit, and of whom it is said: 'Everyone moved by the Spirit is a son of God' (Rom 8:14) and again: 'You are, all of you, sons of God through faith in Christ Jesus' (Gal 3:26). This sonship is not something added to the dignity proper to every human being, it brings the initial creation to its proper end, but by completely transcending it. The faithful are 'called to be united with the Son' within a call which creates all men for Christ.

Sonship in the Spirit does not take its origin from 'human stock or urge of the flesh or will of man' (Jn 1:13); it is characterized by a union of persons. However, it is more real than any other kind, in the same way that the sonship of Christ with regard to his God and Father is fully expressive of a relationship.

The Spirit here plays his habitual role. He is the Spirit of the Father, as father, at the service of the begetting of the Son in the world. He makes the faithful fully persons and makes their relationships divine. The relationship of the faithful with the Father is none other than the Spirit himself, 'the fellowship of the Holy Spirit'. He is the divine action by which God begets his Son and those who are in him.

The newness of the gift

Filial birth in the Holy Spirit is something new, unknown to the Bible of the Old Testament.[18] For the paschal gift of the Spirit is very new; thanks to this gift men become sons of God. The very abundance of this gift is new: '*Fountains* of living water will flow out' (cf. Jn 7:37), 'I will pour out my spirit on *all* mankind' (Joel 3:1; Acts 2:17). The very nature of it is new, for 'the revelation of a mystery kept secret for endless ages, but now so clear...' (Rom 16:26) is not only that of Christ in his passover, but also that of the Spirit given in Christ. John could say: 'There was no Spirit as yet because Jesus had not yet been glorified' (7:39). According to the Apostle, 'when the appointed time came' (cf. Gal 4:1–7), God sent his Son and the Spirit of his Son simultaneously. *The saving mystery of the Son and the gift of the Spirit are both equally new.*

In the Old Testament the outpouring of the Spirit is a promise, intended for the messianic era: 'I shall put my spirit in you' (Ezek 36:27). John the Baptist announced it as a baptism hitherto unknown. According to Luke, Jesus inaugurates his ministry by calling on his anointing by the Spirit (cf. 4:18; Acts 10:38), sign of his messiahship and of the 'year of grace'. The two gifts promised, according to the fourth gospel, that of the body of Jesus and that of the Spirit, are reserved for the day of glorification: 'The bread that I shall give' (6:51), 'the Advocate...whom I shall send to you' (15:26). The coming of the Spirit depends on the passover of Jesus: 'Unless I go, the Advocate will not come to you' (16:7). The unity of the Son and the Spirit is ceaselessly manifested: the Spirit who is the fullness of God enters into the world when 'the fulness of the divinity comes to live in Christ's body' (cf. Col 2:9). Like the resurrection, the paschal outpouring of the Spirit is something new in the world.[19]

Israel lived in a time of childhood which, paradoxically, was a time of age-old slavery, since the messianic heritage had not reached it (cf. Gal 4:1–7). The letter to the Hebrews is definite: 'All these died...before receiving many of the things that had been promised, but they saw them in the far distance an welcomed them,...they were not to reach perfection except with us' (11:13, 40). The Spirit is the blessing promised to the descendants of Abraham, according to the Apostle, the descendant who is Christ. This blessing is brought to the people of God by the risen Christ (cf. Acts 3:25f.). It is received in faith and in communion with Christ (cf. Gal 3:14).

The history of the outpouring of the Spirit *is ongoing*: its beginning is found in the initial creation, its climax in the resurrection of Jesus. God became progressively involved in the world: by creative action, later by the covenant with Israel, and finally by the fullness of the covenant in Jesus Christ. The union between God and man is, in Jesus Christ, different from the covenant with Israel. Furthermore, it is in that Spirit that God became involved in the world. In Jesus Christ, the Spirit in person forms the link between God and man, just as he is the link in the eternal Trinity. This presence is new, unknown in the older covenants. A successive presence runs like a thread through sacred history; however, the final presence is new, with a newness proper to fulfilment; there originates in it what, in time, precedes it.

The ancient covenant was a 'stage'; it had to be taken over by another covenant. Speaking of the new covenant (cf. Jer 31:31), God declares the earlier one outdated; what is old and outmoded is about to disappear (cf. Heb 8:13). The Old Testament had its symbol in the glory shining on the face of Moses, a transient light, a glory which was to disappear (cf. 2 Cor 3:7, 11). But the glory of the New Testament 'is going to last' (2 Cor 3:11). It shines on the face of Christ transfigured in the Spirit (cf. 2 Cor 3:17f.).

'It is going to last' belongs to the vocabulary of the eschatological realities which cannot be transcended and which, by nature, differ from the next-to-last realities.

Salvation history has progressed to the rhythm of God's mystery inserted in the world. It reaches its climax in Christ's passover, when the mystery becomes immanent in creation as it has ever been in eternity. God was first manifested on Sinai; there he promulgated a law through the intermediary of a man, a law composed of numerous precepts and inscribed on tablets of stone. But the Spirit is the law of the New Testament in person, 'the law of the Spirit of life' (Rom 8:2); it is inscribed in the heart of Christ and of those who belong to him. No human intermediary intervenes: for the Spirit is poured into Christ in his very begetting, in his sonship; he is given to the faithful in this sonship in which they participate. Jesus had promised: 'The Spirit of truth will be *in you*' (cf. Jn 14:17).[20] St Paul claims that he possesses the Spirit and thinks that every believer in Christ possesses him. No prophet or just man in the Old Testament ever made such a claim! Speaking of his Precursor 'who was much more than a prophet', Jesus stated: 'Of all the children born of women, a greater than John the Baptist has never been seen; yet the least in the kingdom of heaven is greater than he is' (Mt 11:9, 11). According to the Greek Fathers, this superiority of the members of the Kingdom is explained thus: in the prophets of the Old Testament the Spirit was present by his action and inspiration; in the New, *his presence is personal, just as it is in Christ, just as it is in the Trinity.*[21]

It is in this way that the difference and the newness of grace in the New Testament are characterized: the Spirit dwells in person in Christ and in the members of Christ. In the mystery of the Trinity he proceeds from the Father in the begetting of the Son; he is the Spirit of the Son, inseparable from him. Moreover, Christ is the Son begotten in this world; by this fact, the Spirit is henceforth present in person in this world, since he proceeds from the Father in the begetting of the Son. His presence is inscribed in history simultaneously with the incarnation of the Son; he dwells in Christ and in those who are members of his body in the same manner in which he is present in the Trinity.[22]

The communion of saints

The presence of the Spirit does not only give man the heart of a son, it unites all men by fraternal bonds. Through their initial creation, the need to be together is already inherent in them, they are marked by the sign of the Spirit through whom they are created. But at the climax of history, in Christ in his resurrection, the creative will of the Spirit becomes imperious: he brings about a total oneness, *the oneness called salvation*.

The Gospel is a message of union: 'What we have seen and heard we are telling you so that you too may be in union with us, as we are in union with the Father and his Son Jesus Christ. We are writing this to you to make your joy complete' (1 Jn 1:3f.). Present in all his truth, the Spirit introduces into the world the union that he brings about between the Father and the Son.

From the beginning, the Church is conscious of a mysterious union developing in her. St Paul testifies to this when he speaks of 'a communion with the body and blood of Christ', that is, a communion with the body and blood of Christ and a communion that unites the communicants among themselves (cf. 1 Cor 10:16f.). The unity thus established is not only in spirit, but in the Holy Spirit, in which all are 'mingled in a single Spirit by the fire of love'.[23]

This great communion, which is salvation achieved, has its obvious source in the redemptive passover. Christ 'died and rose again *for us*' (cf. 2 Cor 5:15). In the power of the Spirit, he became a being who is union, giving and sharing himself down to depths that cannot be shared: in his death and in his birth as son. He unites all men in himself by giving himself to them. The grain that dies comes to life again in the form of a sheaf of wheat; the vine is enriched by shoots and fruit – Jesus, self and community, comes to life again.

Man can become in Christ what Christ himself is – source of life and leaven of union, for 'we have become as he is' (1 Jn 4:17). In Christianity, 'if we live, we live for the Lord; and if we die, we die for the Lord' (cf. Rom 14:7). We are never holy only for ourselves; 'the manifestation of the Spirit is given to everyone for profit' (Vatican II, *LG* 12). Teresa of Lisieux had the experience of a grain that bears fruit. During her last illness someone brought her a sheaf of wheat; she picked out the finest ear: 'This ear of corn is the image of my soul: God has entrusted me with graces for myself and for many others'.[24]

The gift of the Spirit is a grace of love. Anyone who loves lives in those whom he loves and wants to make them live in him: 'I...feel like this towards you all, since you have

shared...both my chains and my work...You have a permanent place in my heart' (cf. Ph 1:7). The grace of Paul, by
which he lives, belongs to those who have a place in his heart.
The creative Spirit, who gives to all the power to love,
emphasizes his action in Christ and in the faithful: he increases
their love, helps the desire for union to grow greater and
brings it about, for the Spirit is both the will to love and
creative omnipotence: *his desire for union creates union.* That is
why a Christian who loves sanctifies, in his heart, the others
whom he loves; he lives for God in favour of others, like his
Lord who could say: 'For their sake I consecrate myself so that
they may be consecrated...' (Jn 17:19)

* * *

The grace of the Spirit is not something one owns, it is not the
property of anyone, it is what binds. God himself does not
possess the richness of grace, he *is* Grace. The richness of his
grace consists in the fact that it has *outright existence* in oneness
with him. The Spirit of union is God's mode of being; present
in man, God enables him to live in a divine way. In God an
eternal dialogue is set up between I and Thou, to the exclusion
of mine and thine: he is the Father and Son in the Spirit, that
is, in perfect union.

Even in his humanity – previously earthly – Jesus is
henceforth assumed into the mystery of the Trinity, 'become a
life-giving spirit' (1 Cor 15:45), a being who is entirely self-
giving; the faithful are saved in him, by sharing his mode of
being: pardoned by the fact that God changes them into
beings who are 'given', freed from the law of sin and death (cf.
Rom 8:2) (which encloses them in themselves) by the fact that
God makes them open. The gift of the Spirit tends to make the
believer what Christ is: 'a life-giving spirit'. Grace enables him
to be a source of grace; each believer shares in the sanctification of others according to the power of the Spirit who
sanctifies him. In Christ he shares in the union of the Trinity.
Furthermore, grace is love, simultaneously brotherly and
maternal, in Christ who has become the intimate brother of
mankind, and in the Spirit through whom are born the
children of God. The Church is formed of brethren united in a
single body, and the Church is our mother (cf. Gal 4:26), a

fruitful vine (cf. Jn 15:2). The Spirit plays in Christ and in the Church the role he plays in the eternal mystery where he is a fruitful womb: it is indeed in the Spirit that the Father begets his eternal Son (see below, pp. 151–155).

The Apostle has had experience of the fruitfulness of the gift of the Spirit: 'The grace that he gave me has not been fruitless' (1 Cor 15:10), 'I begot you in Christ Jesus' (1 Cor 4:15); my children, 'I must go through the pains of giving birth to you all over again, until Christ is formed in you' (Gal 4:19). For he has been assumed into Christ dead and risen again (cf. 2 Cor 4:10–12) and, by this fact, he has become 'a life-giving spirit' (1 Cor 15:45).

In the Church there is one woman who sums up the Church and represents her: the mother of Jesus. The faithful think of her, their sister *par excellence*, as their mother too, for the words were said: 'Woman, this is your son' (Jn 19:26). In her the grace of the Spirit wells up in its highest concentration, in its totality as regards the Church. Fully sanctified, Mary is the very heart of the community of grace. The spiritual motherhood of the Church finds in her its fullness and its symbol.

The Spirit flows from the pierced side (cf. Jn 19:34); similarly, in the believer, grace is communicated to others through a wound, through participation in Christ's immolation: 'So death is at work in us, but life in you' (2 Cor 4:12). This is why Paul rejoices in his sufferings, because it is for the Church that he makes up in his own body all that has still to be undergone by Christ for the sake of his body, the Church (cf. Col 1:24). In union with, yet at the same time in dependence on, Christ, the Christian can expiate the sins of others – thus making eternal life available to them.[25]

★   ★   ★

How is it that grace, which is not a thing to distribute but the mode of being of redeemed man – how is it that grace can thus be shared?

The communion of saints is sometimes explained by the image of something poured from one vessel into another. But what an unsatisfactory comparison! A liquid is a thing, subject to the necessary laws of things, whereas man is a person, grace is a uniting reality, very different from quantitive realities.

The communion of saints comes from the mystery of the Spirit of love; therefore, theology has recourse to love to explain this mysterious union: 'Charity puts the goods of each at the disposal of all'.[26] Love is the condition and the cause: 'If we presuppose a union of love with others, then we can hope for eternal life for others, in that we are united to them in love'.[27]

But the love which explains everything does not explain itself. What concerns the Spirit, just like what is characteristic of a person, is shrouded in mystery.[28] By the experience of love, people can nevertheless glimpse the possibility of boundless love.

Even at the psychological level, friendship throws some light on this matter. A person who loves feels favoured with what belongs to the other. St Paul feels himself enriched by the faith and charity of the communities that he has set up (cf. Ph 4:1; 1 Th 2:19f.). Health, beauty, all the qualities in one who is loved: in a child they give joy to the parent, in a bride they give joy to the bridegroom. Each rejoices in the good of those he loves.[29] Disinterested love has this unexpected effect: happy in what belongs to another, one makes it one's own without depriving the other of it.

But the true explanation lies at a deeper level, that of the person. Love not only rejoices in the qualities of others, it is anxious to share its own possessions, even the most personal ones. On earth love succeeds in this to a certain extent; it creates first of all a sharing of that very personal good which is itself: people who love one another do not speak of love in the plural, but of 'our love', the love through which one is united to the other. Between husband and wife who love one another for many years, a union is established which is not merely of the order of sentiment; this union affects human beings in the depths of their person: the 'I' of each is developed in this relationship. We have seen partners incapable of living without each other, so that when one dies, the other is not long in rejoining him or her.[30]

The grace of the Spirit is like this. It is not in the first place a quality which has nothing to do with relationships, like e.g. a clear intellect, a strong will, artistic gifts, health, with which a person is endowed, but which he is incapable of sharing with another. Grace is not first and foremost a possession, but a *bond*; it is the extension to the whole Church of the fellowship of the Spirit. It affects man in the depths of his person, just as the Spirit affects the Father as father, in the begetting of the Son; as he affects the Son in his relationship with the Father. Grace enables man to have a relationship with God, just as the Father and the Son are constituted as persons given to one another in the Spirit. The role of the Spirit always has to do with persons. The communion of saints is less a sharing of possessions than a community of persons.[31]

In the paschal mystery, which is the basis of the communion of saints, Christ gives up everything by dying in order to have everything. But, through the Spirit of his resurrection he *is*, rather than *has*, the fullness of being. In this fullness he becomes fully a person. *Because he is given* to man, he draws him and incorporates him into himself. He lives for the Church; she is thus rich in her Lord, through the love with which she is loved. He enriches the Church by giving himself to her.

The Eucharist illustrates this: when Christ makes the Church his body by allowing her to eat of him (cf. 1 Cor 10:17), the Eucharist belongs to all who belong to him. The Church possesses him and is possessed by him, through the love the Lord has for her. The Lord is for the body and the body for the Lord (cf. 1 Cor 6:13): 'he died for all so that the living should live no longer for themselves, but for him who died and was raised to life for them' (2 Cor 5:15).

What the Spirit brings about in Christ, he accomplishes in the faithful, but at their level. They are 'risen together with him in the power of the Spirit', and their love contributes to cementing the unity of the edifice of which Christ is the corner-stone. Each gives himself and exists for others, *and each by loving another binds him to himself*. The love of a king could make a shepherdess a queen; similarly, the saints, by loving their brethren, bind them to themselves and consecrate them through their holiness. We belong to anyone who loves us in the Spirit. The saints possess us, not by monopolizing us, which would deprive us of our freedom, but because they bind themselves to us by self-giving. Such is their glory; given to others in the Spirit, they are the first in the Kingdom. They share in the salvific lordship of Christ.

Even more than a share in holy things, *the communion of saints is a union of persons*, bound to one another in the gift of self. Those who love one another share their riches. The saint belongs in love to every ordinary Christian; the latter is helped by the saint who loves him, and the saint is rich on account of the ordinary Christian who belongs to him in love. True riches lie in relationship. Such also are the riches of the Persons of the Trinity.

* * *

The communion of saints extends its network of salvation out over the whole world, for Christ is risen and the Church is constituted in the love of the Spirit who gives saints to the whole world. Everyone is in some way baptized, to a certain extent consecrated, by the presence of Christ and of the Church at the heart of humanity. St Paul recommends a spouse who has become a Christian not to leave a partner who has remained a pagan, for 'the unbelieving husband is made one with the saints through his wife, and the unbelieving wife is made one with the saints through her husband' (1 Cor 7:14).

People who are loved are not far from Christ or from the Church which, through their love, is very close to them. They already belong to the Church through the link which binds the Church to them. Can a person be lost, if another person, rooted in Christ, is bound to him? In order to be lost, it would be necessary to be so strongly opposed to love that one could no longer remain attached to that person. But will the refusal to love ever be stronger than the boundless love of the Spirit?

* * *

This power to love, to give oneself, to become attached to others, is possessed by the saints in heaven and exercised by them with regard to those who have not yet joined them 'in heaven, in Christ Jesus' (Eph 2:6).[32] The Spirit is always simultaneously a power of attraction towards God and a power of 'sending' into the world. The movement which exalts Christ to God raises him to life in the world, the glorification of Jesus belongs to the last times, it is a coming: 'I am going away and shall return' (cf. Jn 14:18, 28). The Church in heaven is the intimate companion of Christ in this double yet single movement: it is turned towards earth through glory, that is, through the Spirit which fixes her in God. In the Spirit, the death of the faithful undergoes a total conversion; their relationships with earth are not severed, but deepened. To someone who asked: 'You will look down on us from heaven, won't you?' Teresa of Lisieux replied: 'No, I will come down'.[33] Jesus said: 'I will not leave you orphans; I will come back to you' (Jn 14:18), and Teresa of Lisieux repeated: 'I will come back'.[34]

Such is the work of the Spirit: he gives stability to people by making them open; he strengthens the personality of man by establishing him in relationships, he, the Spirit who makes God radiate in the Trinity.

The apostolic Church

The apostolate is a visible aspect of the communion of saints; it is the activity that translates the light of salvation into evident reality. The dynamism of the communion of saints and that of the apostolate are interrelated, just as mystery and visible institution are united in the Church. Under the inspiration of the Spirit the Church aims at extending to the confines of time and space; the presence of the Spirit is also eschatological in this sense; it wills the extension of the Church to the *ends* of the earth[35] and the *end* of time.

The Spirit is a pervading power. He appears in the form of tongues of fire: the tongue a symbol of communication, fire speaking of divine power. Jesus promises: 'You will receive power when the Holy Spirit comes on you, and then you will be my witnesses' (Acts 1:8). The Spirit sets apart Barnabas and Paul for the work to which they are called (cf. Acts 13:2). The Gospel which 'is the power of God' (Rom 1:16), spreads 'by the power of the Spirit' (Rom 15:19; 1 Th 1:5); it is 'the Good News of the glory' (2 Cor 4:6), but the Spirit is the glory of God. The words of the apostles are 'a demonstration of the power of the Spirit' (1 Cor 2:4): they express 'spiritual things spiritually' (1 Cor 2:13). The one who is the soul of the Church is also the soul of her apostolate.

The apostolic action of the Spirit is developed *within the mystery of sonship*. The apostles are sent in the power of the

Father who raises his Son from the dead (cf. Gal 1:1); St Paul holds the grace of his apostolate from the Son through his resurrection (cf. Rom 1:4f.); *apostolic dynamism is none other than the power of the Spirit who raises Jesus in this world*. The Spirit who is always at the service of the Son, causes him, through the apostolate, to assume a body in the world.

By this very fact, as John testifies, the apostolate is derived from the mystery of the incarnation. This mystery is both consecration and mission to the world (cf. Jn 10:36), in keeping with the double, unique movement of inwardness and diffusion proper to the Spirit. But the incarnation is seen by John at its Easter climax, when mission and consecration are total (cf. 17:19). The apostles are caught up in the paschal consecration of Jesus (cf. 17:19) and in his mission (cf. 20:21f.): the Breath that Jesus breathes on them consecrates them to God and sends them out into the world.

St Paul says he is 'an apostle by calling' (Rom 1:1; 1 Cor 1:1),[36] sent (*apostolos*) into the world by the fact of his being caught up by Christ; he is 'set apart for the gospel' (cf. Rom 1:1), that is, set apart for a mystery, but a mystery spread throughout the world.[37] These formulas are paradoxical, they speak of membership of Christ, of sanctification and at the same time of mission. Paul says that he is attached to the triumph of Christ (cf. 2 Cor 2:14), that God glorifies through him and at the same time sends him to take possession of the world. Anyone who is caught up by the Spirit into the mystery of Christ is at the same time sent by him. There is always this movement of ebb and flow, characteristic of the dynamism of the Spirit.

* * *

The apostolic charism is not something added to Christian grace, it is intrinsic to it. The vocation of the apostle lies within the call to be united with the Son (cf. 1 Cor 1:9), which is the prerogative of all Christians. One is an apostle by one's call, just as Christians are 'saints by calling' (cf. Rom 1:7); Paul is marked out as an apostle by the seal of death and resurrection (cf. 2 Cor 4:10–12) and this is also the seal of baptism. The Breath breathed by Jesus on the apostles recalls the creation of Adam (cf. Jn 20:22): consecration to the apostolate is a creation. Moreover, there is no other new creation save that of sons of God in Jesus Christ. In other words, the grace of the Spirit consecrates a man to the apostolate by making him a Christian; for St Paul, to be an apostle was his way of being a Christian.

From this we can conclude that, if in the Church there are some men specially ordained in view of their apostolate, their ministry is not a simple function added to their life as Christians; they are bishops, priests, deacons, like the first apostles, who were Christians by the fact of their call to the apostolate.

We can also think that the dynamism of the Spirit is apostolic throughout the Church, that every grace, every consecration in the redemptive mystery, implies commission. The Twelve who were 'to be his companions and to be sent out' (cf. Mk 3:14) were the symbol of the whole Church.[38]

* * *

Consecration makes the apostle *a man of the Spirit*, in Christ become a life-giving spirit. His apostolate is the 'administering of the Spirit' (2 Cor 3:8), he forms part of the eschatological realities which constitute the domain of the Spirit. The administering is of such brightness that 'compared with this greater brightness', the ministry of Moses, the brightest there ever was, was as though deprived of brightness (cf. 2 Cor 3:10). God's light temporarily illuminated the face of Moses; in the heart of the apostle it is going to last (cf. 2 Cor 3:10f.): a brightness of a different order, that with which the face of Christ, image of God, shines (cf. 2 Cor 4:4, 6). The apostle knows mysteries formerly unknown, for the Spirit who inspires him reaches the depths (cf. 1 Cor 2:10). Paul, minister of Christ, 'writes...with the Spirit of the living God, not on stone tablets but on the tablets of your living hearts' (2 Cor 3:3). The prophets of old had an influence on the history of their times, but Paul is at the service of the eschatological realities; his Gospel is 'the power of God saving all who have faith' (Rom 1:16). Similarly, the gift of the Spirit brought by Christ, 'the ministry of the Spirit', is completely new.[39]

Under the influence of the Spirit, the apostles proclaim the resurrection of Jesus, his lordship and final coming (cf. e.g. Acts 2:17, 24, 36). What he enables them to proclaim is brought about by the Spirit through their proclamation (cf. 1 Th 2:13). For he raises up apostles and breathes life into them, *in so far as he raises up Christ*, establishes his lordship and brings about the Day: he is always the Spirit of Christ in his resurrection and it is as such that he animates the apostles. He raises Jesus in *this* world 'in the form' of apostles, so much so that Paul can say: 'Christ lives in me' (Gal 2:20), 'Christ is speaking in me' (2 Cor 13:3). He raises him from death 'in the form' of men who by preaching believe in Christ and allow themselves to be incorporated into him. 'By the power of the Holy Spirit' the Apostle *'accomplishes* the Good News' (cf. Rom 15:19; Col 1:25): he contributes to *bringing about in the world the Good News which is Christ in his resurrection* (cf. Acts 13:32f.).[40]

Here we are stating a fact of great importance: *the Spirit accomplishes the mystery in the world by revealing it to the world*. His revealing action is creative, the proclaiming of the mystery is also its coming into existence. It is thus that, already in the Trinity, God manifests himself in his Image by bringing it about, by begetting his Son in the Spirit.

We can draw our conclusion about the newness of grace of the Spirit and of the divine sonship in the New Testament also from the fact that they were unknown in the Old Testament and that they are revealed today. God reveals by accomplishing.[41]

★ ★ ★

The words of the apostles are the principal means of conveying the mystery which is achieved by its very revelation. Thanks to his words, a man can come to meet another and be at one with him. Through the apostles, it is Christ who speaks (cf. 2 Cor 2:17; 13:3), who 'in the form' of the apostles' words is communicated to people; the mystery of Christ is spread through its proclamation (cf. Rom 1:16).

Moreover, the Spirit is inseparable from the Word, he is the voice that conveys the word. He does not only raise up apostles, he makes them speak (cf. Acts 2:4; 4:31; 19:5f.).

From the discourse of a human being, the Spirit makes the Good News the sacrament of salvation in its diffusion and its effectiveness. By the power of the Spirit Christ himself rises again *in this world* in the form of the Church which is his body, in the form of Paul who is an apostle in whom Christ lives (cf. Gal 2:20), in the form too of preaching. The act of preaching (also that of catechesis) has a quasi-sacramental character. It is an action of the Church which, in its entirety, is the sacrament of Christ in his coming in the power of the Spirit.[42]

St Paul compares himself to an earthenware jar holding a treasure (cf. 2 Cor 4:7). This jar carries the finger-marks of the one who is the hand of God and the one who has shaped it, the Spirit who first shaped Christ in his passover. The words of the apostle are divine power for salvation (cf. Rom 1:16), but in extreme weakness (cf. 1 Cor 1:25), for the Spirit triumphs in the humility of the cross. It is foolishness (cf. 1 Cor 1:23), for the Spirit who raises up Jesus in death cannot be grasped by reason. The messengers of the gospel often risk being told 'they have been drinking too much' (cf. Acts 2:13), whereas Christians who count too much on reasoning fail to evangelize. The apostle disowns a wisdom inspired by 'the flesh' and surrenders to the movement of the Spirit: 'In my speeches and sermons there were none of the arguments that belong to philosophy; only a demonstration of the power of the Spirit' (1 Cor 2:4). He makes use of 'spiritual' rhetoric: 'We teach...in the way that the Spirit teaches us; we teach spiritual things spiritually' (1 Cor 2:12f.). What are the terms inspired by the Spirit, if not very simple ones evoked by the Spirit of the resurrection? The power of God in the weakness of man and his words: such is the charism of preaching.

Prophetic inspiration

The words of the apostles are prophetic: it is God (cf. 1 Th 2:13), it is Christ (cf. 2 Cor 2:17; 13:3) who speaks through them; they proclaim the realities of the next world, the mystery kept secret for endless ages, but now within our world (cf. Rom 16:25f.). Moreover, it is the Spirit 'who speaks through the prophets'; it has always been known that a prophet is a 'man of the Spirit' (Hos 9:7).

Moses expressed the wish: 'If only the whole people of Yahweh were prophets, and Yahweh gave his Spirit to them all!' (Num 11:29). Joel (3:1) announces the realization of this: 'After this I will pour out my spirit on all mankind. Your sons and daughters shall prophesy...Even on the slaves, men and women, will I pour out my Spirit in those days'. On the day of Pentecost Peter confirms that the last times, those of the promise fulfilled, have come (cf. Acts 3:17f.). The whole nation, in whom the Spirit dwells, enjoys the prophetic charism: 'They will all be taught by God' (Jn 6:45) and will be able to reveal his secrets (cf. Is 54:13; Jer 31:33f.).[43]

The faith, which belongs to all the people, is a prophetic gift; it is inspired by the Spirit: 'No one can say, "Jesus is Lord" unless he is under the influence of the Holy Spirit' (1 Cor 12:3). Faith perceives the mystery of Christ which is the deep, future mystery of the world. Christ reveals himself to his Church in a lasting way; for his resurrection is always at this moment and always revelation: 'You will see me' (Jn 16:16). The time of revelation is not limited to the apostolic ages; revelation is not closed in the sense that since then revelation has been entirely enclosed in formulas and is henceforth merely transmitted and commented on. Christian revelation remains open. The Church always lives in an encounter with Christ risen in the Spirit. The faith of the first apostles was born in this encounter, it is born afresh in an encounter with the risen Christ and in the grace of the Paraclete who, even today, teaches us and reveals everything that Christ said (cf. Jn 14:26). According to 1 John 2:20, 27, the Church hears in her heart a permanent revelation: 'You have been anointed by the Holy One and have received all knowledge'.[44]

However, the revelation made in former times to the apostles is unique, universal, normative, *and nothing else can be added to it*. Because there are not two resurrections, when Christ comes and reveals himself, neither can there be two Christian revelations. The resurrection of Christ, who is Christian revelation, is expressed in the faith to which it gives rise, that of the apostles and that of today. We might say that faith is the mystery of Christ throwing light on the screen of the Church, thus transforming the Church (2 Cor 3:18). The resurrection of Christ in the Spirit is unique, the coming of

Christ when he reveals himself to the Church is unique, faith too is unique. But the image presented on the screen has a variety of colours; no image is capable of exhausting the divine fullness dwelling corporeally in Christ. Each generation can draw old and new from its treasures which have been at the disposal of the Church since the beginning.

★　★　★

Among the graces of prophecy conferred on the Church, the principal one is the inspiration of Holy Scripture. The Church professes emphatically that the Book was drawn up under the movement of the Spirit: 'When men spoke for God it was the Holy Spirit that moved them' (2 Pet 1:21).

Jesus announced that the Holy Spirit would glorify him (cf. Jn 16:14; 14:26); this the Spirit did magnificently and continues to do so by raising Jesus simultaneously in himself and in the form of the Church, her preaching and her sacraments, especially the Eucharist, in the form too of Holy Scripture. He thus creates a world of real symbols in which the perceptible presence of his Son is brought about in this world.

The charism of the inspiration of the Scriptures, contained in the action of the Spirit who raises Jesus, draws its source from the pierced side whence flow the rivers of the New Testament: the Book is born of Christ's open side like a child born of its mother. But a child leaves its mother's womb, whereas the Scriptures – like the baptized – do not cease to be bathed in the grace of the Spirit. They are read and understood in the Spirit in whom they have been drawn up, and it is the same Spirit who gives life to those reading them.

The Spirit raises Christ in the world of material things by seeking to incorporate these realities in Christ. He incorporates men into Christ and makes them 'the Church which is his body'; he incorporates into Christ the bread and wine and makes of them the Eucharist which is his body; similarly, he incorporates the words of man into the one who is the Word made man. He accomplishes, as it were, a transubstantiation of the human word and thus contributes through the Scriptures to giving a body to the Son in the world.

What the sacred authors write is not merely a word about Christ, but the word of Christ, through the operation of the

Holy Spirit. The Eucharist too is not merely a sign of presence; it is presence itself, through the intervention of the Spirit. The assembly of the faithful is not only united in the name of Christ, it is his body. Paul says that he speaks in Christ and Christ in him (cf. 2 Cor 2:17; 13:3). 'It is (Christ) who speaks, when the Holy Scriptures are read in the Church' (Vatican II, *SC* 7); 'the Gospel is the mouth of Christ'.[45] When the Church writes the Gospels, when she proclaims and assimilates them, she celebrates the memory of Jesus somewhat as in the Eucharist: 'As for me I think the body of Christ is also his Gospel'.[46]

The grace of the inspiration of the Scriptures is a prophetic charism *proper to the faith of the Church*. It is not a flame which was enkindled in former times in Paul, Mark, Luke... for the era of the composition of their writings and which is extinguished today, an isolated phenomenon for a particular age. Apostolic preaching, also inspired (cf. 1 Th 2:13), preceded the writings; it was continued during the period when the writings were drawn up; it continues today, still, as ever, inspired, in the full measure in which it is the expression of the Church's faith. No one, today as yesterday, can proclaim his faith in Christ except under the inspiration of the Spirit (cf. 1 Cor 12:3). The Scriptures form part of primitive, inspired preaching, a preaching given a fixed written form, in order that it may be for ever 'the mainstay of our faith'.[47] Furthermore, the preaching of the apostles is continued in today's preaching.

Between the preaching and writings of apostolic times and the actual proclamation of the faith today, there is certainly a difference. But it is not between an inspired apostolate in former times and an absence of inspiration in today's apostolate. The inspired word is necessary now, ceaselessly to stimulate the Christian community in a world where all are born pagans, and to cultivate within the community itself a faith which remains fragile. But in the historical beginnings of the Church, the word of God had the advantage of a privileged charism, an inspiration, I would say, *a specific authority which made this word a norm for all ages of the Church*. Between the inspiration of apostolic times and that of today there is a difference analogous to that which distinguishes, without

separating, the apostles of the first ages and those of today.
The latter, too, are founders and they too are inspired, but as
successors of the former and in fidelity to their teaching.

Must we not also admit a diversity of inspiration within the
writings of the Old Testament,[48] a different level of inspiration in Old and New Testament? If salvation is accomplished in the course of a history of which Christ is the
climax, it does not seem logical to place the charism of
inspiration at the same level throughout the stages of history,
as perfect inspiration present at the imperfect stage.[49] The Old
Testament was *en route* towards the day of God and the
Messiah. The inspiration of Jesus, the supreme prophet,
differed from that of olden times: 'It was said...but I say...'.
Moreoever, the Spirit acts in the apostles as the Spirit of
Christ.

With regard to the reading of the Scriptures, we know that this
is subject to a collection of rules: to all the rules of grammar
and logic and to others which are required for the interpretation of a text; there is a further rule, proper to Scripture, and
it bears an eminent name: the rule of the Holy Spirit. He is the
law of the life of the Church (cf. Rom 8:2); he is also the law of
reading the Scriptures. 'Scriptural prophecy is never a matter
for the individual' (2 Pet 1:20). Inspired by the Spirit, the
Book is not understood in depth except by inspired readers.[50]

The reader must therefore be open to the action of the
Spirit. 'The word of God living and active' (Heb 4:12) is such
in the measure in which it is lived, in which it can be active:
'God's message is a power... among you who believe it' (1 Th
2:13). The first disposition is therefore a lively faith which
enables one to be open to the meaning derived from the book.
Kierkegaard wanted us to read the Bible 'in the presence of
God', as a fiancé would read a letter from his fiancée. Hence
the importance of prayer which means a welcome given to
grace: 'Fervent prayer is absolutely necessary for an understanding of divine realities'.[51]

The great grace obtained from reading the Scriptures is an
encounter with the Lord Jesus. In all his activities the Spirit is
at the service of the mystery of sonship and its realization in
the world; by the Scriptures he makes Christ come into this
world and brings about his growth by calling men to union

with the Son. It is Christ who is, according to St Paul, the deep meaning of the inspired book; he is 'the spirit', that is, the living and life-giving reality who fills the Bible and without which this book would be only a 'dead letter', a lifeless document. This deep meaning is more than an underlying idea in the text and is intended not only for the understanding of the reader. The Lord Jesus himself is 'the spirit', he is in person the deep meaning which is derived from the reading and revealed to the eye of the reader.

Moreover, it is the Holy Spirit who opens the eye of the believer, that he may see this face in the transparency of the pages. For the Spirit is freedom: he removes the veil and enables us to see freely.[52] The believer thus finds himself face to face with the Lord, exposed to the brightness of his face: the veil falls from his eyes. 'For the Lord (Jesus) is the Spirit, and where the Spirit of the Lord is, there is freedom. And we, with unveiled faces, reflecting like mirrors the brightness of the Lord, are turned into the image that we reflect...' (2 Cor 3:17f.).

Such was the experience of the Apostle, it is that of every Christian ('and of us all...'). No one has ever expressed so splendidly as St Paul does in this text, the work of grace that the Spirit accomplishes in the reading of the Scriptures.

The Spirit and the sacraments of the Church

The whole Church is the sacrament of the outpouring of the Spirit. But she also has special rites of sanctification called sacraments in a more precise sense. Risen in the Spirit, Christ has become the source of the Spirit in the world; founded by the Spirit, the Church is the place where this Spirit wells up; similarly, the individual sacraments are instituted in the Spirit and at the same time they are channels where the Spirit is at work.

The Spirit given in baptism

The messianic gift of the Spirit was announced in the image of water which God would cause to well up from the earth; it was symbolized by the water flowing from the side of Christ. Baptism is the sacrament that typifies this gift. To be 'born through water and the Spirit' (Jn 3:5) is to be born through the Spirit of whom baptismal water is the symbol: 'In one Spirit we were all baptised' (1 Cor 12:13).

Baptism is the rite of beginning, the water of birth in which God is father, creator and saviour through the Spirit; it is the 'bath' of rebirth and renewal (cf. Tit 3:5), which belies mortal old age by linking man once more to his eternal origin, that of the Son who is born of the Father through the Spirit. Birth into earthly life is also a beginning, but a beginning of growing old: hardly has man been born than he moves away from his 'newness'. Baptism is not something in the past which is followed by a succession of years of Christian life: baptismal grace is a constant openness towards the future. Once born through the Spirit, the believer is always being born, he does not emerge from this 'bath of renewal'. Just as in Christ death was reversed through birth, *so the Christian era flows towards the source*, towards the eternal begetting of the Son in the Spirit.

The Spirit acts in baptism just as he raises Jesus to life, that is, in a lavish begetting of Christ : 'in baptism... you have been raised with him' (Col 2:12). He raises up the faithful with Christ by incorporating them in him: 'in the one Spirit we were all baptised' in one body (cf. 1 Cor 12:13).[53] He works so that the Son may be begotten in the world and assume a body there, and so that, in the begetting of the only Son, men may become sons. Here, as always, he is the Spirit of fatherhood and sonship. This Son to whom the Spirit gives a body in the world is therefore both individual and collective. Baptism assembles a people, founds the Church. St Paul sees this sacrament as announced in the passage of the Red Sea, where the Hebrews established themselves as a people 'baptised into Moses' (cf. 1 Cor 10:1f.). Baptismal grace is a power of 'gathering together' and of mutual communion: 'one body, one Spirit...one baptism' (Eph 4:4); it is the 'fellowship of the Spirit'.

The eternal assembly is thus prepared, that of the fullness of the gift of the Spirit. Even now the faithful are taken out of darkness and transferred to the Kingdom (cf. Col 1:12f.); they are saints (cf. Rom 1:7 and *passim*), protected from the retribution which is coming (cf. 1 Th 1:10; 5:9; 1 Pet 3:20f.);

eschatological judgement announced as a baptism 'with the Spirit and with fire' (Mt 3:11), is exercised in their favour. They are incorporated into Christ who is in person the final mystery.

In the meantime, the gift of the Spirit is still only like a 'deposit'; the first union with Christ is at the same time 'a call to union with the Son' (cf. 1 Cor 1:9). Baptism, which is the entry into the last times, is also a door through which to penetrate ever deeper. The fact that the eschatological gift is conferred by a rite using water proves that the Church is born to the Spirit amidst earthly realities, that the heavenly mystery is lived by her on earth, and that the seed of the future, sown in time, has yet to flower, until time is absorbed into the birth of eternity.

Given in confirmation

In order that baptismal grace may be developed, the Church makes use of a sacrament the name of which specifies its function: confirmation.

It is difficult to define what is specific in this sacrament and to distinguish its effects from those of baptism. When confirmation is called *the* sacrament of the Spirit, we risk forgetting that in baptism the believer is already steeped in the Spirit. When we say that baptism is the sacrament of incorporation into Christ, whereas confirmation is that of integration into the Church, we forget that the Church herself is the body of Christ, with which baptism unites the faithful, and that union with Christ and integration into the Church are accomplished in the same movement (cf. 1 Cor 10:17; 12:13, 27; Gal 3:27–29). It would seem that confirmation *adds nothing, but confirms everything*: its grace is that of baptism, but with its dynamism increased. That is why it has been possible, in the course of the history of theology, to attribute to confirmation most of the effects proper to baptism.

Although it does not add anything, confirmation has its own identity. The grace of the sacrament differs from that of baptism in the way in which the adult differs from the child of yesterday, in whom, however, the same human nature was already present. Such is the conclusion which, in the absence of light thrown by Scripture, can be drawn from Christian tradition.

A man grows to maturity when the riches already in him are developed, riches which characterize the person. A baptized child has to advance towards adulthood by a personal blossoming out as a Christian. The Spirit who inhabits him is a power for developing personality, as we have already said. In creating the world the Spirit imprints upon it a movement of evolution towards the climax which is the human person; in this creative movement he draws with him every human being. Jesus himself was led by the Spirit to personal fulfilment in death and resurrection. By confirmation the Spirit is present to help the believer to develop towards this adult age where his union with the Christ of Easter will be more authentic.

In what does this evolution consist? In that he is a person, man is autonomous and capable of union, integrated in a network of relationships. Because of this autonomy and power of union, he is a responsible being with duties towards others enjoined on him. The grace of baptism introduces man into the mystery of salvation which is in Christ, but this mystery is intended for the whole human race; it therefore saves each one individually by enabling him to be joined to the mystery of the salvation of all. The Spirit of confirmation ensures that each believer passes from the age of receiving, proper to childhood, to that of giving, in which the believer shares Christ's responsibility with regard to the Church and humanity: he enables baptismal grace to develop according to the potential for community inherent in a person.

He sets the seal on *membership of the Church*, inaugurated by baptism. In the accounts of Acts 8:14–17, in which theology believes it can grasp the meaning of confirmation, the mission of Peter and John to the newly-baptized in Samaria, and the gift of the Spirit which they confer, signify that these neophytes are integrated into the Church of which the apostles are the leaders, the centre of which is in Jerusalem.

The Spirit strengthens membership of the Church *in order to ensure a share in the responsibilities of the community*; he accustoms the faithful to receive ministries and confers these on them. The laying-on of hands and the gift of the Spirit have this meaning more than once in Acts (cf. 6:6; 13:3).[54] According to Methodius of Olympus, every Christian whose faith is adult assumes the role of the Church as a mother of the human race, one who dispenses salvation. Thus Paul, first born into the Church and nourished by her, becomes in his turn 'Church' and is acquainted with the 'travail of giving birth to those who, through him, have believed in the Lord...'. Does he not say: 'My little children! I must go through the pain of giving birth to you all over again, until Christ is formed in you'?[55]

In the network of Christian relationships, the most fundamental is *that which unites us to the Lord Jesus*. It is always on account of the Son and union with him that the Spirit works on the heart of man. The grace of confirmation is intended to increase faith in Christ in love and hope. This faith, full of love and hope becomes active and urges us to *bear witness* to Christ to the degree that it receives public, social expression.

Confirmation is therefore intended to make a Christian adult. The grace of this sacrament is indeed that of baptism, but baptism from which dimensions of common life are developed. It tends to an effective integration *into Christ saviour of the world and into the Church, universal institution of salvation*. Its charism is service, power of apostolate, courage for a profession of one's faith. Fundamentally, it is union with the Christ of Easter.

If such is the nature of this grace, is it possible to answer the question often asked: at what age is it appropriate to confer this sacrament? During childhood? Later? Baptismal riches mature according to the rhythm of the psychological development of a person. The Spirit 'does not overstep or upset the laws of humanity... he integrates himself into man's potential for virtue and sets it free from within, beginning here, according to the possibilities found here'.[56] If therefore baptism is celebrated at an adult age, confirmation will immediately set a seal on Christian initiation. If baptism is given in early infancy, there would seem to be a place for deferring confirmation until an age when personal potential for virtue is developed.[57]

Spiritual bread

The Eucharist is eminently the sacrament of the Holy Spirit. For it is, more than any other, the sacrament of Christ's passover, from which flow rivers of living water. It is the bread of life (cf. Jn 6:48–51), the life which is that of the Spirit. It belongs to the realities of spirit and life (cf. Jn 6:65) which constitute the domain of the Spirit. St Paul calls it 'spiritual food' (1 Cor 10:3). It is in the power of the Spirit that the Eucharist is celebrated and in this same power it spreads in the Church. In this sacrament, as in everything, the Spirit is at the beginning and at the end; he is the soul of its celebration.

He is at the beginning. It is his prerogative to transform the bread and wine into real symbols of the paschal presence of Christ in the midst of the Church. For it is through him that Christ rises again; moreover, the Eucharist is what we can see in this world of the resurrection of Jesus. The Spirit is creative, it is he who gives meaning to things; it falls to him to bring the bread and wine and the meal to their most intense fulfilment, by making them the bread of eternal life and the wine of the Kingdom. He is creator of all things by attracting them to Christ because 'all things were created through him and for him' (cf. Col 1:16f.). He influences the bread and wine and incorporates them into Christ, making them subsist entirely in him. In the Eucharist, the Spirit manifests clearly that he is at the service of the Son's presence in the world and that he has the power to incorporate into Christ.

It is therefore the Spirit that the Church invokes so that the Eucharist may take place: 'Let your Spirit come upon these gifts to make them holy, so that they may become for us the body and blood of our Lord, Jesus Christ' (Eucharistic Prayer II). Then 'the Spirit comes down on the gifts, *making the mystery of the resurrection of our Lord from the dead a present reality... This Spirit, who has raised him from the dead, now comes down to celebrate the mysteries of the resurrection of his body'.[58]

The Spirit transforms the bread and wine *by the very power which raises Christ to life*, for he always acts in the Church as the power of the resurrection of Jesus. The changing of the bread and wine into the sacrament of the presence of Christ is derived from the mystery of the resurrection, from the mystery of God who, in the Spirit, begets his son in the world.

The transforming action of the Spirit is thus connected with the mission which devolves on him to glorify Christ, to testify in his favour, by manifesting him to the Church (cf. Jn 16:14). The Eucharist is an excellent witness: it attests, by achieving, the resurrection of Jesus in the Church.

It is the risen Christ that the Spirit makes present in the Church – nothing is added to Christ's glorification, which is complete – the Spirit makes him present as in the resurrection itself, so that the faithful enter into communion with him in the passover of salvation. 'In each of the particles (Christ) approaches the one who receives him. He acclaims and reveals his resurrection.'[59]

Nor does Christ come *after* his death, but in the moment of death in which the Spirit glorifies him. Jesus was offered through an eternal Spirit (cf. Heb 9:14); his offering was 'made eternal' in this Spirit. Jesus retains his glory at the summit of his ascent to the Father whither the Spirit led him, that is, in his death: in submitting to the Spirit, even to death, he gives complete acceptance to the Father. The Eucharist is the Easter sacrament, the sacrament of Christ risen to life in death. It is the extension to our space and time of the passover of salvation, so that the Church may take part in it.

To make him present, the Spirit does not destroy the bread, which earth has given and human hands have made, in such a way that we should have to say: 'On the altar there is no longer any bread, there is only the misleading appearance of it'. The Spirit does not put an end to the first creation, he brings it to its final fulfilment. Sin alone breaks with creation, whereas the Spirit transforms it by enriching it and by going beyond the act of creation. He changes the bread and wine by making the best bread and wine imaginable, the sacrament of the eschatological banquet.[60]

But the Spirit does not work alone, he works in conjunction with Christ as well as for himself. It is Jesus who says over the bread: 'This is my body'. His words are said in the omnipotence of the Spirit through whom Christ is the Kyrios: what it decrees it causes to exist. It is thus that the Lord will transfigure our wretched bodies 'into copies of his glorious body'. He will do this 'by the same power (that of the Spirit) with which he can subdue the whole universe' (Ph 3:21).

Latin theology has tended to attribute the Eucharistic transformation to the words of Jesus alone, pronounced by the minister of the Church; Greek theology has been inclined to reserve this role of consecration to the Spirit.[61] In the Old Testament God created by Breath *and* by Word; in the New, every salvific action is the concern both of the Spirit and of Christ in complete unity of action. From this we must conclude that the Eucharist is the common work of them both. Christ is the mediator of all sanctification, but through the power of the Spirit. The words: 'This is my body, this is my blood', pronounced by the Church, form part of the apostolic proclamation; these are the very words of Christ (cf. Rom 10:14; 2 Cor 2:17; 13:3), but they are made effective by the power of the Spirit who conveys them. In sacramental realities – in the Church, in the Eucharist – the action of the Spirit assumes concrete forms: in the Eucharist it is exercised through the ministry of the Church, through which Christ's action is expressed.

If the Church begs the Spirit to come down on the gifts, so that he may transform them, it is not that the Eucharist is one of the graces that the Church obtains by asking for them and according to the degree of her confidence. This descent is of the essence of the institution. The transformation of the bread and wine is part of the memorial established by Jesus and celebrated according to his command. Similarly, the sanctifying power of baptism is inherent in the rite that the Church is commissioned to carry out. The Church therefore pronounces with assurance the words of Jesus: 'This is my body...', but she accompanies them with a humble prayer to the Spirit, for she is totally the receiver, even in the accomplishment of her mission. Her attitude is one of welcoming, her ministry is exercised in humility and prayer. Jesus himself receives power from the Spirit, who is, however, at his service. The Church therefore presents the bread and wine to the Spirit that he may make the resurrection of Christ visible through the ministry of the priest who says: 'This is my body...'.

* * *

The Spirit who makes the Eucharistic celebration possible is also the fruit of it reaped by the faithful. In communicating with Christ whom the Spirit makes present, the Church receives the gift of the Spirit.

St Paul speaks of a spiritual food, a spiritual rock, a spiritual drink (cf. 1 Cor 10:3f.). John's gospel makes use of a strange image which we have already pointed out; 'I am the *bread* of life. He who comes to me will never be hungry; he who believes in me will never *thirst*' (Jn 6:35). Bread which satisfies one's hunger and slakes one's thirst! Although incoherent in appearance, the image is a rich one. Christ is both bread and fountain.

When celebrating the Eucharist the Church relives the experience of John who has seen and borne witness (cf. Jn 19:35). She contemplates the one whom they pierced, she sees a fountain flowing beneath the gate on the right side of the Temple (cf. Ezek 47). Her joy is great when Christ invites her to come to him, to drink of the fountain from his wounded side: 'If any man is thirsty, let him come to me...' (Jn 7:37–38).

It is there, from his open side, that rivers of living water flow. The Spirit is given at the moment of this paschal outpouring, when Jesus in his glorifying death 'sends out the Spirit'. For the Eucharist is the presence of Christ at this moment when in his death God glorifies him in the superabundance of the Spirit. The faithful are sanctified by the Eucharist as they were by baptism: in communion with Christ in his death and glory.

The entire concern of the Church in the celebration of the Eucharist is to enter into communion. The Eucharist is the sacrament of presence, we must welcome Christ and open our hearts to the one who comes. It is the sacrament of Christ in his sacrifice, we must offer the sacrifice, not by repeating it – it cannot be repeated – we must offer it by receiving it, by sharing in it. It is the eminent sacrifice of the outpouring of the Spirit, we must let ourselves be overwhelmed by the Spirit. 'Take this, all of you, and eat... drink...'; the entire role of the Church is given direction by this invitation.

By her acceptance the Church is transformed. The Spirit came down on the bread and wine and made them the body of

Christ in his sacrifice. He comes down on the Church and makes her the body of Christ in his sacrifice. Received by the Church in union with the Christ of Easter, the Spirit brings about this identifying union with Christ in his passover. The Spirit and Christ together sanctify the Church in an action, the interplay of which is uninterrupted.

The Spirit's action on the Church is different from that on the bread and wine. With regard to these lifeless elements, his power is imperative, not awaiting any consent. But towards the Church, almighty power is loving: it solicits, attracts and transforms by making the Church a bride. This union is one of inexpressible intimacy; Christ and the Church share what cannot be shared: they are two in one unique body, in the same death and in the same filial birth. Such is the work of the Spirit who is perfect communion.

The other sacraments

The other sacraments are also instituted in Christ and his Spirit; they too are celebrated in union with Christ in his passover, and they are fountains of the Spirit.

The Church places at the disposal of the Christian who is a sinner a sacrament that has been called a second baptism, a sacrament that purifies him from his sins.

To understand *the sacrament of reconciliation*, we must first know what sin is, and to understand sin, we need to know what holiness is. Holiness is not primarily conformity to a collection of laws, nor even virtue, nor even the sum-total of the virtues. Holiness is the Holy Spirit possessed by a person who is one in faith with Christ. Sin is the opposite, it runs counter to the Spirit, it is opposed to union. According to St Paul, sinful man is deprived of God's glory (cf. Rom 3:23), he is deprived of the Holy Spirit. Unmoved by the power of the resurrection, he shuts himself in on himself by refusing union, he separates himself from Christ and falls from grace (cf. Gal 5:4).

A sin of this kind is not forgiven by the fact that God could efface it, for it is not only a stain. It is not forgiven by the fact that God could decide to forget it, for it is not only an action of the past of which one might take no further account. Sin does not exist in itself, but there are sinners; God saves them from their sin by converting them to union. He forgives sin through the gift of the Spirit by opening the heart of the person to this gift. Holy Spirit is the name for pardon, just as he is the name for God's holiness: 'The Holy Spirit...is our forgiveness' (Prayer over the Gifts, 7th Saturday of Easter).

It is Christ who dispenses the gift of the Spirit, he is the mediator of pardon. At the beginning of John's gospel, Jesus is present as the Lamb of God on whom the Spirit rests and who takes away the sin of the world (cf. Jn 1:29–33). At the climax of the account we are reminded of the paschal Lamb, none of whose bones will be broken. From his open side flows water, the symbol of the gift of the Spirit. The end of the gospel is thus related to the beginning: Jesus takes away the sin of the world because he is the all-holy Lamb, filled with the Spirit and giving the Spirit.

The gift of the Spirit is an Easter grace, an entry into union with Christ in his glorifying death, a power which ensures the passage from the flesh to the Spirit. The prodigal son said: 'I will arise and go to my father' (cf. Lk 15:18). The hour had come for passing from this world to the Father (cf. Jn 13:1). Jesus also says: 'Come now, let us go' (Jn 14:31), for 'I am going to the Father' (Jn 14:12; cf. Jn 16:28). The Spirit sets the Christian who has sinned once more on the road to the passover of Jesus; he renews his filial relationship, his union with Christ to whom the Spirit first granted to die 'for God'.

The risen Christ entrusts to the Church his power to forgive sins: 'Receive the Holy Spirit. For those whose sins you forgive, they are forgiven' (Jn 20:22f.). This Johannine account corresponds to other texts by which Jesus commissions the Church to evangelize, by preaching to all nations 'repentance for the forgiveness of sins' (Lk 24:47): she forgives sins by evangelizing, converting and making Christians. The Spirit is the forgiveness of sins in that he is the power that raises Jesus from the dead 'to justify us' (Rom 4:25). Moreover, we know that this power of justification is exercised in the world in the form of evangelization (cf. Rom 1:16f.).

The whole Church is a sacrament of evangelization and therefore of forgiveness of sins; by all her activities she calls to conversion and brings it about in the power of the Spirit. God puts in the mouth of the Church the words of reconciliation, efficacious words that produce the reconciliation they proclaim (cf. 2 Cor 5:19). In this ministry of evangelization and reconciliation the sacrament of penance is a privileged moment. The role of the Church is not reduced to pronouncing a formula of absolution by which sins can be forgiven or which states that God ceases to impute them to the penitent. It is by evangelizing, converting, reconciling that the Church forgives sins. When she says: 'Your sins are forgiven', she completes the bringing of *the Good News which justifies the sinner by converting him.*

That is why the sinner is not the only one who must be open to the Spirit so that his sins may be forgiven. The Church, first and foremost, must submit to the Spirit in order to exercise her mission of reconciliation; she must be a 'converting' Church, above all in the person of those who are especially ordained for the ministry of reconciliation. It is to them in the first place that Jesus says: '*Receive* the Holy Spirit!'

★   ★   ★

A close kinship unites the *sacrament of order* with that of confirmation. The latter helps the baptized person to become an adult Christian, it involves him in the Church's responsibilities. Ordination makes a Christian more than adult: in the language of the first centuries it makes him an elder. The Spirit entrusts to him the whole Church of God (cf. Acts 20:28), assigns to him the totality of the ministry, involves him wholly in the service of the apostolate, thus integrating him into the heart of the Church which is the covenant of salvation, the organ of presence and contact between Christ and the world.

Like the grace of confirmation, that of ordination is contained in the gift received in baptism; it steeps the Christian in the Christ of Easter and in the Holy Spirit. It does not merely confer an 'office', as people have said in recent years: by placing a Christian at the centre of the Church, sacrament of salvation, the Spirit makes him another Christ. A priestly vocation is Christian, it is 'a call to communion with the Son'. Peter and Paul were not first of all Christians and then, over and above that, apostles: their way of being Christ's disciples was to be apostles. For Paul the call to the apostolate did not differ from the grace of conversion: 'God chose to reveal his Son to me, so that I might announce...' (cf. Gal 1:16). The Spirit of his apostolate was also the grace of his sanctification: 'God himself...has marked us with his seal and given us the pledge, the Spirit, that we carry in our hearts' (cf. 2 Cor 1:22). Jesus was speaking of the apostles as such when he said: 'I consecrate myself so that they too may be consecrated' (Jn 17:19). In the sacrament of order, as in that of confirmation, the Spirit produces a complex effect which cannot be broken up into its elements: he consecrates a Christian to Christ in his death and glory and thus makes him a sacrament for salvation. Sanctification and mission are inseparable, just as sonship and the mystery of the redemption are in Jesus.

The Spirit thus conferred is that of Christ in his passover, which consecrates him in the Father and makes him Lord for the salvation of the world. He makes the priest the symbol of Christ 'the head of the Church' (Eph 1:22), that is, he intends him to be the servant of all the faithful for their salvation.

Because of the unity between personal consecration and ministry, the priest is sanctified when he exercises his ministry; he is evangelized when he evangelizes, he is consecrated to God when he makes others 'an offering, made holy by the Holy Spirit' (Rom 15:16).[62]

* * *

The Church counts the *marriage* of her faithful among the sacraments, recognizing that it was instituted in the love of the Spirit and that it is the source of the gifts of the Spirit.

It is sometimes said that on their wedding day the bride and bridegroom mutually give each other this sacrament. Not only do they give it to each other, they enter into it for its abiding celebration. Some sacraments are permanent; such is the Eucharist which lasts as long as the sacramental species exist, such above all is that other community, the Church, fundamental sacrament of Christian life. Similarly, the 'conjugal community' is an abiding sacrament, a permanent source of sanctification.

The Spirit is the fountainhead of this sacrament. Through

him God has created man and woman; through him who is love and union God gives rise to the love and union between them; through him who tends to make everything personal, the relationship of the sexes becomes a covenant, a personal relationship. The Spirit has created a world of symbols, among which marriage is unrivalled: 'a great mystery', applying to Christ and the Church (cf. Eph 5:32).

Every marriage, whether Christian or not, contains this reflection of the union of Christ and the Church.[63] But in the case of Christian partners, the symbol is more real, richer in its mystery. Between the symbol and the reality the connection is closer. The Spirit who creates everything 'for Christ' wants to bring the first creation to the point of final fulfilment in Christian married couples.

The grace given in every sacrament is also an unremitting call to welcome this grace. The gift received in baptism invites the believer to allow himself to become ever more Christian: 'Be clothed with Christ' is St Paul's recommendation (cf. Rom 13:14) to those who have already been clothed with him (cf. Gal 3:27). Similarly, the 'conjugal community' calls for continual celebration, continual deepening. Married couples who are Christians from the beginning of their marriage have to become ever more Christian through the power of the Spirit, to come ever closer to the mystery of Christ and the Church of which they are the symbol.

The grace of this sacrament, like all the activity of the Spirit, creates persons: a grace of intimate personal relationship. 'Husbands must love their wives as they love their own bodies; for a man to love his wife is for him to love himself... A man must leave his father and mother and be joined to his wife, and the two will become one body (one flesh)' (Eph 5:28, 31). Body, flesh: these words relate to a person;[64] the formulas 'one body', 'one flesh', speak of a relationship so intimate that it is indestructible. This is how Jesus understood marriage: as a union of persons so closely knit by the creator that man has no right to sever it.

Indissoluble by nature, according to the image of it given by the union of Christ and the Church, marriage is nonetheless vulnerable and threatened, as is every reality on earth. In relating it to the eschatological model, in making it a sacrament, the Spirit has not changed its nature; he vouches for its indissolubility. In the power of the Spirit, Christian couples have the duty to become ever more husband and wife; more than other people, they have the grace and the duty to make their 'conjugal community' effectively indissoluble.[65]

The indissoluble bond of marriage is not a juridical, impersonal reality, a bond existing in its own right, independently of the people united by it. Its importance is not derived from a contract that the sacrament consecrates and makes unchangeable. The bonds of marriage cannot be dissociated from conjugal fidelity; indissolubility is a gift and a duty which concern the married couple at that personal depth called by Scripture 'the heart'. Though given by the creator, indissolubility must be unceasingly converted into reality; just as a human being is a person through God and yet must not cease to 'create' himself. In the union of Christ and the Church, as in the union of the Father and the Son, the indissoluble bond has a name, it is called the Holy Spirit. In marriage too the bond is of the order of spiritual realities; it is a union of persons, born in the encounter of a man and a woman, a union which never fully attains completion. The grace of the sacrament deepens love through divine charity, making it capable of braving everything that might tend to separate the couple.

The love which establishes the 'conjugal community' is also the law which governs it. What is true of the whole Church is true of a Christian family. The law for a Christian life is the Holy Spirit, that is, divine charity, no other law is imposed unless it is related to charity. The Apostle states emphatically: the faithful have been freed in Christ from laws, whatever they may be, that are exterior to the person, they are subject only to this exacting law of freedom – the Holy Spirit and his love. Every other demand imposed in conjugal morality is insignificant compared with being one in love.[66]

* * *

There is a sacrament in the Church for the faithful afflicted by illness; *the anointing of the sick*. The words anointing conjures up in itself the gift of the Spirit and his power. The Council of Trent states on this point: 'Anointing very aptly represents the grace of the Holy Spirit with which the soul is invisibly anointed'.[67] It is said first and foremost of Jesus that he was anointed with the Spirit and with power (cf. Acts 10:38).

God is close to the poor, to people in their weakness and in their trials. It is to them that the Good News of the Kingdom is announced. The heart of God's Messiah was with the poor; at the sight of them 'Jesus was moved with pity'. In his death he is united with people in their deepest misery. In this death of the Son, God becomes intimately close to man in his helplessness. A sacrament is given to the Church which expresses the privileged presence of God and his Christ to man in his sickness.

However, it is through the Spirit that God is present to the world. The Spirit is the finger of God, it is through him that the Lord Jesus touches man in his weakness. The anointing of the sick is a sacrament of the Holy Spirit and his love.

Tradition sees in the text of James 5:14f. a description of this sacrament: 'If one of you is ill, he should send for the elders of the church, and they must anoint him with oil in the name of the Lord and pray over him. The prayer of faith will save the sick man and the Lord will raise him up again; and if he has committed any sins, he will be forgiven'. The prayer of faith asks for the salvation of the sick person; the anointing has the same purpose (cf. Mk 6:13; Lk 10:34): the patient will be saved, the Lord will raise him up again. These words recall the cures worked by the Lord: he 'took her by the hand and helped her up' (Mk 1:31), 'Stand up and go on your way. Your faith has saved you' (Lk 17:19). The salvation brought by Jesus to the sick was simultaneously a healing and the forgiveness of sins (cf. Mk 2:5; Lk 7:48, 50). It is the same in this sacrament. The unique grace of the Spirit is intended for the sanctification of the sick person and for his recovery; *this is what is at work in the resurrection of Jesus*: an eschatological gift, for the salvation of the whole person.[68]

It is therefore in the nature of the sacrament to bring the sick person physical comfort which may even lead to healing. But the sacrament does not act like medicine. Medicines repair the harm done to physical powers, acting at surface level. The action of the Spirit touches the roots. Just as the love with which a person is loved can enable him to find strength and the joy of life again, so the grace of this sacrament reaches to the heart of man, *it comforts the sufferer as a person*. From this starting point, its action may have repercussions on his physical strength. It is one of the characteristics of the Spirit to act on the person. It is in this way that Christ was raised from death, beginning with the mystery of his person, when God begot *his Son* fully through the power of the Spirit. It is in this way too that the Eucharist is 'the medicine of immortality and the remedy by which we escape death',[69] because it acts on the person of the believer, introducing him into union with the Risen Christ.

The finger of God touches the Christian at his very core which is simultaneously the highest and the lowest point. The Spirit inhabits the person of the believer and acts on him. By reaching the sufferer at this point grace sanctifies him, by forgiving sin, while at the same time bringing him comfort.

Living according to the Spirit

The Spirit who is the source of Christian life is also the norm directing it. He is in person the law of the New Testament.[70] St Paul exhorts us: 'Since the Spirit is our life, let us be directed by the Spirit' (Gal 5:25). There is a great nobility about the law which governs Christian morality: this law motivates God himself in his action, and Christ in his resurrection lives by it: 'the law of the spirit of life in Christ Jesus' (Rom 8:2).

This law is *personal*. It is itself a person, a divine person! Furthermore, it is concerned with man in the centre of his being, in his 'I'. It builds up the person and creates union between God and man. The Spirit is always a personalizing force.

The Mosaic law was external to the person. It was promulgated from the top of a mountain, it was expressed in a code with numerous precepts. The new law is *one*, affecting us in the unity of our person. It is *interior*: the Spirit who is the inwardness of God is poured into our heart. The law of holiness is interior to such an extent that a Christian is holy in his very being.[71] It is promulgated, made known, only by its presence in the heart: 'The anointing he gave teaches us everything... and as it has taught us, so we must stay in him' (cf. 1 Jn 2:27). However, because our earthly condition distracts us too often from this interior anointing, the law needs to be expressed in words and taught by human beings.

Written laws contain precepts; they do not give the strength to observe them; being written in the will, the new law *makes it dynamic*, for the Spirit is strength. The will produces acts, just as a plant ripens its fruit, as a mother gives birth: 'The Spirit brings fruits of love, joy, peace, patience, kindness' (Gal 5:22). Such birth may be painful, but the force that brings it to birth is powerful.

Although the law is imposed on man, it *makes him free*, for 'where the Spirit of the Lord is, there is freedom' (2 Cor 3:17). One who is 'directed by the Spirit' poured into his heart, obeys the law of his own heart. Doubtless he is obeying the will of another, that of God, but this will is within him and has become his own wish: he does what he wants. Because this law deep within him is a strength, it frees a Christian from adverse powers and from his own weakness in which he has hitherto been imprisoned. No one is as free as a person who has the desire, and the strength, to do his duty.

Before writing the law of the Spirit in the heart of a believer God engraved it in Christ, glorifying him in death: this law is of the Spirit, *of Christ and of the resurrection*. Once more we find that indissoluble unity of the Son and the Spirit into which the Church is baptized. Holiness consists in submission to the Spirit who is at work in Christ's passover, flowing out with Christ in this passover: 'Since you have been brought back to true life with Christ, you must look for the things that are in heaven... You have died, and the life you have is hidden with Christ... You must kill everything in you that belongs only to earthly life' (Col 3:1–5). The same Spirit that 'ripens' his most beautiful fruit in the Christ of Easter, bears fruit in the faithful through works of love, patience, kindness... (cf. Gal 5:22).

The Spirit is a *law of death* in the heart of a man of flesh: 'Those who walk by the Spirit do not gratify the desires of the flesh. For the desires of the Spirit are against the flesh... Those who belong to Christ Jesus have crucified the flesh with its passions and desires' (Gal 5:17, 24 RSV). But the Spirit brings *birth* out of this death. It is the new law of sonship, the power of God who raises his son to life in an eternal begetting. Children are born to God through their consent to this law which is resurrection and life (cf. Rom 8:2, 11). Fidelity to the law of the Spirit is not merely a pledge of resurrection but a 'birth-giving' process. Through fidelity to this law, a Christian passes from his initial birth in baptism towards fulfilment. Paul pursues his course to try to capture Christ, 'to know him and the power of *his* resurrection' (cf. Ph 3:12). 'What does it mean to try to capture him? What Paul has previously said: "to take my place in the resurrection of the dead" '.[72] The Spirit's power to raise to life opens up a way into the interior freedom of the faithful and, in their sanctification, he begins to make the resurrection of Jesus visible in the world.

The way is endless, *Christian morality is open-ended*, the work of the making of man into a person is continuous, for we shall never assimilate completely either the power of the Spirit offered to us or the sonship of Jesus. The end already partially reached remains ahead of man, until the Day of the Lord and complete union with the Son. A boundless desire is awakened in us. The spirit does not cease to sigh (cf. Rom 8:26). In Christianity the desire is sacred, it is the repercussion in our hearts of the presence of the Spirit and of infinite union with him: 'The Spirit and the Bride say: "Come!" ' (cf. Rev 22:17). Even in the blissful encounter with Christ, the desire, although satisfied, can never be exhausted, for the Spirit, through whom all is consummated, is an eternal beginning (see below, pp. 145–148).

The whole of Christian morality is characterized by the definition of the Spirit: *oneness*. The three essential virtues are unifying: faith is open and welcoming, charity is union, hope seeks with assurance for complete union. It is the Spirit of oneness that arouses faith in Christ, he himself is charity and animates hope (cf. Rom 5:5). His action is always concerned with persons and he creates being united with one another on a personal level.

Specific moral demands are motivated by the network of relationships in which the believer is involved. The Apostle forbids fornication, not by appealing to the dignity of a man who tries to control his passions, but in the name of his membership of the body of Christ (cf. 1 Cor 6:12–20). For the same reason he forbids divisions among Christians (cf. 1 Cor 1:13; 11:18, 20) and telling each other lies (cf. Col 3:9–11). Everything is regulated by the law of unity.

A life of charity

Agapē (love) is a keyword in Christian morality, it has the same meaning as oneness or communion. Like the Spirit, of whom it is the imprint in our hearts, it contains the whole law: 'The whole of the law is summarized in a single command: Love...' (Gal 5:14; Rom 13:9). It is the synthesis of perfection, because it is the imprint in our hearts of the Spirit who is the holiness of God. As an eschatological virtue (cf. 1 Cor 13:13), *agapē* is the source of all virtue; for the first thing that motivates the Christian is the last thing to be attained. Faith which is open and welcoming is fostered by a movement of charity, in hope it is again charity that seeks total oneness: 'Charity believes all, hopes all' (cf. 1 Cor 13:7). Here, as elsewhere, the Spirit is at the end and at the beginning.

Because of the central place occupied by charity, we must repeat that *Christian morality is freedom*. Love does not only set free from the restraint of external laws – 'the fruit of the Spirit is love, joy...against such things there is no law' (Gal 5:22f.) – love is identified with freedom. Subject to the Spirit's law of love, man can do what he likes; he is simultaneously submissive and free, obliged to be free: 'You were called...to freedom' (cf. Gal 5:13f.). When the law is identical with the Spirit who is freedom, submission to the law merges with freedom. Liberating for the one who loves, charity is also liberating for those loved. In a society of brethren, everyone is free.

The law of charity is *perfect happiness*, it bears within it this reward: one who loves asks only to love. The Jews compared the Mosaic law to a yoke. Jesus says that his yoke is gentle and his burden light (cf. Mt 11:29). The weight of a law which is love gives support as much as it is supported. Here too the Spirit who is charity is at the beginning and at the end.

The law of charity *is not established as a morality for super-*

beings. The Spirit of love, infinite power, is also God's humility. His fruits are: 'patience, kindness, trustfulness, gentleness' (cf. Gal 5:22). Charity is always ready to serve: 'Serve one another...in works of love' (cf. Gal 5:13; Eph 4:2; Col 3:12). The purpose of the law is not so much to form models of virtue, but rather people who know how to love (cf. 1 Cor 13:3).

In a morality consisting of observances, man can boast of his meticulous fidelity (cf. Lk 18:11). In a morality concerned with virtues, he can congratulate himself on the perfection acquired. 'Charity does not boast' (cf. 1 Cor 13:4). For 'the love of Christ which urges us' (cf. 2 Cor 5:14) is that of Christ, it is the Spirit of God poured into our hearts. Charity is therefore a gift, it is received with humility. Moreover, this gift is dynamic: the observance of the law is imposed on us, it is observed by our accepting it in its dynamism. No one can boast, *the merit of a Christian consists in receiving*. Humility is the fundamental attitude in which helpless man accepts the power of the Spirit. The Spirit, it is true, involves a Christian in undertakings (cf. Eph 2:10), some of which are out of the ordinary. But moral success is not so much in what is achieved as in what is attempted, in our consent to the Spirit who expresses his desire through the heart of the believer. *The value of man is in his humble aspirations*.

A law which is interior promulgates itself and *allows us to discern*, in the circumstances of life, the good to be done and the evil to be avoided. It is a movement which provides the light to illumine the way ahead. 'Transform yourselves through renewing your spirit (in accepting the Spirit), in order that you may discern what is the will of God, what is good, pleasant and perfect' (Rom 12:2; 1 Th 5:19–21). The conscience is formed and refined in the practice of charity: 'That your love for each other may increase more and more and never stop improving your knowledge and deepening your perception, so that you can always recognize what is best' (Ph 1:9f.). Hence the importance, for the discernment of the duties of a Christian, of integration into the Christian community where charity is deepened and right decisions come to maturity.[73]

In Judaism, Pentecost had become the feast of the Covenant

and of the gift of the Law;[74] on this day Christians celebrate the outpouring of the Holy Spirit. The relationship is perfect. The fullness of time has come: the gift of the Spirit is both the eternal Covenant and its law.

A life of faith

The love of the Spirit poured into our hearts is directed first and foremost towards Christ. The Spirit always works in favour of the Son in the Church as well as in the Trinity. By the power of the Spirit, people become open to Christ and put their faith in him. The Acts of the Apostles juxtaposes the words 'Spirit' and 'faith': Stephen and Barnabas are 'filled with the Spirit and with faith' (Acts 6:5; 11:24). No one can make a profession of faith, 'no one can say, "Jesus is Lord!"' unless he is under the influence of the Holy Spirit' (1 Cor 12:3). According to 1 John, the presence of the Spirit in our hearts is the guarantee of faith in Jesus.[75]

This power enabling us to believe is the power exercised by the Holy Spirit when raising Christ from the dead. The action which exalts Christ in his lordship submits man to the Lord by 'the obedience of faith' (Rom 1:5), 'every thought is our prisoner, captured to be brought into obedience to Christ' (2 Cor 10:5). When Thomas believes, Jesus becomes in actual fact *his* Lord and *his* God. Faith is the glorification of Jesus giving light in the heart of the Church (cf. 2 Cor 4:6).

Furthermore, faith acts in the believer as a power of creation and of resurrection: 'You have been raised up with him (Christ) through your belief in the power of God who raised him from the dead' (Col 2:12). From this we can understand that salvation is given not only by reason of our faith, but in the very act of faith itself (cf. e.g. Rom 1:17; 3:22; 10:9; Gal 2:20; 3:2, 5, 14). Whereas 'sinners are deprived of the glory of God' (Rom 3:23), God raises up Christ 'for our justification' (cf. Rom 4:25); he creates believers, that is, people who are justified through his action in glorifying Jesus.

Hence the complex unity of action between the Spirit and Christ is once more apparent. The Spirit leads man to accept Christ through faith, and it is in his acceptance of Christ that the believer is subject to the vivifying and justifying action of the Spirit. The Spirit is cause and effect, he is at the beginning and at the end: no one believes in Christ except through the Spirit (cf. 1 Cor 12:3) and it is through faith that we receive the promised Spirit (cf. Gal 3:14).

The Spirit who stimulates our faith is love; that is why faith and charity are intimately connected. Faith goes out to Christ (cf. Jn 7:37), receives him (cf. Jn 1:12), allows itself to be grasped by him and grasps him; it is carried along by a movement of love. it is born in the immense act of love in which the Father gloriously begets Christ, that is, in the Holy Spirit. Belief begins at the same time as love, and the surest means of preserving this faith is a great love for the Lord, and life in the Spirit, the cause and 'confirmation of our faith'.[76] Because faith is inseparable from charity, it flourishes in the Church, for God pronounces his Word in the charity of the Spirit, and it is in charity that it is received.

★ ★ ★

The first sacrament of faith used to be called *phōtismos*, enlightenment. Baptismal water is light, it cleanses by enlightenment. The man born blind was sent by Jesus to Jesus – 'Siloam is translated the One sent' (cf. Jn 9:7) – to find spiritual water enabling him to see. The sacrament of faith is a spring of knowledge and a fountain of youth.

According to St Paul, a believer has possibilities of knowledge of which an unspiritual man is deprived (cf. 1 Cor 2:14): he is spiritual (cf. 1 Cor 2:15; 3:1; Gal 6:1), he has access to the 'things of the Spirit' (cf. 1 Cor 2:13). God confers on him 'a spirit of wisdom and perception of what is revealed to enlighten the eyes of his heart' (cf. Eph 1:17f.); he enables him to grasp in his own depths the realities of which the Spirit has knowledge, the knowledge of the depths of God (cf. 1 Cor 2:10).

The divine mystery is not first revealed by stating truths, by 'dictating' them to our intellect: God comes out of himself in the Spirit who is his ecstasy and encounters man in the depths of his person, *where intellect and will are unified at their roots*. The faith which he stimulates is an act which cannot be dissociated from an understanding will, a loving intellect, a conscious union in which the believer grasps the mystery which grasps him: you 'have all received knowledge' (1 Jn 2:20).[77]

Enlightened at a depth to which earthly knowledge has no access, this insight supposes and brings about a renewal of man at his roots. Having perceived in himself a new kind of knowledge, St Paul draws this conclusion: 'The old self has passed away, a new self is here' (2 Cor 5:17; Col 3:10). The creative Spirit enlightens while he creates.[78] He imparts knowledge of the mystery of Christ while he brings about union with the resurrection through which this mystery is accomplished: 'To know him and the power of his resurrection' (Ph 3:10). According to John 14:20, Jesus promises: 'On the Day you will know...'. It is not without reason that Christ's passover, shared by the Church, is called the Day: it is impossible to see in the dark (1 Th 5:4f.). The Spirit of the resurrection of Jesus transforms the believer's intellect into spirit,[79] and raises it to the level of Christ become spirit. 'Stephen, full of the Holy Spirit'...sees 'the glory of God and Jesus standing at the right of God' (Acts 7:55).

A life supported by hope

Man's first contact with eschatology, that of faith, awakens him to a hope in a union which is fulfilment.

Hope is a movement of desire and certainty. The *desire* leads to Christ: 'Persevere through hope in our Lord Jesus Christ' (cf. 1 Th 1:3), they are 'converted to God... and are now waiting for his Son, whom he raised from the dead, to come from heaven' (cf. 1 Th 1:9f.). *Certainty* is based on an encounter, already taking place, with the Lord with whom we still however desire the definitive encounter (cf. 1 Cor 1:9): 'Christ among you, your hope of glory' (Col 1:27).

The dynamism of this desire is the Spirit present in the hearts of the faithful;[80] again the Spirit brings about actual union with Christ who gives certainty. The first fruits of the Spirit are given (cf. Rom 8:23; 2 Cor 1:22; Eph 1:14); thanks to these, a believer already belongs to Christ (cf. Rom 8:9), and through them 'we...groan inwardly while we wait...' (cf. Rom 8:23), certain of our salvation (cf. Rom 8:16f., 23–30). Present in the form of a seed, the Spirit expands towards his own fulfilment, he who is in essence fulfilment. His presence has the same double effect as that of Christ: it awakens desire and establishes assurance of final justification, for the love of the Spirit poured into the heart is this justification anticipated. 'The seal of the Spirit' (cf. 2 Cor 1:22; Eph 1:13; 4:30) is the mark of our belonging to the last times and of our setting out towards them. That is why, even now, hope establishes in a believer the joy and peace that is to come: 'May the god of hope bring you such joy and peace in your faith that the power of the Holy Spirit will remove all bounds to hope' (Rom 15:13).

The path of hope advances therefore from a first union with the risen Christ towards total oneness with him in his resurrection. It advances similarly from the first fruits of the Spirit towards the gift of him in its fullness. Here the virtue of hope manifests once more the unity between the Spirit and Christ that we have so often stated: one body and one Spirit, just as you have been called into one and the same hope (cf. Eph 4:4). Hope begins in the glorified Christ, in the Son whom the Father begets for us in the Spirit. *Beginning with the divine sonship of Christ, we proceed towards it in the Spirit through whom sonship becomes a reality.* We 'who possess the first fruits of the Spirit' (and of sonship), we too groan inwardly as we wait for 'the sonship of the fullness of the Spirit' (cf. Rom 8:23).

This path is traced out in creation from its beginnings. The world is born in the shadow of the Spirit who hovers over its origin, it is thus created in Christ and for him (cf. Col 1:15–17). A confused but irrepressible hope makes it pulsate. St Paul, who had a feeling for the Spirit, sensed that the whole creation was groaning as it waited impatiently to share in the freedom and glory of the children of God (cf. Rom 8:19–22). Created in the Spirit and called to the fullness of sonship, the world will be restless until the day when it will rest in the mystery of sonship which is its origin.

Hope makes for a future where its anchor is already fixed (cf. Heb 6:18f.). It moves, in the dynamism of the Spirit, towards a salvation already grasped by faith and inhabited by love. This is the reason why hope is often named last, after charity (cf. e.g. 1 Th 1:3; 5:8). It is charity itself, but in the form of a vessel getting under way towards its own fulfilment.

The Spirit of prayer

Prayer is one of the forms of expression of hope and of the presence of the Spirit.

In the early ages of the Church, so marked by an abundance of the charisms of the Spirit, Christians were distinguished by their almost continual prayer.[81] It was from these assemblies for prayer that the Church received the name *ekklēsia*: 'When you come together as an assembly (*en ekklēsia*)', St Paul says, speaking of assembling for prayer (cf. 1 Cor 11:18).

The believer is invited to pray by the presence of the Spirit in his heart. This presence itself is prayer, just as it is love: the will of the Spirit tends irresistibly to union as a river flows towards the sea; moreover, prayer is a quest for union. Paul perceived the presence of the Spirit in himself as a desire (Rom 8:6, 27), an instinct for supplication, an inexpressible groaning (cf. Rom 8:26). The Spirit is vocation, a permanent calling repeated in uninterrupted invocation. St Paul's 'pray without ceasing' (cf. 1 Th 5:17) corresponds to the nature of a life animated by the Spirit.

When a Christian begins to pray, he accepts the presence of the Spirit in him. Grace makes him ask for grace.[82] Prayer, hymns, praise, a liturgy that is lived (cf. Rom 12:1; 1 Pet 2:5), all these are spiritual (cf. Eph 5:18f.; Col 3:16). 'Pray in the spirit!' (Jude v. 20), 'pray all the time, asking for what you need...from the Spirit' (cf. Eph 6:18).

The Spirit, who is the grace of prayer, is also its answer. He is the eschatological gift which penetrates the heart of man: 'If you then, evil as you are, know how to give your children what is good, how much more will the heavenly Father give the Holy Spirit to those who ask him' (Lk 11:13).[83] The Spirit who gives us the gift of prayer, is given to us in prayer. Here, as elsewhere, he is at the beginning and at the end.

When a Christian prays, he is already heard; prayer is in itself its own answer. A man at prayer is subject to the movement of the Spirit who is the gift of salvation; he prays in that union which is the reality of salvation. He can consider his prayer, however poor it is, as a sign of the covenant with God. When the Spirit empowers a person to say: 'Abba! Father!', he causes him to be born a son of his Father. 'Prayer itself introduces us to familiarity with God'.[84] Our request is forestalled by being heard, at least by an initial hearing, for prayer begins in the grace already granted, and this is amplified by the consent given to it by prayer. A man of prayer can live in peace – fruit of the Spirit (cf. Gal 5:22) –, his salvation is assured.

It may happen that a believer does not know the precise meaning of his desire: 'What we should pray for as is fitting, we do not know'.[85] The Spirit who is at work is not a word, he is an instinctive way of life (cf. Rom 8:16), he expresses himself in inexpressible groanings (cf. Rom 8:26). Moreover, according to John 3:8, the grace of sonship, in which man is embraced by fatherly love, is incomprehensible, and this is the grace that, without knowing it, he is asking for in all his supplications. But God knows the desires of the Spirit, he discerns what the Spirit is asking for in his groanings: that our union with the Son may be realized so that the Son may be the first-born of many brothers (cf. Rom 8:29). The Spirit is present in the hearts of the faithful as he is in God, and thus he is prayer: as Spirit of God in his fatherhood, Spirit of sonship. Prayer is a slow evolution, making the sons of God into persons.

What should we ask for in prayer? This question is now secondary. The essential is to give ourselves up to the answer which comes to us, to ask that God should do what he likes. In the Spirit of fatherhood with which he is filled, God loves to be a Father, to give life to his Son and to each of his faithful. Jesus 'offered up prayer and entreaty...to the one who had the power to save him out of death, and he was heard...and he was made perfect' (Heb 5:7, 9). He asked to be saved from death and was heard in the fullness of his life *as son*, in the Spirit of the resurrection. *God hears (prayer), he is saviour, since he is the Father who begets to life eternal.* The Church prays in the passover of Jesus; the Spirit who sighs in the hearts of the faithful is the one who makes Jesus a permanent prayer, 'offered to God in an eternal Spirit' (cf. Heb 9:14), eternally heard by the Father who glorifies him in the Spirit. The Church is an assembly for prayer, because she lives in the passover of Christ. She is heard as she penetrates more and more into this paschal union, until the day of celebration of the wedding of the Lamb to which she aspires: 'The Spirit and the Bride say: "Come!" ' (Rev 22:17).

The Spirit, suffering and death

One of the most striking paradoxes of the mystery of the Spirit is expressed in the image of the blood and water which together flow from Christ's side. Blood is the sign of immolation, water the symbol of the Spirit. A strange similarity unites the Spirit of life, glory and joy with suffering and death.

It is in suffering that some Christians have had the clearest experience of the Spirit. Jesus promised his presence in times of persecution (cf. Mt 10:20 parr.); the Thessalonians 'took to the gospel with the joy of the Holy Spirit, in spite of the great opposition' all around them (cf. 1 Th 1:6); St Paul's joy is overflowing in all his tribulations (cf. 2 Cor 7:4). Peter's first letter insists: 'It is a blessing for you when they insult you...because...you have the Spirit of glory, the Spirit of God resting on you' (4:14). Joy is the radiation of the presence of the Spirit, as the Apostle confesses: 'It makes me happy to suffer for you' (Col 1:24). Glory is one of the names of the Spirit as he is manifested; moreover, it is the lot of anyone who is united with the passion of Christ (cf. Rom 8:17). Paul is proud to boast about his sufferings, knowing that from them comes hope, and that hope has its power in the love of the Spirit (cf. Rom 5:3–5). Suffering, hope, love of the Spirit are links in the same chain which connects a believer to his future (Rom 8:15–17).

It seems that the similarity which prevails between grace and the trials suffered by a Christian corresponds to one of the laws of the action of the Spirit. Suffering is born and grows in the world in the measure in which people awaken to consciousness and love, and as they grow in personality towards the spirit, that is, towards the Holy Spirit. Christ, in his sonship, which is the climax of the history of creation and salvation, attains the climax of his achievement in the fullness of the Holy Spirit and of suffering. Could we say that it is a signature of the Holy Spirit to his work of creation and salvation? The signature is illegible, suffering is a problem that cannot be solved by reason. The signature cannot be effaced, the glory of the Kingdom will not obliterate it, it transfigures the stigmata of the Crucified One, it raises Christ to life without abolishing the mystery of his death. The signature is illegible and ineffaceable, for the Spirit is a mystery and his imprint on the world is eternal.

If it is true that suffering is for our reason a question to which reason provides no answer, the problem of suffering has nevertheless a meaning in a life of love, in a life animated by the Spirit. The riddle is resolved existentially, suffering does not seem absurd for a Christian who loves: he knows that his life is rich. Nowhere else does the Spirit reveal himself as creative more than in suffering and death where 'he calls into being what does not exist' (Rom 4:17), where he fills with meaning what seems to be absurd.

Doubtless no one will be able to explain this close connection between the Spirit and suffering, but we might say what the former is, and take note of the latter. Moreover, we do know that the Spirit is love and that love has an affinity with suffering.

★ ★ ★

Death, even more than suffering, is, in the eyes of someone who has no faith, the seal of the absurdity that marks creation. Yet nothing is as rich or as overflowing with meaning as the death of Christ, for the fullness of the Spirit is in that death.

The Christian was born to the life of the Spirit when he was baptized in the death of Christ (cf. Rom 6:3). His entry into the full life of the Spirit will coincide with a total union in death with the Lord: 'If we die with him, then we shall live with him' (cf. 2 Tim 2:11).

'If we die with him!' Is it possible to die 'in twos', to be two together in the same death? It is possible to share a thing with someone, or to work together in an activity external to the person; but death is not a thing or an activity of this kind. The death of a person is that person in his dying. He dies alone, for he himself dies. Earthly love tries to deny this fact when, as sometimes happens, it dreams of a shared death, yet in his dying a person is independent of others.

Christ however transforms the death of human beings and thus saves them. In his own self he has reversed the meaning of death. He did not suffer it passively, even though he died nailed to the wood of the cross;[86] at this supreme moment of the grace of the Spirit, 'he offered himself...through the eternal Spirit' (cf. Heb 9:14); what he achieved, he himself brought about. His dying was also his passover, his passage to the Father; Jesus allowed himself to be wholly caught up in the filial movement, his whole human being was assumed into the Word who is 'for God'. The redemptive death is Jesus in this dying, Jesus advancing towards the Father in infinite love, that is, in the fullness of the Spirit. In his dying, Jesus is the Son, abandoned to the infinite movement of the Spirit who bears him towards the Father; Son and saviour in death, Son and saviour in the Spirit. It is here that the fullness of the Spirit is within creation; it is here that he is at the service of men, the Spirit of sonship, the Spirit of union, to gather them together into the mystery of sonship.

Jesus saves men by uniting them with his death in the fullness of the Holy Spirit, by gathering them together here through the power of this Spirit: he had 'to gather together in unity the scattered children of God' (Jn 11:5f.). He draws them into the movement which raises him up to the Father: 'When I am lifted up from the earth, I shall draw all men to myself' (Jn 12:32). He unites them in himself in his own dying, in this perfect movement towards the Father, that is, in the fullness of the Spirit.

As far as God in concerned, man is intended to die. He is not destined for immortality, for a life from which death is excluded. Created for Christ (cf. Col 1:16), he is destined to be one in death with him. He is a being-intended-to-die, but to die a death which leads to total oneness, that is, a death which is eternal life in the Holy Spirit.

Death is to be found at the heart of the plan of creation: the creative, salvific action of the Spirit culminates in it. It seems to be meaningless, an emptiness void of sense, and yet it is full of grace through the Spirit who creates by calling man to communion with the Son, thus giving meaning to everything. Death is a passage to life in common with Christ, 'our sister Death', and it is fitting that we should praise God for her.

The sacraments prepare the faithful to 'die-with' Christ. The grace of baptism unites men in a single body, in the same death: 'In one Spirit we have all been baptised in one body' (cf. 1 Cor 12:13; Eph 4:4): 'it is in his death that we have been baptised' (cf. Rom 6:3; Col 2:12). Such is the effect of the Eucharist where the faithful form a single body in communicating with the death of Christ, thanks to this 'spiritual bread'.

Death in communion with Christ is the final experience a believer has of the presence of the Spirit. According to St Paul, this presence is expressed in the form of charity (cf. Rom 5:5); *similarly, its final expression is in the form of Christian death.* We are familiar with the relationship which exists between love and death; anyone who loves lives in a state of immolation; it does happen that a Christian wants to die that his love may be fulfilled: 'I want to be gone and be with Christ' (Ph 1:23). Christian death is the movement of a perfect love, that of the Spirit of the Son carrying Christ to the Father, a love in which the believer is caught up: 'If we die with him'. That is why to die is to be born. Formerly, the believer was born of water, symbol of the Spirit; now he is born by dying in the power of the Spirit.

In the death of Christ and his faithful, the Spirit plays the part that is his in the mystery of the Trinity. He is the love through which the Son is born of his Father and carried towards him. For Christ and his faithful, death is the birth of completeness; it is the sublime movement carrying them out of this world to God.[87] In the Trinity, the Spirit is *one* person within two, and thus brings about unity between them. Christ shares with the believer his own dying: two in a single death, they are united in an inconceivable unity. What bond can be compared with that of a single death experienced by two together? The promise made by Jesus is accomplished: 'On that Day (of their common passover) you will understand that you are in me and I in you' (cf. Jn 14:20). To die in communion is an act of perfect love and the root of eternal happiness. *This death is the form of the total presence of the Spirit in Jesus and in the believer.*

The Pauline formula of 'dying-with', according to which the same death, that of Christ, is shared by many, becomes crystal clear. The passover of Jesus is the fullness of sonship, in the fullness of the Spirit who carries him to the Father. The faithful are caught up in this same dying, this same movement, in the unique filial Spirit.

★   ★   ★

Many people are not ready to leave their earthly life in a death like this. In spite of the grace they have had, to anticipate their salvific death, in baptism, in each Eucharist and throughout life (cf. Gal 2:19), they will not be capable of yielding immediately to such pure love. At the moment when their life is no longer that of earth and not yet that of the Kingdom, they will remain attached, as though in a no-man's-land. The dynamism of their spiritual freedom is too weak to cover the whole passage from the flesh to the Spirit, the departure from this world to the Father.

The door of this passage serves, even on earth, as introduction into life: Christ, and baptism in the Spirit he sends. Christ is the purgatory of human beings in their death; the Spirit is their fire. He burns the stains by sanctifying, by opening hearts to the love of the Kingdom. He proves that he is unmerited love, granted even to those who, on earth, were unable to make a sufficient response to him.

For this last grace, which brings eternal happiness, he plays one of his finest roles, that of consolation. The Church which asks 'always to rejoice in his consolation'[88] is heard above all at the hour of death. Man, created for relationships, finds himself emptied of self and a prey to despair once he is alone. Without communion with the Spirit, suffering is a prison, death complete solitude. The Spirit is the supreme consoler, he changes death into the most inconceivable of communions. It is thus that the Father consoled the Son in his death by glorifying him in the Holy Spirit.[89]

Joy and peace in the Spirit

This last consolation was announced a very long time ago. It is a delicious fruit and it ripens slowly: 'The fruit of the Spirit is...joy and peace' (cf. Gal 5:22). The presence of the Spirit brings radiance and peace: 'The Kingdom of God is...joy and peace in the Spirit' (cf. Rom 14:17), 'the disciples were filled with joy and the Holy Spirit' (Acts 13:52). In the joy of the Spirit the Church sings 'spiritual canticles' (cf Eph 5:19; Col 3:16). This joy can overflow to such an extent that one might think it is the effect of drinking too much (cf. Acts 2:13). Jesus himself rejoiced in the Spirit (cf. Lk 10:21).

There is also a worldly joy (cf. Jn 16:20) as well as a worldly sadness (cf. 2 Cor 7:10) – the two are closely connected. Joy in the Spirit is of a different order, it can flourish where there is reason for sorrow. Jesus promises that the sadness of his departure will be changed into joy (cf. Jn 16:20), just as his own death will be transformed into life in the Spirit. When he disappeared from the sight of the disciples – although he was their only hope – they returned to Jerusalem full of joy (cf. Lk 24:52). This joy does not have the same roots as earthly joy: it resembles the very different power and life seen in the helplessness of death.

A tree is judged by its fruit. Therefore, if the Spirit bears fruit in the faithful in joy and peace, we can conclude that this is God's joy. Similarly, we can recognize divine charity in him, it is he who increases love in our heart. How could he not be eternal joy since he is the outpouring of exuberant life? Full life is the joy of living. The Spirit is the exultation of God, omnipotent love, the desire for infinite communion and its realization. He is the paschal joy of Jesus, his birth ever new, the encounter with the Father, the embrace of Father and Son. Endowed with the treasures received in his passover, Christ gives the Spirit, he brings peace and the disciples rejoice (cf. Jn 20:19–22). Spirit, peace, joy: different names for a single gift. Risen in the Spirit, Jesus has become in person 'the Kingdom which is peace and joy in the Spirit'.

For a Christian, joy is an imperative: 'Rejoice!' the Apostle repeats four times (Ph 2:18; 3:1; 4:4 twice). But no one can produce his own joy, it is given in communion: '*Rejoice in the Lord!*' (Ph 4:4). Now it is a beginning, at its early stages, an initial union. It points towards its own fulfilment, the veiled presence of the Lord promises the unveiling. This nearness of his presence is also a source of joy: 'Rejoice! The Lord is near!' (Ph 4:4–5).

The triumph of the Spirit

One day the meeting with Christ which we await in hope will be final. God will be 'all in all' (1 Cor 15:28) in his Kingdom where the Spirit will hold undisputed sway.

What is the Kingdom of heaven? A heavenly place? A state of complete happiness? Certainly a state of complete happiness; since the Spirit is the happiness of God. But heaven is also a *place*, a 'Kingdom of peace and joy in the Spirit' (cf. Rom 14:17). Christ is in person this Kingdom, he is the place where those whom the Father calls to 'be joined to his Son' (1 Cor 1:9) are gathered together; he is the centre in which they exist – 'You are (exist) in Christ' (cf. 1 Cor 1:30) –, where they are created according to eschatological newness: 'If anyone *is* in Christ, he is a new creature' (cf. 2 Cor 5:17). In the measure in which the faithful are in him, they live even now in heaven: 'He has given us a place in heaven in Christ Jesus' (Eph 2:6; cf. 1:3). According to John 14:20, Jesus said: 'On that Day (that of the eternal Easter) you will understand that *you are in me* and I in you'.

The Spirit tends to make everything personal. He urges people to transform the earthly space into a network of relationships. His love abolishes distances which separate: he makes the most distant person a neighbour of Christ and the faithful. When he brings creatures to their final end, he makes one completely personal space by assembling everyone into a single body, that of Christ: 'In one body and one Spirit' (cf. Eph 4:4).

To this heavenly space corresponds a *time* which, similarly, is specifically of Christ and of the Spirit. St Paul calls this the 'now' of salvation, of which St John also speaks when he says: 'on that Day'. Even on earth, Christians live united with Christ in his death and resurrection at the exact moment of its realization (cf. Rom 6:3–10; Gal 2:19f.; Col 2:11f.). In the Kingdom of heaven, people are wholly taken up into the today of Christ, in his passover of death and glory where Christ becomes eternal.

Thus time too becomes a personal entity. It is identical with the death – that of Christ – which is the most personal reality there is; it is also identical with another very personal reality, birth, that of Christ in glory. Heaven therefore can be given a date, the hour of the passover, simultaneous with the death and resurrection of Christ; the heavenly meal is the celebration of the 'accomplished' passover (cf. Lk 22:16), that of Christ.

Such time is not fleeting, it does not pass away as does time on earth, it reaches a climax; though its duration is permanent, it is not immobilized. The orbit of its movement has a wide sweep, it shares in trinitarian time which is that of the eternal begetting of the Son in the Spirit.

God builds the heaven of human beings into the heaven which is that of the Father himself: in 'the Son of his love' (cf. Col 1:13), on whom his favour rests. He builds it by raising his Son from the dead, that is, in begetting him in the Spirit. Heaven is the work of the Father who, in the power of the Spirit, begets his Christ and who, in this unique action of the Spirit, captures men by incorporating them into his Son, making them 'come to life together with him' and thus he gives them a place in heaven in Christ Jesus. From the beginning, everything was created in Christ and for him, and in him all is completed; the action of the Father, in the power of the Spirit, is concerned wholly with the Son and culminates eternally in him. Heaven is the extension of the mystery of sonship. Its space is the body of Christ, its time is that of the begetting of Christ. The Spirit is everywhere at work: it is in him that the Son assumes a body in the human race and that the space of heaven is created; it is in him that the Father begets his Christ and the time of heaven is unfolded. Heaven, its space and its time, is simultaneously of Christ and of the Spirit.

In the Church there is a sacrament the celebration of which contains and illustrates the mystery of heaven: the Eucharist is the authentic banquet of the Kingdom of heaven, but celebrated in an earthly manner. People scattered all over the world are, in the Eucharist, assembled in a single place, the body of Christ. They are assembled by the Eucharist across the centuries and live at the single moment of Christ's sacrifice, that of his glorifying death which is the event of their salvation. In heaven, as in the Eucharist, space and time become personal and find their synthesis in the mystery of Christ.

★   ★   ★

The Spirit is the agent of a history of which heaven is the final outcome and the climax. He is the breath of God in that twofold movement of breathing in and breathing out; as such he gives life to the history of salvation.

On the one hand he is the key of love which opens, he is

ecstasy and outpouring. Through him God comes out of himself in making his Son man; he goes to the uttermost limits of self-abandonment, submitting to our condition of flesh and sin (cf. Rom 8:3), in suffering and death. In this 'first-born of all creation' the Spirit creates a world and people who are scattered throughout time and space. But the Spirit is also an omnipotent movement of consolidation and of immanence. In the Trinity the Spirit brings the Son back to unity with the Father; he brings the incarnate Son to the extremity of the human condition, that is, death, and into glorious communion with the Father. He assembles the human race in the unity of the body of Christ, simultaneously with his death and resurrection.

Sacred history is constituted by this ebb and flow; it has its repercussions on the eternal trinitarian movement, that of the Father who, in the Spirit, comes out towards the Son and embraces him in the unity of the Spirit. In the early stages of history, it is the outpouring that seems paramount, yet even then the whole cycle exists through the call to union. At the climax of history, it is unity that is emphasized; in the death of Christ, the Son and everyone else have become a multitude and are brought to the Father at the same time as God is committed without restraint to Christ and to people without number. This climax, where the twofold action of the Spirit becomes one great movement, we call heaven.

★ ★ ★

Then the Church will easily be recognized in the definition: one body, one Spirit. By the bonds of the Spirit she had always belonged to Christ (cf. Rom 8:9); but the reign of the Spirit had not been felt in all its power; union with Christ was as much a hope as a reality. Now, in the fullness of the Spirit, the Church and Christ form only a single *body*.

The Easter glory of Christ, the grain of wheat which dies, consists, according to John 12:23f., in bearing much fruit. The same happiness is promised to the disciple (cf. 12:26; 15:8). Already on earth a Christian does not live only for himself (cf. Rom 14:7); 'The grace that he gave me has not been fruitless' (1 Cor 15:10). Christ makes each one what he himself is (cf. 1 Jn 4:17), a life-giving spirit; his disciples also bear fruit which lasts (cf. Jn 15:16); Paul's glory was to beget men in the world for their eternal life (cf. 1 Cor 4:15; Ph 4:1; 1 Th 2:19). In heaven, more than ever before, the grace of each will be a source of grace.

On earth *the communion of saints* remains limited in its effects. People remain wrapped in themselves in the measure in which they do not rise above an existence according to the flesh. On earth Jesus himself was like a solitary grain of wheat. But in death the 'wrapping' falls away and the Spirit realizes a union such as is inconceivable on earth. Just as the grain lives anew in the form of blade and sheaf, Christ raises up the community again. The faithful risen with him are transformed in the Spirit who opens them to the gift of self and to mutual acceptance. What Christ is in glory, what heaven is for human beings – space of their life and happiness – they become for one another, according to the spiritual potential of each. In Christ and in the Spirit God reverses the order of sin and makes others become heaven for one another. *They will live through one another, they will live for one another*, in the Spirit through whom all is received and given.

Furthermore, the greater grace of one will not arouse jealousy on the part of the others, but rather their gratitude, for it will benefit them. Nor will grace make the one who possesses it proud, for it has its roots in the body of Christ who is the common ground of all, and in the Spirit who sustains it: 'All the elect will discover that they owe to each other the graces that merited a crown for them', Teresa of Lisieux said.[90] If a rose could rejoice, it would be full of gratitude to the soil which bears it; and the soil would be happy and proud to see a rose blossom from it. Glory and complete happiness are complementary. The Spirit is communion, that is why he is the glory and the happiness of heaven.[91]

At the beginning God said: 'Let us make man in our own likeness'. This one God speaks in the plural: – 'Let us make' – he completes creation in his likeness: men are henceforth a multitude and a single body in the Spirit who gives them life with his breath. They have reached their goal, created in the likeness of the divine mystery where each Person lives in relationship with the others.

* * *

In the communion of saints the radiating power of holiness reaches its supreme intensity in the one who is the Christian woman *par excellence*: in Mary, the mother of Jesus. *In her the whole Church is summarized and crowned.*

In John's gospel, Mary is not called by her own personal name, she is given the name of a function: she is the woman (cf. 2:4; 19:26), she is the mother (2:1–5; 19:25). In the Book of Revelation (chapter 12), the Church appears in the image of a woman, mother of Christ. Mary is a symbol. The words: 'Woman, this is your son' (Jn 19:26) refer to the Church, the beloved disciple is entrusted to Mary, representative of the Church. Jesus had already had recourse to images of motherhood: that of the grain bearing abundant fruit, that of the fruitful vine. Now the image is a living one, symbol and reality coincide: Mary personifies the Church, the disciple is entrusted simultaneously to Mary and to mother-Church. But to speak of the 'motherhood of the Church' is to describe by another name the communion of saints. In Mary, symbol of the Church as mother, is concentrated the richness of the communion of saints. The Holy Spirit triumphs in her and makes her a perfect icon of the Church in her mystery of unity, which is first of all the mystery of the Spirit himself.

The Spirit who tends to make everything personal has not made the Church a homogeneous crowd. Spouse and mother, she is individualized and realized in persons and is found anew, in differing degrees, in each believer. Church history, throughout its path from the beginning to the end, has come to be concentrated on the person of Mary in whom the Spirit displays the whole of his activity in the Church. This history goes back to the beginning of the world. According to Christian faith, humanity ever since its origin has been sown with messianic seed.[92] For the Spirit, in whom God creates human beings, is the Spirit of God in his fatherhood; through all his activities he tends towards one single end: to cause the Son to take a body within the world. Already in the Old Testament Christ had his Church, a people united to him by the flesh and into which he was to be born; a Church who is mother, a Church Christian according to the flesh, a Church spiritual according to the Spirit who shaped her (cf. Gal 4:29). The Church of the New Testament is no longer the mother of Christ, she is his associate. She is united to him in the passover, and, in this communion of death and resurrection, she is sanctified in the Spirit of Jesus and at the same time she is sanctifying, the mother of mankind for their eternal life.

At the foot of the cross, Mary is the image and reality of the two Testaments. The Church of the Old Testament, mother of Christ through the action of the Spirit, is fulfilled. In Mary she conceives in her flesh through the power of the Spirit. On Calvary she is the presence of this earlier Church with God's Christ. The whole nation of Israel in its motherhood of flesh and blood and all the faith of Abraham and his descendants, faced with the unfathomable will of God, are found united in Mary. In her Israel stands at the foot of the cross. At this climax of fidelity Israel passes, without repudiation of itself, into the New Testament: Mary is associated with Christ in his Hour. She is joined to Christ in death to the flesh; the Old Testament Church, united to Christ in the flesh, dies to herself; and Jesus speaks of a new spiritual motherhood, which is that of the Church of the New Testament. Sacred history, from its beginning, when God established enmity between the serpent and the woman, to the resurrection from the dead, discovers its synthesis in this humble woman, eternally radiant in the Holy Spirit.

By placing Mary at the heart of the Church, by making her the very kernel of the Church, the Spirit unveils the meaning of his own activity. Mary, mother of Christ according to the flesh, his associate in the work of salvation, mother of those who are sons of God in Christ, is, as it were, the human counterpart of the Holy Spirit. He is the Spirit of sonship; all his activity, like that of Mary, tends to give a body to the son in this world: in Christ and in men who are his brothers. The mystery of the Spirit, like that of Mary, is intimately associated with the mystery of the Son.

* * *

The *resurrection of the dead* forms part of the mystery of heaven. In it the communion that God establishes in Christ and in the Spirit comes to fulfilment. Jesus saw the resurrection of the dead inscribed in the covenant concluded with Abraham, Isaac and Jacob (cf. Mt 22:31f.). In the light of the passover of Jesus, it appears as the completion of salvation (cf. Rom 8:23), of that salvation which is eternal communion between God and man in Christ Jesus.

On earth it is by means of the body that a fabric of relationships is woven; when the body dies this fabric is torn apart. But God overturns the scourge of death. In Christ and in union with the Spirit he transforms death into eternal resurrection and thus creates an indestructible fabric of relationships. The resurrection from the dead is the seal of the covenant between God and man and that of the covenant of men among themselves.

Thanks to baptism, the believer is initiated, even in this life, into the mystery of his future resurrection. He is clothed in the Christ of glory (cf. Gal 3:27); he becomes one body with him in the same Spirit (cf. 1 Cor 12:13): he makes but one in Jesus Christ, one single body, with all those who are 'sons of God in Christ Jesus' (cf. Gal 3:26–28). St Paul knows that he will be clothed with this same body when he leaves his earthly life: 'We know that when the tent that we live in on earth is folded up, there is a house built by God for us, an everlasting home not made by human hands, in the heavens' (2 Cor 5:1).

A mysterious resurrection! God assures us of it, for Christ is risen for us (cf. 2 Cor 5:15), that is, that we might rise again in him (cf. 1 Cor 15:12–22); the pledge of the Spirit of the resurrection of Jesus has already been given to us (cf. 2 Cor 5:5). But in itself the final resurrection remains a mystery: in presupposing death to the earth, it is inconceivable to the earthly mind.

However, the resurrection of Jesus throws some light on this. For the faithful will be transformed 'by the power of *his* resurrection' (cf. Ph 3:10, 21); they will be raised up together with him, according to the expression frequently used, caught up in the unique action of the Father who, in the Spirit, gives life to his Son: 'If the Spirit of him who raised Jesus from the dead is living in you, then he who raised Jesus from the dead will give life to your mortal bodies through his Spirit living in you' (Rom 8:11).

The resurrection of Christ results from the mystery of his being begotten as Son: it is said in Psalm 2 that he rose from the dead: 'You are my son, today I have begotten you' (cf. Acts 13:33). The Spirit who awakens the dead is the Spirit of divine sonship; by raising people from the dead the Father introduces them into the fullness of sonship. St Paul awaits, on the same day, bodily redemption and divine sonship: 'We who possess the first-fruits of the Spirit, we too groan inwardly as we wait for sonship, the redemption of our bodies' (Rom 8:23). At the end of life a Christian reaches his full birth, thus returning to the beginning of the world: the begetting of the Son in the Holy Spirit. The Spirit of the resurrection of the dead is the Spirit of the Father as father, the Spirit of the begetting of the Son.

Never again will man depart from the moment of his birth. The resurrection is the synthesis and the climax of creation, beyond which one cannot go, in the permanent today of the Easter birth of Christ (cf. Acts 13:33). *Henceforth the eternal begetting of the Son in the Spirit is immanent within the world*: the world is steeped, at this its own climax, in the eternal trinitarian movement. The joy of being born, of receiving ceaselessly from the Father in the Spirit, of living always at one's beginning, this joy is part of heavenly bliss.

To the question: 'What sort of body will they have when they come back?' (cf. 1 Cor 15:35), St Paul answers: 'What is raised is imperishable ...glorious...powerful, the spirit'. The Apostle sums up his thoughts by concluding: 'They will rise as *spiritual* bodies' (cf. 1 Cor 15:42–44).

But what is a spiritual body? The two words appear to be contradictory. Always paradoxical in his work, the Spirit triumphs in what appears to be the opposite of his spiritual nature: in corporeal beings. However, Spirit and body are close to one another.[93] According to the accurate thought of the Bible, man is not a soul that possesses a body, he is a living body. Man's body is the man himself expressed as integrated into the world, man considered in a network of relationships. Even in its earthly condition, the body is to some extent spiritual, the source of mutual relationships. But this source is defective; the person is imperfect, in need of redemption (cf. Rom 8:23). Although man *is* a body, one can also say he *has* a body, what is certain is that a person cannot be identified merely as a body. Moreover, 'to have' is an imperfection in the person; to possess something is not to have a relationship with it. The Spirit must recreate the body and make it completely personal.

In the power of the Spirit, Christ 'became a life-giving spirit', a being fully in relationship, fully in gift of self, the source of life just as he himself has life. People 'raised up with him' in the same power of the Spirit will no longer live 'according to the flesh'; the body will no longer be a defective instrument which closes them in on themselves while linking them with others. The resurrection from the dead is a mystery of reciprocal intimacy, of mutual gift of self: *it is the mystery of the communion of saints in its highest truth*. Each one will share, according to the measure of his grace, in the resurrection of Christ whose glorious body contains the whole Church and who said: 'On that Day you will know that I am in you and you in me'.

The resurrection of the dead is the keystone of the work of creation, where all the stresses of the architecture come together and become stable. It is the masterpiece of the Spirit who is communion and creator of communion. The long work, the purpose of which was the begetting of the Son in the world, is completed in the resurrection of the dead. The Spirit is both the untiring movement of the world and its rest. The creative action comes to a calm climax, when all becomes spiritual, personal and filial. Then 'God will be all in all', because he will be in the world what he is in the eternal mystery: the Father who begets the Son in the Spirit.

5

The Spirit of the Father and the Son

Theologians distinguish the divine mystery in itself and this mystery in its manifestations in the course of salvation history which they call the 'economy of salvation'. So far we have tried to come to know the Spirit by following the traces of his presence in creation, in Christ who is the climax of creation and in the Church which is the body of Christ. But what is the intimate mystery of the Spirit? After this preliminary re-search, is it possible to penetrate into the depths of his trinitarian being?

Some have been of the opinion that the perspectives opened up by salvation history could never lead us into these depths. Not content with making distinctions, they dissociate the two aspects of the mystery and do not believe that a bridge would allow our thinking to cross from one side to the other.[1] But no theology proceeding by way of dissociation can claim to go back to the master of all theology, to the Spirit who is communion and who creates everything with a view to communion. Theology finds itself obliged to think in terms of synthesis. In the knowledge of the Christian mystery where everything bears the mark of the Holy Spirit, distinctions which separate constitute a grave error. To divide is always to sin against the Holy Spirit. Distinctions are necessary for our limited understanding, but they must always be at the service of synthesis, and they have their meaning only in their integration into the whole.[2] In our reflections on the Holy Spirit we cannot therefore distinguish, by separating them, between the mystery in itself and the 'economy of salvation'.

The Spirit is glory, he is the divine radiancy. From the fact that he is diffused in the world, he is manifested, just as the sun is seen by the light which it diffuses. The mystery comes out of itself and at the same time leads back: it comes towards men while making them come to it; while communicating itself to them, it gives them experience of itself, it makes itself known by them. What should we know of the Spirit, if his activities did not reveal him or if he differed radically from his manifestations?

In Jesus Christ the Spirit is present just as he is in himself and he manifests himself there just as he is in his eternal truth. There is no divine mystery other than that which is in Christ, in whom dwells the fullness of the divinity (cf. Col 2:9). Christ is complete revelation just as he is complete salvation.[3] If the mystery of the Trinity differed from its manifestation in Christ, could Jesus say: 'Who sees me, sees the Father' (cf. Jn 14:9)? Would he be God-with-us, the image of the invisible God? He is the imprint of the substance (of God) (cf. Heb 1:3), the burning bush of the divinity, Jacob's ladder which reveals heaven so that man can know about it. We can state nothing true about the deep mystery of God unless we begin with Christ, and unless we begin with Christ we can say nothing about the person of the Holy Spirit.

St Paul identifies the Spirit given to the faithful with the Spirit proper to the eternal Son: 'When the appointed time came, God sent his Son...God sent *the Spirit of his Son* into our hearts' (Gal 4:4, 6). The Son was sent just as he is in his eternal mystery, and similarly with the Spirit. What is specific in the New Testament is contained in the personal coming of the Son and the gift of the Spirit in person, so that the mystery of Christ cannot be dissociated from the mystery of the Spirit, nor can the Spirit in his trinitarian being be dissociated from the Spirit as he is given to us in Christ. *Moreover, the Christ of glory, source of the Spirit for the faithful, is not exterior to the Trinity.* In his passover Jesus was wholly taken up into the mystery when the Father announced in the Spirit: 'You are my son; today I have begotten you'. Just as Christ is in truth the very Word of God, the relationship between the heavenly Christ and the Spirit is that of the Word and the Spirit. The activities of the Spirit in Christ and in the world are rooted in his personal mystery and find their explanation there. 'The Spirit is truth' (1 Jn 5:6); he wears no deceptive mask; his manifestations are the expression of his intimate being.

The Spirit, a person

There is a movement apparent in the Bible, in the Old Testament, which is intensified in Judaism at the approach and beginning of the Christian era, that of a gradual process of the Spirit being regarded as a Person. Earlier, he was regarded simply as a power emanating from God. Later, the Spirit becomes the subject of numerous activities: he speaks, cries out, exhorts, is distressed, weeps, rejoices and consoles.[4]

According to St Paul, the Spirit penetrates the depths of God (cf. 1 Cor 2:10f.); he cries out in us 'Abba! Father!' He testifies that we are children of God (cf. Rom 8:16); he intercedes with God (cf. Rom 8:26f.); he distributes gifts to each one as he wills (cf. 1 Cor 12:11). He is not only the action of another and the gift made by another; he acts and distributes his gifts as a person who is free in his decisions. He constitutes a triad, together with God (the Father) and Christ (cf. 1 Cor 12:4–6; 2 Cor 13:13), so much so that the personal meaning of the Spirit is forced upon us, just as for the Father and Christ.[5] He is truly a person.

St John stresses the personal characteristics of the Spirit with great emphasis. The Spirit is the Paraclete, the advocate who comes to the help of the disciples. He answers to a personal pronoun, a masculine pronoun,[6] whereas *Pneuma* is a neuter noun. He teaches, he reminds (cf. 14:26); he testifies in favour of Jesus (cf. 15:26; 1 Jn 5:6), reveals him (cf. 16:3) and glorifies him (cf.16:14). Side by side with Jesus, who is also a Paraclete (cf. 1 Jn 2:1), the Spirit is 'another Paraclete' (cf. 14:16), a person just as Jesus is a person. He is sent by the Father and by Jesus (cf. 14:26; 15:26; 16:7); but an impersonal reality cannot be sent. His presence will ensure the presence of Jesus among the disciples (cf. 16:7) and he will take what belongs to Jesus to reveal it to them (cf. 16:14).[7] In John 14:16–23, Jesus announces a triple coming: that of the Paraclete (cf. v. 16), that of Jesus (cf. v. 18) and that of the Father and Jesus (cf. v. 23). 'Here we have one of the clearest statements about the Trinity in the New Testament.'[8] A very impressive parallel can be established between the activity of the two Paracletes, Jesus and the Spirit;[9] the Spirit is presented as the subject of an action on the same grounds as Jesus, and this proves at the same time the intimate relationship which unites the Son and the Spirit, while at the same time distinguishing them. Words reported earlier by the Synoptics describe the Spirit as the subject of actions: 'The Spirit will teach you what you must say' (Lk 12:12). This action is parallel to that of Jesus: 'I myself shall give you an eloquence and a wisdom that none of your opponents will be able to resist or contradict' (Lk 21:15).

But what a mystery this person is! And what a mystery is this God whose Spirit is a person! The Spirit is will, activity, love. In God everything is person: divine operation itself is a person. In men activity is the expression of their personality; but in the Spirit action and person are merged: he is the action of the Father and the Son.

Although our thinking is incapable of imagining such a person, we can discern in the Spirit the two characteristics basic to every person: namely, an existence in his own right and the dynamism of the relationships in which that person exists. Scripture describes him as subject of his actions, existing therefore in his own right, and as a mystery of communion. However, this second aspect is stressed with such evidence, the 'relational' nature of the Spirit is so forceful that one might think that the other aspect (that of existence in his own right) is cancelled out. The Spirit is the unique operation of the other two Persons, their common will: he is *one* Person in two others, he exists in his own right but as absolute gift of himself, given to the other two Persons. We are confronted with a mystery which is certainly that of Love.

Here the paradox of the Spirit reaches its climax. This divine Person is powerfully asserted as he effaces himself in total communication of himself. This paradox is the root of the others already often mentioned: that of power and life displayed in renunciation, triumphant in immolation. This effacement is reflected in the images by which the Spirit is presented. He is breath, power, water and fire: impersonal images. He is never presented as 'I' *vis-à-vis* the Father and

Christ; he is within them; he is in person the mystery by which they live, by which they are the Father and the Son in absolute unity.

Personal dignity is possessed in its fullest truth by the Spirit so that he is at the origin of all that is personal in the world and in God, for it is in his Love that God begets, that there is a Father and a Son. If, therefore, the aspect of relationship, gift of self, is affirmed so vividly of him that it appears, as far as our understanding is concerned, to eclipse the other aspect, that of individual existence in his own right, this means that a person is most fully a person in the gift of self, that *relationship is even primordial, that it constitutes the height and depths of a being.*

If this is so, we can answer the question often asked: what is 'the salvation' for which Christ died and which is proclaimed by the Christian message? Throughout the present reflection on the Holy Spirit, we have been forced to the certain conclusion that salvation is to be found in relationships, in communion between God and man (cf. 1 Jn 1:3). Christ died to introduce man into communion with the Holy Spirit.

The Spirit of the Father

Before the coming of Jesus Christ, people were ignorant of the fact that, in the intimacy of his mystery, God is a father. The future apostle Paul adored the true God but did not know that God has poured himself out in a Son; he had a revelation of this fact 'when it pleased God to reveal his Son to him' (cf. Gal 1:15f.). The fatherhood of God was revealed in the world when it was brought about there, when, in Jesus Christ, God became in creation what he is in himself, essentially the Father who begets the Son. In Christ and his passover people learn furthermore that this God is also their own father.

In earlier times the Spirit was known as power and holiness; he was called the Spirit of God, in whom God is omnipotent, through whom his holiness is revealed. It was not known that he is the Spirit of the Father, that omnipotence is exercised and holiness manifested in God's fatherhood. Such is the new light that the revelation made in Jesus Christ casts on the mystery of the Spirit: *he is the Spirit of God in his fatherhood.*

Christ does not only reveal the fatherhood of God, he teaches us that it is in the Spirit that God is a father. Jesus is born as the divine Son through the power of God who is the Spirit (cf. Lk 1:35); he is proclaimed Son of God, for the Spirit rests on him (cf. Mt 3:16f.; Jn 1:33f.); he is established in the fullness of sonship (cf. Acts 13:33; Rom 1:4) when God raises him from the dead in the Holy Spirit (cf. Rom 8:11).

This God and Father, however, is the same as the God of the Old Testament, and the Spirit in whom God begets is not different from the one through whom God creates everything. Even then they recognized in God the father of Israel and the father of creation; but henceforth people knew that the source of his work in the world and in Israel is in his fatherhood with regard to Christ. They had always known that the Spirit is the operation of divine power, but they did not know that all God's activity in the Spirit has its origin in the begetting of the Son.

In his creative and salvific activity in the world, the Spirit has always appeared to us as the radiancy of God, as a 'power by which God "opens" himself '.[10] It is first of all in the depths of his eternal mystery that God pours himself out through the Spirit; it is in him that 'this Son is the radiant light of God's glory and the perfect copy of his nature' (Heb 1:3). The Spirit is the omnipotence of God, the one who carries out all the divine works. It is therefore in him that God's specific work, that of divine fatherhood, is accomplished. For the Spirit is the fullness of being and of life; it is in this fullness that God raises up a being and a life of fullness: his eternal Son. The Spirit is infinite love; it is in him that God accomplishes the essential work of love: the begetting of the 'Son that he loves' (Col 1:13). 'The Spirit is the breath of God, the one who pronounces the Word';[11] he is the voice of the Father who pronounces the Word; the Word wells up, is conveyed by the Breath; the Father begets his Son in the Holy Spirit.

We have often stated that in all the work of creation and salvation the Spirit acts in a simultaneous movement of ebb and flow; he attracts to God and he leads back to him the beings that God creates outside himself in the Spirit. Within the eternal mystery God wells up out of himself in a Son in the love of the Spirit, and it is in the power of this love that he recalls his Son back to unity with him.

Therefore it is in the Spirit that there is a Father and a Son; by reason of the third person, there exists a first and a second. In creation the Spirit tends to make everything personal, but it is first at God's own level that the procession of persons begins in an eternal love. God *exists* in the Spirit, it is his nature to come out of himself in Love by begetting his Word in the Spirit.

The love which human beings experience provides an image of the role played by the Holy Spirit. The one who loves is borne towards the other, he becomes open and comes out of himself to give himself and, in self-forgetfulness, becomes more fully himself. In the Spirit God leaves himself and is carried towards the Son and himself becomes what he is: the Father. Furthermore, love brings about the existence of the other in love: God similarly begets, in Love, the eternal Son. The person who loves wants the other to have life, he wants this to the point of wishing to *exist* for the other and in him; it is thus that, in the Spirit, God *exists* for his Son, he *exists* in him, becoming Father in begetting the Son.

*   *   *

The trinitarian mystery overflows into the work of creation. God creates by begetting the Unique One in the Holy Spirit; the eternal generation of the Son is reflected in the form of creation. All God's activity in the world is fatherly, given its thrust by the Son whom he makes, in Jesus Christ, 'the first-born of all creation' (cf. Col 1:15). The Spirit who hovers over creation is that of the Father who pronounces over Jesus Christ: 'You are my son; today I have begotten you'.

Creation is a trinitarian work, brought about by the co-operation of Father, Son and Spirit; each participates in it according to his nature: the Father in that he begets, the Son in that he receives all from the Father and returns everything to the Father, the Spirit in that he is the one through whom the Father begets, in whom the Son is begotten and returns everything to the Father.[12] God gives a human face to his Son, through Jesus, by an action which is that both of father and creator; in his fatherhood worlds are created with regard to Christ: 'He (Christ) is the first-born of all creation, for in him were created all things...Before anything was created, he existed, and he holds all things in unity...because God wanted all perfection to be found in him' (cf. Col 1:15–19). Creation does not only culminate in Christ in glory and in the fullness of his sonship, but it also has its origin in him. That is why creation is good and shares in sonship, because it was created by the Father in his fatherhood, out of Love for his Son. In Christ who inhabits the Trinity, this creation is 'within' God; at its height and in its roots, it enters into the eternal begetting of Christ of whom it was said: 'Today I have begotten you' (cf. Acts 13:33).

The Spirit of the Father and the Son

According to the consistent teaching of the New Testament writings, the Spirit is the third Person in trinitarian order, an order that theology has no right to reverse. Although he is as it were the ground of the divine mystery, the synthesis of its attributes of power and holiness...he does not come before the Father or the Son. He is the Spirit of them both and no Person comes from him; his personality is entirely defined by his relationship with the Father and the Son.

Scripture uses an accurate word to characterize the relationship of the Spirit with the Father: 'The Spirit of truth who *proceeds* from the Father' (cf. Jn 15:26). This word means that the Spirit has his source in the Father and it implies that he does not issue from him by birth. It is a fact that the Spirit is never presented as the One Begotten by the Father, as is the Son in whom he delights. He is the power of the Father, he is his will, he is the outpouring of life: we do not say of a person that he begets his own life, that he reproduces himself through his power and his will. Power, will, love, issue from someone without reproducing him. The Spirit is not born of the Father, his relationship with the Father is different from that of the Son: 'he proceeds from the Father'.[13]

However, his relationship with the divine sonship is very intimate. He proceeds in the begetting of the Son, he is the Spirit of the Father in his fatherhood. The entire activity of the Father is to beget the Son, and although God does not beget the Spirit, it is nonetheless in his fatherhood that he is the source of the Spirit.

In the earthly life-history of the Son, that is to say in Christ, the Spirit and the Son are inseparable, their union is clear and permanent. The whole action of the Spirit is concentrated on the Son whose birth in the world he brings about, whom he makes son throughout his life, death and resurrection. From his birth on earth until the climax at Easter, the sonship of Jesus is displayed in the Holy Spirit; he is truly Son, since he is in truth the man of the Spirit. If then it is possible to ascend from a knowledge of Christ to that of the mystery of the Trinity – than which there is no other, or more sure way – we must conclude that the Father begets in the Spirit, that *he* is the Spirit of the Father in this begetting, that he 'proceeds' in this relationship of Father and Son.

He does not beget and he is not begotten, but he is the Spirit of fatherhood and sonship. He is power in its eternal operation; he is love in its fecundity; he is the ecstasy of God, the self-giving of the Father in his fatherhood; he is the glorification of the Father, the one through whom the Father is glorified in his Son. We must repeat emphatically: the whole mystery of the Father is to beget his Son; if therefore the Spirit proceeds from the Father whose whole mystery consists in begetting, and if he himself is not the Son, *he must therefore be this begetting*. Although human language fails us, it would seem that one could say: the Spirit is the action of the Father as father, he is the begetting.[14]

In the light of this, the words of John (cf. 7:39) become clear: 'There was no Spirit as yet (in the world), because Jesus had not yet been glorified'. Certainly, the Spirit was already active in the world, he was not, however, present as he is in God. But in the passover of Jesus the eternal begetting of the Word was fully 'accomplished' within creation: 'The fact that he is risen from the dead is stated in Psalm 2: You are my son; today I have begotten you' (cf. Acts 13:33). By the fact that this begetting is brought about henceforth in the world, the Spirit, who is this begetting, is present in creation as he is in God.

In the mutual relationship of the Father who begets and the Son who is begotten, the Spirit who is this begetting is possessed by both, Spirit not only of the Father but also of the Son.

The Father shares with the Son all the riches of his being, his power, his holiness...Moreover, God's treasure is the Holy Spirit; the treasure is possessed in common. In begetting in the Spirit, the Father enables the Son to be in the Spirit, enables him to exist when his action is completed. It is thus that, in raising Christ from the dead in the Spirit, he makes him a life-giving spirit (cf. 1 Cor 15:45). The Father begets in his perfect likeness; the Son would not be the image of the Father if the Spirit, in whom are expressed all God's attributes, were not also the Spirit of the Son. In salvation history Christ rids himself of the condition of a slave (cf. Ph 2:7), that of sinful flesh (cf. Rom 8:3), and becomes the perfect image of the Father (cf. 2 Cor 4:4; Col 1:15), when he is overwhelmed by the power and the glory of the resurrection, that is, by the Holy Spirit: risen, he becomes like the Father in the fullness of the Spirit. The Son is the eternal image of the Father in that he is begotten in the Spirit and in that he possesses him in his fullness.

If the Spirit is possessed in common, in an identical fullness, *he is nevertheless possessed differently*. For the Father begets in the Spirit, whereas the Son is begotten in the Spirit. The Father is the source flowing into the Son; all is given by the Father and all is possessed in common; nothing distinguishes the Son, except that he is the Son and not the Father, and that *he possesses the Spirit by receiving him*. The treasure is possessed in common, but with the difference that distinguishes the Father and the Son.

To receive everything is also to share in the power to send forth the Spirit. The Father holds nothing back, he does not deprive the Son of any of his prerogatives.[15] Moreover, could he communicate the Spirit without conferring the power to send him forth? The Spirit is breath, breathing; he would not be the 'Spirit of the Son' (cf. Gal 4:6), his breath, if the Son did not send forth this breath. It is possible to keep for oneself a material good, but the Spirit is not a possession, he is entirely gift. The Father does not possess him except by giving him, similarly, the Son possesses him by giving him. The Spirit is ecstasy, outpouring from the source; he therefore inhabits the Son only by flowing from him. He is divine love, he cannot be given to the Son without the Son loving him too, that is, without the Son sending forth the Spirit.

Here too the resurrection of Christ casts a decisive light on the matter. When the Spirit overwhelms him, Christ becomes not only a spirit, 'he becomes a life-giving spirit', the fountainhead of the Spirit for the faithful. Even in the followers of Christ, to whom he gives life, the Spirit is radiancy; he makes them sources of grace. When Jesus communicates the Holy Spirit, who is forgiveness of all their sins, the disciples begin to preach him and forgive sins (cf. Jn 20:22f.).

As long as Jesus has not ascended to the Father, he cannot give the Spirit (cf. Jn 15:26; 16:7; 7:39). The Spirit will be at his service when Jesus himself is fully within the mystery of the Trinity, assumed into the glory of sonship, even in his body which is the sacrament of our salvation: *to be the source of the Holy Spirit is therefore a privilege of sonship*; Jesus will be fully in possession of it when he is recalled to his own eternal mystery (cf. Jn 17:5). This means that he *will have the Spirit at his service in virtue of his sonship*, that the Spirit who proceeds from the Father issues also from him, in that he is the Son. When Jesus says that he 'will send the Spirit of truth who issues from the Father' (Jn 15:26), he recognizes implicitly that the Spirit, whose source is in the Father, wells up also from the eternal Son, since Jesus will be able to give him when he is glorified and fully resumes the privilege of sonship.

Jesus is more explicit when he says: 'the Holy Spirit whom the Father will send *in my name*' (Jn 14:26). 'The "name" expresses what is deepest in the person of Christ, his quality of Son. The formula "in my name" is an indication of the perfect communion between the Father and the Son in the mission of the Spirit: the Father is the origin of this mission; the Son will therefore send the Spirit "from the Father" (15:26); but the Son too is the principle of this sending: it is "in the name of the Son", *in virtue of his union with the Son*, that the Father will send the Spirit; the Father and the Son are both the principle of this mission of the Paraclete.'[16]

Therefore, the Son shares all the Father's glory, that of possessing and that of sending the Spirit. He is the 'Spirit of the Son' (cf. Gal 4:6) as well as the Spirit of the Father. When the fullness of time comes, when the Son enters into the world just as he is in the eternal mystery, then the Spirit appears too, the Spirit *in person* just as he is in the eternal mystery. Both are 'sent' simultaneously (cf. Gal 4:4–6), the Son and the Spirit who wells up in him.

Equal in possession of the Spirit and the power of sending him, the Father and the Son are however distinguished by reason of the fatherhood of the one and the sonship of the other. The Father is the source who enables the Son to possess and send the Spirit: the source gives the power to be a source.[17] Jesus presumes this order in the Trinity when he says in John 15:26: 'I shall send to you from the Father the Spirit of truth who proceeds from the Father'. He uses similar language when he says that *his* word is that of the Father and not his own (cf. Jn 14:24; 17:14). The Father who begets the Word is the source, the words come from him, *yet it is Jesus who utters them.*

Because the Father begets in love, he empowers the Son to love him. He enables him in Love to be the source of Love. It is thus that parental love awakens love in a child, and it is in this awakening to love that the parents continue to beget the child until his personality blossoms. Reciprocally, the child's love stimulates love on the part of the parents. By loving, the eternal Son arouses the love of the Father who however begets him in this love. Jesus could say: 'The Father loves me, because I lay down my life' (Jn 10:17), because I perform this act of supreme love. By this fact the Son is not inferior to the Father, although he receives everything from him; because, for his part, he stimulates in the Father the love through which he is the Father. The Spirit oscillates between them in a unique movement of ebb and flow, through which the Father begets, through which the Word is begotten. This has been compared to a kiss in which mutual love is expressed and aroused.[18]

The person of the Spirit is therefore constituted in the relationship of the Father and the Son. That is why we must call him the third Person; in the Father and the Son, differently in each, *he is in person the begetting.* Clearly, human words are always inadequate to express the mystery; but in recognizing in the Spirit the eternal begetting, such as it is in the Father and in the Son, we have voiced important facts about the person of the Spirit.

We need to note that when Scripture says that the Spirit proceeds from the Father and that he is sent by Christ, we must not picture him as leaving the Father and leaving the Son. Love does not absent itself from a heart that loves. While making man ecstatic, love causes him to go down into himself, to depths hitherto unknown. The Spirit proceeds from the Father and the Son where fatherhood and sonship are brought about, while remaining the intimate depths where the movement of the Trinity is at its beginning and at its final end, that is, in the Father and in the Son.

At the end and at the beginning

The Spirit is the third Person and no other proceeds from him. As the third, principle of no other person, is he the last, is he sterile? Or is he indeed the third because in him the depths of the divine mystery are completed, open out and are glorified? It is certainly thus that he is the third Person: as both climax and depths. Not that he raises himself above the Father and the Son, but he is in person the divine mystery, common to the Father and the Son, the one in whom they are Father and Son.

Theology speaks of a gyratory movement, a circular dance,[19] in which the rhythm of the Trinity is the same as at its beginning, in which the third Person is already present and active in the Father and the Son, but nevertheless proceeds from them.

In the work of creation and salvation, the Spirit is the eschatological gift, the agent of final accomplishment; yet everything begins in him. This movement is clear in Christ in whom the work of creation and salvation is recapitulated and completed. Jesus rises from the dead as Son of God in the fullness of the Spirit, he who was at first conceived Son of God in the Spirit. Jesus, as Lord, risen from the dead, has the Spirit at his service, he sends him, the waters of the Spirit flow out from his side, he is the 'Lord of the Spirit'; but it is the power of the Spirit that makes him Lord, it is the Spirit who empowers him to bestow the Spirit. Similarly, the Church is fount of the Spirit, but because she is sanctified in the waters of the Spirit. The Eucharist is the great sacrament which makes the bread from the earth into the bread of grace. At the beginning and at the end we always find the all-embracing presence of the Spirit 'who...holds all things together' (cf. Wis 1:7). Moreover, Jesus, in his human existence and his life-history, the Church and the Eucharist have been shaped by the trinitarian mystery and make the Spirit known to us.

The Father is the beginning; however, from the beginning the Spirit plays the role proper to him. For the Father begets in virtue of infinite divine perfection, that is, in the Spirit who is in person this perfection. The omnipotence, the holiness, the life which are at work in the begetting of the Word are summed up in infinite love, that is, in the Spirit. The eternal begetting of the Son is the Father's act of love; and the Spirit is this love in action. He wells up, is established as Person, in the action that constitutes his very self: in the begetting, in the relationship of the Father and the Son bound to each other in him. While 'proceeding' in this relationship, mutual love is in itself its cause; love in Person is constituted in the achievement of his love.[20] With us too, love has its explanation in itself: we love because we love. Love spread throughout creation is the sign of the mystery of the Spirit.

On the one hand the Father is therefore *the* beginning and the Son is *the* end to which nothing is added; but the Spirit is *at the* beginning, in the Father who begets; he is *at the* end in the One Begotten. While proceeding from them, he does not come after the Father or after the Son, for it is in him that they are Father and Son. He is in the fatherhood of the Father in whom he has his source, and in the sonship of the Son from whom he wells up. The mystery of the resurrection of Jesus is an illustration of this: the Spirit is himself the power of the resurrection which enables Christ to be the channel of the Spirit.

Compared with the personality of the Father and that of the Son, that of the Spirit would seem less pronounced. However, it is he who is the principle of everything concerning persons; he is the Person who establishes persons. In him the Father begets the Son and the Son is begotten; in him they are persons. People have said of a human person: 'the "I" and the "thou" do not exist before love, they are directly constituted by it'.[21] It is first of all in the divine mystery that it is thus: the otherness of the Father and the Son and their mutual communion, these characteristics, constitutive of the person, are initiated in the love of the Spirit.[22] No person is without love, and the Spirit is love.

★ ★ ★

The Spirit plays this role of making everything personal in creation, of which he is the mainspring. In sowing love there, he raises creation to its highest point where, in man, it reaches the dignity of person. Two stones are distinguished only by the different space they occupy and are united only by their nearness to one another in space; but two people who love one another constitute different entities and communicate with one another by reason of their otherness. Love is the 'place' of their encounter; love brings about the person. This is a triune situation: an 'I', a 'thou', two termini and a mutual communion. These termini are kernels, centres of existence, firm, invincible, and yet entirely receptive to one another. Love sown in the heart of man is in the image and likeness of the mystery of the Spirit.

In Jesus the Spirit accomplishes perfectly his role of building up persons. He endows this man with the dignity of the person of the eternal Son. In his death and resurrection, when the Spirit is displayed in him without limit, Jesus is fully revealed as the person he is: he is 'proclaimed Son of God in all his power according to the spirit of holiness' (cf. Rom 1:4).

Because everything is made personal by the Spirit, in God and in man, it is to him that credit is given for having founded a religion not of fear but of confidence: 'The spirit you have received is not the spirit of slaves bringing fear into your lives again: it is the spirit of sons, and it makes you cry out: "Abba! Father!" ' (Rom 8:15).

If God is not personal, he is to be feared, and familiar dialogue and communion with him are impossible. Hence the fear of idolatrous religions and religions of the Powers and forces of nature of which St Paul speaks (cf. 2 Cor 2:15, 20), which would reduce man to fear and slavery (cf. Gal 4:1–10). In the Spirit who makes personal, everything encourages trust and communion.

★ ★ ★

In the Old Testament God revealed himself in his unity, then he manifested himself in Jesus Christ as a trinitarian mystery. Sometimes we represent God to ourselves according to this progressive revelation, as if the three Persons were constituted after there had been, *at first*, only one God. There is a theological tradition which distinguishes between a divine nature, which is one, and three Persons constituted after this nature. Unity, holiness, power and love are the 'attributes' enumerated as belonging to this nature... Such a distinction makes it easier to talk about God, but it does not correspond to the reality revealed in Jesus, and it ignores the central role of the Spirit. *In God there is no nature which becomes fruitful in Persons*: there are three Persons, *it is God's nature to be Trinity*. Of these three Persons one is the Holy Spirit in whom God begets; he is the 'common property' and the bond of unity between the Father and the Son; *in him the attributes of God are personified* (see above, p. 20, and below, Chapter 3, note 8).[23]

Although he is the third Person in an enumeration, the Spirit is not for this reason the last, he is not inferior to the others; he does not come after them, *he is in them. He is the mysterious base of the keystone*. Neither the Father nor the Son would exist without the Spirit. Each Person exists in relationship to each of the other two. If it is true that no Person proceeds from the Spirit, he is nonetheless the divine fruitfulness through which all is accomplished. Since the third Person is also at the beginning, there is no place for a fourth: the circle is closed, the movement is perfect, it is eternal.

One single God in the Spirit

In possessing in common the indivisible Spirit, the Father and the Son are at the same time distinct and united. The Spirit is 'common to them both',[24] yet he establishes their otherness. He is the meaning of the mystery which is both plural and singular.

The Spirit is one person in two others.[25] In begetting, the Father communicates his Spirit who, while given to the Son, does not cease to be the Spirit of the Father. 'The Son of his delights' (cf. Col 1:13) loves with the very tenderness of the Father. By becoming love in person, the Spirit does not separate, but unites the two entities which are constituted in him. The Father expresses himself by saying: '*I* beget you'; the Son by saying: '*I* am in my Father'. In the Spirit they say: '*We* are *one*' (cf. Jn 10:30). It is the same with the love of two human beings: they feel their love as a third power which enhances their otherness and at the same time unites them in communion. Moreover, they do not say 'my love' or 'your love', but 'our love'.

However, the love of two human beings is not absolutely one; it can die out in one heart and continue to exist in the other. But divine love is possessed indivisibly by the Father and the Son. The Spirit is in person the will, power, holiness and action of the Father and the Son; he is love in person, the life of the one and the other. Although the Father and the Son are distinct, their power is one, their love is one. *There is no bond to be compared with that constituted by a single person within two others*. Just as the person is indivisible, so the Father and the Son are inseparable. Their union is complete, brought about in the absolute unity which is proper to a person. God is therefore one, not by reason of an impersonal divine nature, but because he is Father and Son in the Person of the Spirit. The Spirit is God's unity in person.

Once more we must repeat: the Spirit is at the end and at the beginning; he proceeds from the unity of the Father and the Son, yet he brings about their unity.

Jesus recalled this eternal unity: 'My Father and I are one' (Jn 10:30). He alluded to it when he said: 'My works are not mine, my words are not my own' (cf. Jn 5:36; 9:4; 10:37; 14:24; 17:14). These works, these words, were indeed those of Jesus, but in an indivisible communion in which nothing is proper to one or the other, save to be Father and Son; all their action is common to them in the Holy Spirit.

The Spirit is called the bond of unity, just as St Paul says of charity that it is a bond (cf. Col 3:14). Such a bond is not a thing, it is a power and a movement; the Spirit is borne from the Father to the Son and from the Son to the Father in a simultaneous ebb and flow. This 'to-and-fro' does not cancel itself out, although it is simultaneous; it is the very reciprocity which leads to it. Our imagination cannot picture such a movement, but the idea is already familiar to us: we find this

movement re-echoed in the activities of the Spirit in the world
and in salvation history. When God creates, he awakens a
being outside himself; but he awakens him by a 'call' to exist.
Jesus knows that he is consecrated to his Father and at the
same time sent far out into the world (cf. Jn 10:36); he comes
out of God and yet he is 'for God' and goes towards him (cf. Jn
8:42 and *passim*; 1:1, 18; 13:1). He is the Son in this double
yet single movement. In his passover Jesus is exalted to heaven
and thus comes into the world (cf. Jn 14:18, 28), to fill it with
himself (cf. Eph 4:10). St Paul knows that he is 'an apostle
(sent) by calling' (cf. Rom 1:1; 1 Cor 1:1), he is sent into the
world 'by a call' towards the mystery of Christ. Everywhere
we see the movement of the Spirit making God come out of
himself in a Son whom he leads back to his Father.

Unity does not abolish 'the many', the one is brought about
in the other and by the other; the Spirit is the principle of
both. The *one* is poor, closed, insular, as long as it is not
'plural'; the many, too, are fragmentary, scattered, solitary, as
long as they are not one. The richness of the one is in the many
it unites; the success of the many is in the unity it brings
about. The unity of God is not enclosed by frontiers; it proves
its transcendence, consecrates its infinity, by going beyond the
insignificance of the one as it exists in creation. It is the
epitome of communion; it is characteristic that an infinite love
excites otherness and is enchanted by it, embracing it in unity.
The Spirit – if one may say so – brings about an 'explosion'
into persons and an 'implosion' into unity.

He is single and yet *he is diversified even in himself in the
Father and the Son*. To be the Spirit of the Father as father is
not the same thing as to be the Spirit of the Son as son. O
strange, mysterious Holy Spirit! He is absolute unity yet
diversified in himself!

We were surprised at the paradoxical manifestation of his
presence in the Church, where he creates the unity of the body
of Christ by making it rich in diversity (see above, pp. 67–68).
The final explanation of this paradox is to be found in the
nature of the Spirit who is in himself one yet diversified. The
multiple unity which is proper to the Spirit also strengthens
the conviction that has been forced upon us since the
beginning of this present study: the Holy Spirit is like the

ground of the mystery of God, of this God who is single yet multiple.

★   ★   ★

The Spirit assures us not only of the unity of Persons in one same mystery, but also of *their equality*. The inequality of human beings is the consequence of the fact that they do not share the possession of power or material goods or even those of the spirit. In God all is communion. The Father and Son enjoy in common the unique wealth of the Holy Spirit. This treasure is not itself a possession that one has for oneself, for the Spirit is ceaseless gift; the Father and the Son are rich in the Spirit, not by possessing him for themselves, but by giving him to each other. It is true that the Son is begotten, that he receives all from his Father, and that the Spirit is given to him; he is not for that reason inferior to his Father, for he is full of this Spirit, whom he sends back to the Father who is Father in the Spirit. Where they differ, their perfect equality is brought about by the love which makes them one.

An important lesson is thus proposed to us. Equality does not result from the suppression of differences, it is brought about by mutual love. The trilogy of liberty, equality and fraternity would indeed be admirable and full of the breath of the Spirit if, instead of always being sacrificed, fraternity were the first to be lived out. We know that, without love, liberty is claimed only at the expense of others, and similarly with equality. Where love reigns supreme, *diversity creates equality* by sharing and by rendering mutual service.

The maternal role of the Spirit

Scripture speaks of a Father in heaven and of a Son; it never has recourse, in speaking of the Spirit, to images borrowed from the difference between the sexes or from family relationships. The Hebrew word for the Spirit, *Ruah*, is feminine, but breath, the reality expressed by it, is impersonal. In the Old Testament, power predominates in the recognized attributes of the Spirit. Neither breath nor power suggests a representation of the Spirit in feminine, maternal form. The New Testament, in its turn, knows of no such representations.

It is nevertheless true that the activities of the Spirit, in God and in history, present striking analogies with the role of a mother.

Christ's faithful are sons of God in communion with the Son; but this communion and this sonship are brought about *in* the Spirit: 'Unless you possessed the Spirit of Christ you would not belong to him...everyone moved by the Spirit is a son of God' (Rom 8:9, 14). Might we not express this role of the Spirit with the help of the image of motherhood? It belongs to the Father to procreate in his likeness (cf. Rom 8:29), but the children made in his image are born to him in the Spirit, and it is in the Spirit that they grow and live as sons. God transcends human realities: he is neither man nor woman; yet we say that he begets, that he is our father. Moreover, his children are born and live *in* the Spirit, as in a mother's womb.

In the birth of the faithful to grace, divine fatherhood is not manifested in symbols: there is no sacramental image of the Father, for the sacraments are mediators, whereas the Father is the origin. But two symbols evoke the Spirit through whom God begets – and they are maternal: the Church and baptismal water. When God creates a language, that of the sacraments, he therefore uses maternal images to express the role of the Spirit.

The Church is Zion proclaimed, mother of nations (cf. Ps 87), our mother, the 'Jerusalem on high' (cf. Gal 4:26), the woman with the twelve stars who gives birth to the brethren of Christ (cf. Rev 12:17). Furthermore, the Spirit and the Church are partners in one and the same activity: the Church is inhabited by the Spirit; children of God are born of the Spirit and of the Church in virtue of a single motherhood; the early ages of Christianity even considered their baptismal fonts, where people were born of the Spirit, as the maternal womb of the Church.[26]

Baptism is the 'water of re-birth in the Holy Spirit' (cf. Tit 3:5); in baptism we are born of water and the Spirit: 'Unless a man is born through water and the Spirit, he cannot enter the kingdom of God' (Jn 3:5). The idea that *water is a symbol of motherhood* lies dormant in human consciousness. It was in a watery medium, it would seem, that life germinated on earth; it is in the liquid centre of the womb that the foetus develops. In Christianity, this symbol has been raised to the dignity of a sacrament: the faithful are born of water and the Spirit, for whom water is the symbol. Each of the Persons in the Trinity plays his characteristic role in baptismal birth: 'But now you have been washed clean, sanctified and justified through the name of Jesus Christ and in the Spirit of our God' (1 Cor 6:11). Sanctification is the work of the Father: 'You have been washed clean, sanctified...';[27] it is accomplished 'in the name of Christ', mediator of salvation, and *in* the Spirit', as in his vital domain.

This birth is for ever. The Son and the sons by grace are rooted in the moment when the Father begets them in the Spirit.[28] The formation of the children of God throughout the course of their life on earth is a recurring birth, and by this very fact it is the sphere of the Spirit. He nourishes them with 'pure spiritual milk' (cf. 1 Pet 2:2), makes them come to know the Father (cf. Gal 4:6) and recognize the Brother who is the Lord (cf. 1 Cor 12:3). He makes them love their other brothers (cf. Gal 5:22), teaches them to pray (cf. Rom 8:15, 26), trains their consciences 'to recognize what is best' (Ph 1:9f.), purifies them of their faults and makes peace prevail. The Spirit is called 'of all Consolers best' (*Consolator optime*: Sequence for Pentecost). Is there any role more motherly than a consoling one? 'Like a son comforted by his mother will I comfort you' (Is 66:13).[29]

According to John's gospel, the disciples inherit, at the death of Jesus, two gifts which are not unrelated: the Spirit and Mary, the mother of Jesus, image of the Church as mother to whom the disciple is confided.

What happens to the children of God is first fully brought about in Christ. The Spirit came down on Mary, he covered her with his glory in order that in her God might become the father of a man: 'So the child will be holy and will be called Son of the Most High' (Lk 1:35). This account has no connection with the Greek myths about love between a god and a woman. The Spirit is not a substitute for a human father;[30] he establishes Mary as mother of God. *She is, as it were, the 'human lining' of the Spirit*, assumed into the role which is proper to the Spirit.

God recognizes as his Son the one over whom the Spirit hovers (cf. Mk 1:10f.) and whom the cloud of glory encircles (cf. Mk 9:7). The apocryphal *Gospel of the Hebrews* interprets these texts as speaking of a maternal presence of the Spirit.[31]

More than is the case with any other child of God, the Spirit takes charge of the formation of this unique Child. He leads Jesus through his life on earth to the fulfilment of his existence as Son. It is through him that Jesus knows God as his Father, recognizes the Father's will and is subject to it, is ceaselessly raised in prayer to the Father, finally to rejoin him in death 'offered in an eternal Spirit'.

The resurrection is an incomparable birth revealing the full truth of the sonship of Jesus. Moreover, it is in the Spirit that the Father raises Christ from the dead; the Spirit is like a divine womb in which the Father begets 'the Son of his love' (cf. Col 1:13). Whereas in an earthly birth the child leaves its mother's womb, Jesus lives his filial mystery fully when the Spirit surrounds and envelops him for ever with his power and glory and makes him the Christ-spirit.

Moreover, Jesus is the eternal mystery made visible (cf. Col 1:15), the entry to full knowledge of God. If he was conceived as Son of God in the Spirit, if he is raised up as Son of God in the Spirit, we can conclude that, in his eternity, the Word is born of the Father in the Spirit and never leaves the womb in which he was begotten. If the Spirit plays a maternal role in Christ and in the faithful, it is because, first of all in God, he is the mysterious womb, loving and fruitful, in which every work is accomplished, the first of which is the eternal begetting of the Word.

In the Old Testament, the Trinity had not yet unveiled its mystery; there people spoke of the Lord God and of the Spirit of God. When the Trinity was revealed in Jesus Christ, a new language was coined which speaks to us of the 'Father' and the 'Son'. But the name of the Spirit has remained unchanged, the name which does not characterize him as a person. To counteract this lack of precision, it is fitting to introduce into the trinitarian formula the preposition which suggests the role of motherhood and also makes the personal nature of the Spirit clear by praising the Father and the Son *in* the Holy Spirit.[32]

God is neither masculine nor feminine. Yet he has created human beings in his image, therefore he is in some way like them: 'God created man in the image of himself, in the image of God he created him, male and female he created them' (Gen 1:27). The riches of man in his virility and those of woman are possessed by God, but infinitely surpassed; none of the qualities, some thought more masculine, some more feminine, is the monopoly of one or other Person in the Trinity. All is common to them, all is unlimited power, outpouring of life, loving with infinite tenderness. The Father begets in love, the Son is begotten in love, but the Spirit, in person, is the love through which the Father begets. The image of motherhood is the special prerogative of the Spirit. It is in this role that his person is constituted.

Although this analogy concerns only the Spirit, God is for us as much a mother as a father,[33] because the Spirit of motherhood is in the Father and the Son. God has even become the brother of men in his incarnate Word. But fatherhood belongs to him especially as Father; only the incarnate Son is the brother of the children of God; only the Spirit is the womb in which God possesses the fecundity of a mother, in whom he begets the Son and his brothers.[34]

* * *

Christ and the Spirit are the life of the Church. She must allow Christ to play in her a role of Lord, and the Spirit a role of motherhood. The faithful who have a ministry of ruling in the Church can call on Christ as head, lord of the Church. However, they must not forget that Christ is lord in the power of the Spirit who is maternal.

In the exercise of her ministry of ruling, the Church is condemned – a sign of the fact that salvation is still incomplete in her – to use certain forms of government akin to the powers of this world. While invoking the lordship of Christ, she must refer also to the Spirit whose power is humble and maternal: thus she will avoid modelling her power on that of the 'princes of this world...who crucified the Lord of glory' (cf. 1 Cor 2:8). Christ was given 'as head to the Church' (cf. Eph 1:22), in death to himself and in the humble, loving power of the Spirit. The only power in the Church is spiritual, that is, it is exercised in the charity of the Spirit. A practice of ministry which ignored the aspect of the Church as mother would be sinning against the Holy Spirit and against Christ the Lord.

* * *

In the one Church, constituted of two principles, Christ and the Spirit, ministries are entrusted to men and women. Is it their prerogative to exercise them indistinguishably, or should they be distributed to the faithful according to the fact that some are for men and others for women?

Equal in their dignity as children of God (cf. Gal 3:26–28), they remain men and women, symbolizing in different ways the double principle that constitutes the Church: man is symbolically closer to Christ as head,[35] woman as mother is closer to the Holy Spirit of God. Who has placed in man's hands the ministries of ruling in the Church? Is it Christ's will, is it the nature of things or the contingencies of history? Whatever be the answer given to this question, it is undeniable that the real power in the Church is spiritual, it is that of the Spirit whose role is to love, to give life from within and to 'fill the universe' (Wis 1:7), while remaining unnoticed. There is one activity of the Church on earth that is of a purity which is spiritual, eschatological, and therefore invisible: the communion of saints, which has a very strong maternal character (see above, pp. 77–78). One day ministries of ruling will no longer be exercised, only the love of the Spirit will continue to exist, the Spirit who carries these ministries and makes them fruitful. Moreover, woman in her role as mother is a clearer symbol of the power of the Spirit.

Therefore woman has the right and the joy to recognize a greater symbolical affinity with the One who, even in the mystery of God, is at the beginning and at the end, who gives life to everything and who is the glory of God. A similar bond unites woman to the Church-as-mother through which the world is sanctified; this bond unites her to Mary in whom the Spirit is manifested as in an icon, in whom too the universal motherhood of the Church is expressed.

In research into woman's role in the ministries of the Church, we must be careful not to do harm to her privileged relationship with true power, that of the Spirit, who, at the same time, is the humility as well as the glory of God.[36]

The Spirit, the humility of God

All true love is humble. It is in the nature of love to be sacrificed when face to face with the beloved; if love is very great, it is capable of a surpassing humility. The Spirit, infinite love, is infinitely humble. He is humility personified.

In all his activity *he effaces himself* in favour of others. Within the eternal mystery, he is divine fecundity and yet no Person proceeds from him. He is the key that 'opens' God, but it is the Son who is begotten and who becomes incarnate, and it is in the image of the Son that the world is created. The Spirit is the revelation of the Father and the Son, but he himself remains inexpressible. He is at the service of the incarnation but does not become incarnate; the Father sends the Son and, in the Son, he sends the Spirit, who does not send anyone. He is the eternal glory, but it is the Father who is glorified; it is the face of Christ that is illuminated. He is the gift, but not the giver. He gives only the power to give the gift itself; it is in the love of the Spirit that the Father and the Son and the Church have the Spirit at their service. He is communion, the 'place' for encounter; but it is the Father and the Son who meet one another in him, who are encountered by the Church. He works anonymously; when the Father and the Son speak, they say 'I'; the Spirit never expresses himself in this way. Yet it is through him that the Father, the Son and the prophets speak.

The activity of the Spirit is *disinterested*. As a mother who is at the service of life, the Spirit never works to his own advantage. He is the action of the Father who begets through him, for whom he obtains numerous children in the Son. He acts for the Son who, in him, is loved by the Father and in whom he incorporates the faithful. Through the glorifying power of the Spirit, Christ is established 'Lord of the Spirit', the one who distributes spiritual gifts. The Spirit thus places himself at the service of a lordship of which he himself is the principle. He testifies in favour of Jesus. He is the power through which the lordship of Jesus is proclaimed by the apostles and professed by the faithful (cf. 1 Cor 12:3); he is not

the object of the proclamation or of the profession of faith.[37]
He enables the faithful to know the Father and invites them to
make the invocation: 'Abba!' (cf. Gal 4:6), but, at least in
Scripture, he is not invoked. As a master of prayer he prays,
but according to the mind of the Father (cf. Rom 8:27).

He is infinite power; he is the immeasurable will of God.
Whereas absolute power makes man proud, *the power of the
Spirit is exercised by loving*, in humility. The commandments in
which the divine will is expressed are intended not to impose
God's domination, but to ensure man's freedom: 'the sabbath
was made for man' (cf. Mk 2:27).

The Spirit is humble and *he makes those he inhabits humble*:
the Father, Christ, the faithful. God comes out of himself in
the Spirit and is lost in his Son. In the Spirit he ventures out of
his transcendence and creates the world. He lives in creation
and is united with it in a strange alloy of gold and clay; finally
he concludes with creation a covenant such that, become man,
he can no longer be separated from his creature. During
Christ's life on earth, God becomes the neighbour of the small
and lowly; he seeks contacts with what is even a contrast to his
holiness: contact with sinful man. Matthew attributes to the
presence of the Spirit the mercy and discretion of Jesus: 'he
warned them not to make him known'. This was to fulfil the
prophecy of Isaiah...'*I will endow him with my spirit*...He will
not brawl or shout, nor will anyone hear his voice in the street.
He will not break the crushed reed, nor put out the
smouldering wick' (12:16–20). The holiness of the death of
Jesus, which is extreme submission, is attributed to the eternal
Spirit (cf. Heb 9:14). The Spirit of the resurrection for ever
consecrates this humility, for Jesus rises again without leaving
the mystery of his death. The stigmata of the passion, with
which he remains marked, are the multiple seal of the Spirit
and of an eternal immolation. It is from these wounds that the
Spirit is outpoured, so that the Church may be reunited with
Jesus in his immolation.

While remaining the humility of God, and because he is this
humility, the Spirit is power and glory. He is the radiancy of
God, his total ecstasy even in the death of his Son. Humility
and omnipotent glory are words diametrically opposed; they
prolong a list, already lengthy, of the paradoxes of the Spirit,

but the love which they express, carried to its climax, reveals perfect harmony.

Conclusion

The Spirit is a mystery. The statement appears on the first page of this book, and doubtless readers have had it forced upon them on the long road they have been prepared to travel. The human heart has reasons of which reason knows nothing, but how much more mysterious is the heart of God in his infinite love!

The Spirit is not, however, unknown. For God has lighted a lamp, Jesus Christ, which burns in our world with the ardent presence of the Spirit. Having lighted it, he placed it on a lamp-stand, raising it on high, when he raised up Jesus Christ from the dead in the fullness of the Spirit, that he might fill the Church with his light.

Henceforth the faithful know the Spirit: 'The world can never receive (him), since it neither sees nor knows him; but you know him, because he is with you, he is in you' (cf. Jn 14:17). They can contemplate the glory of God on the face of Christ, that glory which is the Holy Spirit. In their communion with Christ, they even possess the Spirit and live through him: 'You know him, for he is with you and dwells in you'.

The Spirit who is God's secret is also his ecstatic power through which God, without leaving himself, has come out into the world and spread his presence, first of all in creation, then in the midst of men, through successive covenants, and finally in Christ and in his Church. This outpouring of the Spirit might be compared with the thrust of a spiral which rises up from the perfect movement of the circle and which, in the power of this movement, is released and tends ever to reproduce afresh the same circle outside itself. It advances by repeating itself, ceaselessly coming back on itself, yet without contradiction, in forms each time new, but nevertheless similar. In the same way the Spirit seeks to reproduce in the world, in forms varied and yet alike, the unique interior mystery of God. He moves in an incessant ebb and flow. He is expressed in terms apparently contradictory, he who is mystery and revelation, a power which is glorified in weakness, the glory and humility of God. Theology is thus obliged to speak of him in a continual cascade of paradoxes and constantly to repeat itself. This is what we have done, at the risk of tiring the reader.

In spite of the spiral's endless revolving on itself, it ascends with assurance towards a goal, towards a centre which is that of the circle whence it rises. In each of its revolutions it advances towards a precise point where it will come to rest at the top of its thrust. So it is with the power of love through which God comes out of himself. This power does not wander aimlessly, its strength is not blind: it is borne instinctively towards a single pole. It is towards Christ that God creates the world in the power of the Spirit. It is towards him that the Spirit directs sacred history. It is into Christ that God incorporates men, in the love of the Spirit, in order to make them the Church. He raises up sons in his Son, blessing them 'in his Beloved with all spiritual blessings' (cf. Eph 1:3–6).

The obvious truth that is clear from all research into the mystery of the Spirit is in this relationship between the Son and the Spirit. All the interventions of the Spirit are polarized by one single purpose: to 'produce' the Son in the world; all divine energy is invested in this 'production'. In each work accomplished in the world, God is the Father begetting the Son in the Spirit, and in all his activity he is the Spirit of the Father as father, the Spirit of the Son as son. The power of the Spirit is displayed in the passover of Jesus according to its mighty sweep which is unlimited; it thus brings the mystery of sonship to its climax in the world. Henceforth the eternal begetting of the Son is accomplished within creation. It is there that the activity of the Spirit reaches its summit, from which and for which God creates everything.

Perhaps it would be permissible here to make the following reflection. At least according to the testimony of Scripture, the

Holy Spirit never claims for himself the homage of worship; yet there does exist one which must be especially pleasing to him: the love the Church has for her Lord Jesus, the zeal she shows in the service of his coming into the world. For all the yearning of the Spirit is directed towards the realization of the mystery of sonship among men: 'The Spirit and the Bride say: "Come!". Let everyone who listens answer, "Come!" ' (Rev 22:17).

When the spiral is released from its original circle, it expresses, by retracing it in manifold fashion, the perfect movement from which it rises. Similarly, the Spirit attempts to *bring about* outside God, and thus to *reveal*, the interior activity of the eternal mystery. The passover of Jesus is the revelation of this mysterious activity as well as its realization in the world. God takes Christ up into the fullness of the eternal begetting: 'He raised Jesus from the dead, as is said in Psalm 2: You are my Son, today I have begotten you' (cf. Acts 13:33). However, it is in the Spirit that God thus glorifies Christ.

The resurrection of Jesus, which is the realization in the world of the eternal mystery of the Father and the Son, reveals that *it is in the Spirit that God is father*, that the Spirit is the eternal action, the power, the holiness, the love and the glory in which God begets his Word. That is why we thought we could say that he is *in person* the eternal begetting. He is the mystery proper to the Father and the mystery proper to the Son. Without being either the beginning or the end of the trinitarian movement, he is at the beginning and at the end, acting in the Father as father, in the Son as son, and it is he who brings about the union of them both. All is accomplished in him who is love, infinitely powerful, the single action of the Father and of the Son. Moreover, he is called the third Person because he is constituted in the relationship of the Father and the Son. At the same time we confess that he is not inferior to them, that he does not come after them, for it is in him that they are Father and Son.[1]

Therefore there is no reason to be surprised that all the attributes of God are made personal in him. He is in person what constitutes the majesty of God: power, holiness, life without end, glory, infinite love. The Spirit is the ground of the mystery of God.

This statement is essential. But, having formulated it, we have only spoken about the Spirit; we have not yet expressed his mystery. We have even confessed that he is inexpressible. The Spirit will ever remain the incomprehensible secret of the divine being.

★   ★   ★

To come to a knowledge of things relating to Christianity, there is fortunately a way other than that of theological reflection: the way of the heart which communicates with the mystery. It is there, in the depth of ourselves, that our eyes, as Christians, are opened: 'May the God of our Lord Jesus Christ, the Father of glory, give you a spirit of wisdom and perception of what is revealed, to bring you to full knowledge of him. May he enlighten the eyes of your heart so that you can see...' (Eph 1:17f.). The most authentic knowledge is that of a loving heart. Theology itself, for fear of error, must be rooted in this basic knowledge. Like all Christian activity, it is referred to the practice of the theological virtues. In Christianity, everything has in communion its beginning and its completion.

In his goodness, the Spirit communicates himself and thus makes himself known. He comes and dwells in the Church, he impregnates with his dew the hearts of the faithful,[2] and their hearts come to knowledge through this love. Although he is the foundation of the mystery, he is intimately known, just as the vast ocean is known by the sponge that lives in its depths.

The Christian even has a language in which this knowledge about communion is expressed, a language without words, through which the Holy Spirit tells of his presence. 'The love of God has been poured into our hearts by the Holy Spirit who has been given to us.' The Spirit is love, he is expressed in the faithful through the love that he enkindles in them.

At the age of eighty-seven, shortly before his death, the philosopher Ravaisson confided: 'I am leaving without having said my last word. We always leave without being able to finish our task'. But a believer in Christ has the privilege of saying this last word which contains the meaning of life and everything, and even the meaning of God. A young Christian, often quoted in this book, pronounced it with her last sigh, and in the very Breath of God: 'Oh! I love Him...My God...I love You!'[3]

Throughout life a Christian prepares himself for this final experience of the Spirit. He prepares himself for it by loving and, in loving, he begins to know the Holy Spirit of God.

Notes

Chapter 1: Inexpressible yet intimate

1 H. Urs von Balthasar, 'Spiritus Creator' in *Skizzen zur Theologie* III (Einsiedeln, 1967), pp. 95–105; in Fr. in *Lumière et Vie* 67 (1964), pp. 115–126.

2 The idea that God or Christ speaks *through* the Spirit is traditional: cf. *1 Clem.* 22, 1 (*SC* 167, 138): 'Christ...exhorts us through the Holy Spirit'. For the analogy between the Spirit and the voice that conveys the word, see Maximus the Confessor, *Quaestiones* 34 (*PG* 90, 813): 'Just as one cannot say that the word is the voice, similarly one cannot say that the Word is the Spirit'.

3 Exegetes are hesitant about the original meaning of the word *ruah*. At first it meant either the wind (cf. R. Koch, *Geist und Messias* [Vienna, 1950], pp. 4–11) or breath (P. van Imschoot, *Théologie de l'Ancien Testament* [Tournai, 1968], p. 23).

4 'In Scripture, *Ruah* everywhere means an event': M. Buber, quoted by M.-A. Chevallier, *Souffle de Dieu. Le Saint-Esprit dans le Nouveau Testament* (*Le point théologique* 26; Paris, 1978), p.14.

5 St Gregory of Nyssa, *Life of Moses* (*SC* 1, 112): 'In this way we learn that every concept formed by the understanding in order to try to attain and to discern the divine nature succeeds only in fashioning an idol of God'.

6 St Simeon the New Theologian, *Hymns* (*SC* 156, 151).

7 *Idem, ibid.* (*SC* 156, 153).

8 'In his nature inaccessible, he allows himself to be understood because of his goodness': St Basil, *On the Holy Spirit* 9 (*SC* 17, 146).

Chapter 2: The Spirit of God

1 Cf. also 'The Spirit of Yahweh came on Jephthah' (Jg 11:29), 'came on (Othniel)' (3:10), 'came mightily upon (Samson)' (14:6, 19)...

2 Luke attributes healings to the 'power (that) came out of (Jesus)' (6:19; 8:46). In his thinking this power is not unconnected with the Spirit (4:18; 24:49; Acts 1:8; 10:38).

3   In Ezek 37:1 a parallel is already established between the hand of God and the Spirit: 'The hand of Yahweh was laid upon me and he carried me away by the spirit of Yahweh'.

4   What St Cyril of Alexandria says is in keeping with Scripture: 'The Spirit is the power and natural action of the divine substance. He performs all the works of God': *Thesaurus*, assert. 34 (*PG* 75, 580; cf. 72, 608).

5   Logically, after speaking of the Spirit of power, one should speak of the Spirit of holiness. But in the resurrection of Jesus power and glory are so closely linked that I have decided not to treat them separately.

6   The Hebrew word *kabod* suggests the idea of weightiness, importance: Abraham is 'very rich' (literally, 'glorious') because he possesses 'livestock, silver and gold' (Gen 13:2).

7   D. Mollat in *Dictionary of Biblical Theology*, 2nd ed. (London, 1973), p. 203.

8   According to a possible translation of 2 Cor 3:18.

9   St Gregory of Nyssa, *Hom. in Cant.* 15 (*PG* 44, 1117): 'That the Holy Spirit should be called glory, no one examining the question could disagree if he considered the Lord's words: "I have given them the glory you gave to me" (Jn 17:22). He gave them this glory effectively when he said: "Receive the Holy Spirit" ' (Jn 20:22). The glory of which St John speaks: 'Father, glorify your Son' (17:1) corresponds effectively to the Spirit of whom St Paul speaks.

10 Several MSS have: 'The Spirit of glory and power, the Spirit of God'.

11 It is first found in Is 63:10–14 and Ps 51:13.

12 It is difficult to be precise about the symbolism of the dove. The flight of the dove coming down from heaven on Jesus is doubtless an element of this symbol. The image of a bird occurs naturally to the wish to represent 'in bodily shape' (cf. Lk 3:22) the coming of the Spirit who is heavenly.

13 (For the translation see below, note 21.) In this archaic, pre-Pauline text introduced by the Apostle into his letter, we rediscover the themes of the Spirit, power and holiness. The term 'spirit of holiness', unknown in other New Testament writings, is known from Palestinian literature of this time. Here it designates either the Holy Spirit or (and this seems to me more likely) holiness, the effect of the Spirit, and inherent in Christ.

14 In Mk 13:11; Jn 14:26 he is called the Holy Spirit. St Basil, *On the Holy Spirit* 9 (*SC* 17, 145): 'Holy Spirit is *par excellence* the name proper to him'.

15 This is without doubt the foundation of an essential theological principle, of great importance for the life of the Church but often misunderstood: in Christian realities there are no distinctions which separate, all is communion; the very distinctions are often a source of communion. It is sin alone that creates distinctions which separate.

16 *Donum Dei Altissimi* in the hymn *Veni Creator Spiritus*. St Hilary calls

him 'the gift': *De Trin.* 2, 1 (*PL* 10, 50); see St Augustine, *Enchiridion* 40 (*CCL* 46, 72): 'The Spirit is called "gift of God" '. – Like every image, that of the gift is imperfect: it is static, whereas the Spirit is action, the act of giving. Moreever, the Son also is given (Jn 3:16; Rom 8:32): he is the gift the Father makes to men by begetting him for men in the Spirit. The Spirit is the act of giving, inseparable from the gift.

17 2 Cor 13:13 seems to be liturgical in origin.

18 Liturgy of Pentecost. In the hymn *Veni Creator*, the Church acclaims the Spirit as 'the living spring, the living fire, sweet unction and true love'.

19 St Irenaeus, *Adv. haer.* IV, 20, 7 (*SC* 100, 649).

20 This text is concerned with Christ in glory, in whom God causes 'the fulness of divinity, to live in his body. In him you too find your fulfilment' (Col 2:9).

21 The usual [e.g. JB] translation 'through his resurrection from the dead' does not correspond to the literal tenor of this pre-Pauline text, nor to early Christian thinking, in which the resurrection of Jesus was seen as an eschatological event.

22 Job 27:3: 'As long as a shred of life is left in me, and the breath of God breathes in my nostrils...'.

23 In these texts due allowance must be made for poetry. However, poetry is not just fiction; the poet sees to the heart of things. It has been said, in formulas that require qualification: 'the breath (of creatures) is not really their own; it is only what Yahweh lends them, Yahweh's own breath': R. Kittel, *Die Psalmen*, 4th ed. (Leipzig/Erlangen, 1922), p. 341. – 'The breath of the Spirit of God is like the respiration of the world': E. Koenig, *Theologie des Alten Testaments*, 4th ed. (Stuttgart, 1923), p. 209. Both quoted by R. Koch, *Geist und Messias* (Vienna, 1950), pp. 14, 21.

24 This definition, Semitic in character, does not mean primarily that God is a pure spirit but that he is full reality, transcendent fullness. Cf. E. Schweizer, *TDNT* VI, pp. 438–439 and note 720. See also R. Bultmann, *The Gospel of John: A Commentary* (Oxford, 1971), p. 191.

25 If, then, God gives the Spirit, it is himself who is communicated; the grace of the Spirit is 'a sharing in the divine nature' (cf. 2 Pet 1:4). St Augustine, *Sermo* 128, 4 (*PL* 38, 715): 'The gift of God is equal to God himself, for the gift of God is the Holy Spirit'. Earlier, St Irenaeus, *Adv. haer.* V, 1, 1 (*SC* 153, 21): Christ makes 'God descend into man through the Spirit'.

26 Cf. e.g. E. Jacob, *Theology of the Old Testament* (London, 1958), p. 136.

27 We know that Gen 1, where the Spirit hovers over the waters, is of more recent origin than Gen 2.

28 F. Baumgärtel, *TDNT* VI, p. 367: '(God's) *ruah* has fashioned history'.

29 M.-A. Chevallier, *Souffle de Dieu* (Paris, 1978), p.32.

30 Acts makes use of the verb *anistanai* when speaking of the prophet raised up by God for his people (3:22; cf. 7:37) and of Jesus whom God

raised up in raising him from the dead for his people (3:26; 13:33f.).

31   J. de Fraine and A. Vanhoye in *Dictionary of Biblical Theology, op. cit.*
      (note 7), p. 228: 'in the concrete and global anthropology that we find
      in the Bible, man's heart is the very source of his conscious, intelligent
      and free personality, the place of his decisive choices'. 'The soul
      corresponds to our *I*': X. Léon-Dufour, *ibid.*, p. 566. 'The reference to
      a "sin against the body" in 1 Cor 6:18 probably refers to a sin against
      the whole human person': *idem, ibid.*, p. 54.

32   J. Guillet, *ibid.*, p. 570: 'the essential experience is that the spirit of the
      believer is inhabited by the Spirit of God which renews it (Eph 4:23)
      and which "joins itself to it" (Rom 8:16), to awaken in it a prayer and
      filial pleading (8:26)'.

33   L. Cerfaux speaks of cases where 'the small letter tends to become a
      capital letter': cf. *The Christian in the Theology of St Paul* (London,
      1967), p. 310.

34   *Tos. Sota* 13, 2: 'When Haggai, Zechariah and Malachi, the last
      prophets, died, the Holy Spirit disappeared in Israel'; cf. H. L. Strack
      and P. Billerbeck, *Kommentar zum Neuen Testament aus Talmud und
      Midrasch* I, pp. 127f.; III, p. 133. Such is perhaps the meaning of the
      answer given by the disciples of John the Baptist: 'We were never even
      told that there was such a thing as a Holy Spirit' (Acts 19:2).

35   According to rabbinical Judaism, the voice of God was no longer heard
      in Israel; the word of God, formerly pronounced by the prophets, was
      relayed by the *bath qol*, the echo of the voice.

36   The TOB interprets Col 1:19 ('God wanted all perfection to be found in
      him') thus: 'The fullness of divinity (Col 2:9), i.e., all that God wants to
      communicate of himself to us in Christ, to introduce us and bring us to
      perfection in him; the term (the fullness) would then be very close to
      pneuma (Spirit)'.

37   He is so completely the Spirit of promise that everything promised by
      God in view of salvation can be called spiritual. Isaac, born according to
      the promise, is 'the child born in the Spirit's way', as opposed to 'the
      child born in the ordinary way' who was not the object of the promise
      (Gal 4:28f.).

Chapter 3:   The Spirit of Christ

1   By these words the Apostle intends to make it clear that the Christ of
     glory is the living and life-giving reality of history. Compared with him,
     the Old Testament with its law and institutions is only a dead letter, a
     lifeless document, if it is separated from its profound reality, which is
     Christ.

2   St Simeon the New Theologian, *Catech.* 33 (*SC* 113, 257) uses this
     image to express the role of the Spirit in revelation: 'The door is the
     Son...the key to this door is the Spirit'.

3   When the Synoptics speak of a visible descent, made precise by Luke:
     'in bodily shape', they are affirming the reality and the fullness of the

presence of the Spirit. The account of the baptism is in the literary form of a revelation, the scene described reveals that Jesus is the man of the Spirit. The account is not intended to present in the baptism the first outpouring of the Spirit in Jesus.

4 St Basil, *On the Holy Spirit* 16, 39 (*SC* 17, 180f.): 'He was first present to the flesh of the Lord when he anointed him and made him his inseparable companion... Then all the activity of Christ was unfolded in the presence of the Holy Spirit... They were inseparable when Jesus performed his miracles... He did not leave him after his resurrection from the dead'.

5 J. Guillet in *Dictionnaire de Spiritualité* 4, 1250: 'Because the presence of the Spirit is...natural in Jesus, the gospels do not often stress the fact, they emphasize it only at decisive moments, to show that this presence accompanies Jesus throughout his existence and explains his action'.

6 'At the moment when Jesus says that the Spirit will be sent, he promises that he himself will come': St Cyril of Alexandria, *In Joh.* IX (*PG* 74, 261).

7 The identity between the Spirit of God and that of Christ appears also in Acts 16:6f.: 'Having been told by the Holy Spirit not to preach the word in Asia...they reached the frontier of Mysia, they thought to cross it into Bithynia, but the Spirit of Jesus would not let them'.

8 In the first centuries A.D. the Spirit was often seen as the heavenly aspect of Jesus. 'The Holy Spirit was often conceived of as the invisible, pre-existent reality, in some way the divine side of Christ': F. Bolgiani, 'La Théologie de l'Esprit Saint de la fin du premier siècle après J.-Chr. au concile de Constantinople (381)', *Les Quatre Fleuves* 9 (1979), p. 41. Cf. my book *The Resurrection* (London/New York, 1960), ch. III, especially pp. 91–107.

9 There are Christologies which make no reference to the Spirit: they are all characterized by a lack of depth. One such is a theology which does not integrate the resurrection, the work *par excellence* of the Spirit, into the mystery of redemption. Such too are especially the modern images of Jesus which, in the absence of the Spirit, ignore his filial relationship to God and the breadth of his mission.

10 M.-A. Chevallier, *Souffle de Dieu* (Paris, 1978), p. 234: The disciples 'said simultaneously: "It is the Christ" and "he has received the fullness of the Breath". For them these were two ways of saying the same thing'.

11 The same words 'image' and 'likeness' express in Gen 5:3 the relationship of son to father. In Col 1:15, the word 'image' is associated with 'first-born'.

12 The verb 'to reveal' (*apokaluptein*) suggests that this appearance is of Christ in the power and glory proper to the Day of the Lord.

13 See L. Cerfaux, *Christ in the Theology of St Paul* (New York/Edinburgh/London, 1959), Book 3, ch. 5, especially pp. 465–466.

14 This glory and likeness are manifested in various ways. Death too is full

of glory; in his death Jesus is likewise the image.

15　St Ambrose, *In Luc.* 7, 19 (*CCL* 14, 221) associates this account with the text: 'The power of the Most High will cover you with its shadow'.

16　St John Damascene, *De hymno trisagio* (*PG* 95, 60).

17　This justice itself is misunderstood as commutative justice, instead of in the biblical sense of 'God's justice' which is the helpful holiness of God exercised in justifying (cf. Rom 3:26).

18　It is improbable that Jesus ever understood his death as a ransom paid to God. His death is part of God's design in the coming of the Kingdom: 'The Son of man is going to be handed over into the power of men' (Lk 9:44). In this text, which is very likely to be authentic, the formula 'he is going to be handed over' – a theological passive, as the exegetes say – expresses the Father's will. The Eucharistic words and the giving of the bread and the chalice clearly indicate the meaning of the death of Jesus: he was *given up for*, i.e. *in favour of* the many. The kingdom of God is established in him, through his death, and the disciples are invited to be united with him and so to take their place in the Kingdom. As for the ransom paid (Mk 10:45b), many exegetes see this as an addition to the words of Jesus as they are reported in Lk 22:27: 'Here I am among you as one who serves'. However this may be, it is not a question of a ransom paid *to God*. In his self-giving the Son of man is given up in favour of the many. Cf. A. Schenker, 'Substitution de châtiment ou prix de la paix?' in *La Pâque du Christ, mystère de salut* (*Lectio Divina* 112; Paris, 1982), pp. 75–90.

19　The letter to the Hebrews often testifies to this 'becoming' through which the mystery of Jesus and that of salvation is accomplished: cf. 1:4; 2:17; 5:9; 6:20; 7:22, 26.

20　The question often asked: Did Jesus know he was the Son of God, did he attribute this eternal majesty to himself? is wrongly worded. He knew God as his Father, and can never have known him in any other way. But to recognize in God his Father, and himself to proclaim himself the Son of God are two psychologically different things, even though they are based on the same reality.

21　We know that this name is the one used by a small child for its father, such a familiar name that it did not seem fitting in a prayer addressed to God.

22　This should not be translated 'having won' (before his entry) but 'winning redemption' through this entry. 'The aorist tenses *eisēlthen* and *heuramenos* express one and the same action': C. Spicq, *L'Epître aux Hébreux* II (Paris, 1953), p. 257. Cf. Acts 1:24, 25:13.

23　St John Damascene, *De fide orth.* 3, 24 (*PG* 94, 1089).

24　The definition of prayer as *elevatio mentis ad Deum*, the raising of the mind to God, may be formulated in its application to the death of Jesus as *elevatio entis ad Deum*, the raising of his being to God.

25　The death of Jesus constitutes a single mystery with the resurrection, to such a degree that sometimes the proclamation of salvation consists only of a mention of the resurrection. Cf. Acts 13:32; Rom 1:1–5; 1 Th 1:9f.

26 The 'Lamb *of God*' who takes away sin is the *heavenly* Lamb (cf. Jn 6:33, 41, where 'bread of God' corresponds to 'bread from heaven'). Jesus is the heavenly paschal Lamb, his liturgy is celebrated at the level of God.

27 If the begetting in the Spirit is understood according to its trinitarian realism, this formulation of the mystery of Christ is in keeping with the dogma of Chalcedon (one divine person in two natures, human and divine). It expresses it in terms of biblical inspiration and trinitarian character. It includes both the personal mystery of Jesus and the mystery of salvation. It takes into account the 'becoming' in which Jesus was involved during his life and in his death.

28 To express this spiritualization, St Ambrose uses a formula which needs to be properly interpreted: 'The body of Christ is the body of the divine Spirit because Christ is spirit': *De mysteriis* 9, 58 (*SC 25bis*, 190). According to St Cyril of Alexandria, Christ forms a unity with the Spirit so perfect that the name 'Holy Spirit' can be used to designate Christ: cf. S. Lyonnet, 'S. Cyrille d'Alexandrie et 2 Co 3, 18', *Bib* 31 (1951), pp. 25–31.

29 May we be allowed to use this language, following several of the Fathers and in the sense in which the Apostle distinguishes two phases in the existence of Jesus, one earthly, that of the condition of a slave when he is nevertheless already the Son, and that of glory when he is endowed with all the attributes of the divine condition (Ph 2:6–11; Rom 1:3f.)!

30 See above, note 28.

31 L. Bouyer, *The Eternal Son* (Huntington, Ind., 1978), p. 401: 'The Father eternally generates His Son, not only as before His incarnation, but also as the Word made flesh'.

32 Cf. my *The Mystery of Christ and the Apostolate* (London/New York, 1972), pp. 19–45.

33 Sent in the Spirit, not by the Spirit. For it is the Father who begets, who sends; he does so in the Spirit.

34 Scripture makes particular use of two concepts to express Christ's glorification: that of exaltation and that of resurrection. The first says that Christ was raised to heaven, i.e. was assumed into the life of God; the other indicates that Christ comes into this world, which however he has left 'according to the flesh'.

35 These two texts contain obscurities but are clarified by the context of the primitive tradition of 'Jesus' descent into hell'. This interpretation has recently been disputed; it is however retained by commentators on 1 Peter: cf. L. Goppelt, *Der erste Petrusbrief* (Göttingen, 1978).

36 St Ignatius of Antioch, *Phil.* 9, 1 (*SC* 10, 151): 'He is the door to the Church, through which Abraham, Isaac, Jacob, the prophets and the apostles of the Church make their entry'.

37 *Idem, Rom.* 2, 2 (*SC* 10, 129).

38 'To know the power of *his* resurrection,...you have been raised with him' (Ph 3:10; Col 2:12).

39 The dream of Joachim of Flora, which still has its sympathizers today, is simply ridiculous. To wish that the kingdom of the Spirit should now succeed that of the Son is to wish to dismantle the Trinity.

40 Flavius Josephus, *Ant.* 8, 4, 1.

41 It would seem that it is Christ who is called upon as witness. In 1 John the same pronoun 'he' (*ekeinos*) refers to Christ.

42 With possibly one exception, in Jn 2:1–11, where it is 'meant for the ablutions that are customary among the Jews' and symbolizes the realities of the Old Testament which are about to be transformed.

43 The account of the man born blind is rich in symbolism. Jesus begins by calling himself the light of the world (cf. 9:5), and then sends the blind man to the pool of Siloam, the name of which, according to the evangelist, is messianic (cf. 9:7). 'Jesus sends the blind man to the pool which bears his name and where his action will make itself felt by baptism': M.-J. Lagrange, *Evangile selon S. Jean*, 3rd ed. (Paris, 1927), p. 501.

44 It is often said that the blood and the water prefigure the Eucharist and baptism. This interpretation can only be secondary. Why should the evangelist have named the blood before the water, since baptism precedes the Eucharist? The sacramental explanation can hardly be said to be prepared for by the context of 7:37–39. Moreover, it does not explain the solemnity of the testimony: 'he knows that he speaks the truth...so that you may believe (have faith)'. According to 1 Jn 5:6, faith consists in believing that Jesus 'came by water and blood', as a being who is heavenly (water) and at the same time truly human (blood). Cf. my book *The Resurrection* (London/New York, 1960), pp. 87f.

45 In John's gospel words and things sometimes have a double meaning, for visible reality is a face with an invisible reverse side. The world is a symbol. The breath that Jesus sends out is probably (as in 20:22) the symbol of the divine Breath that he communicates.

46 'The recalling of the open side (cf. Jn 20:20f.) reminds the reader of the account of the piercing of his side whence came out blood and water (19:34) and at the same time of the words announced by Jesus: "From his breast shall flow fountains of living water" ': J. Kremer, *Pfingstbericht und Pfingstgeschehen* (Freiburg, 1973), p. 227.

47 When John speaks of the sending of the Spirit – 'The Advocate whom I shall send to you' (15:26) – we must not think of the gift of the Spirit as a sent reality that is *exterior* to Christ.

48 Although the Spirit is not named here, Eph 4:7–13 testifies to the same conviction that, in his exaltation to heaven, Christ is the author of the graces of the Spirit. Cf. Rev 22:1.

49 The word 'Paraclete' designates counsel for the defence, an advocate.

50 A. Jaubert, 'L'Esprit dans le N.T.', *Les Quatre Fleuves* 9 (1979), pp. 26f.

51 Cf. I. de la Potterie, *La Vérité dans S. Jean* (Rome, 1977), I, pp. 391–395.

52 From ancient formulas of the Christian faith which go back to the beginnings of the Church we know, in fact, that the resurrection and salvific lordship of Jesus were publicly proclaimed (the kerygma), whereas faith in the incarnation was expressed in the liturgical hymns sung in the Christian communities. Cf. Ph 2:6f.; Col 1:15f.; 1 Tim 3:16.

53 Cf. Wis 1:6; 7:22. Like Wisdom, the Spirit fills the whole world (1:7; 7:24; 8:1; 12:1). Wisdom, like the Spirit, is at work in everything (7:21, 27). 'Wisdom is a breath (spirit) of the power of God' (7:25). The Spirit and Wisdom play an identical role in 1:4f. and 9:17.

54 I. de la Potterie, *op. cit.*, I, p. 326.

Chapter 4:   The Spirit in the Church

1 Jesus has just said: 'The hour has come when the Son of Man will be glorified'. He adds: 'Amen, amen, I tell you: if the grain of wheat...'. In John the formula 'Amen, amen, I tell you' ratifies the truth of a previous statement: the allegory of the grain of wheat confirms and explains the statement: 'The hour has come when the Son of man will be glorified'.

2 Luke knows that Jesus was exalted to God in his resurrection (Acts 2:36) and given possession of the Spirit in this exaltation (Acts 2:32f.).

3 According to Ex 12:16; Num 28:26, Pentecost was the harvest festival. At least from the second century B.C. it was further regarded as the anniversary of the Covenant (*Jub.* 6:17–23). In the first century A.D. it began to be associated with the gift of the Law. In these different aspects, the relationship between the Spirit and Pentecost is important: the Church is the harvest born of the death of Jesus and brought to fruition in the Spirit, who creates the New Covenant of which he himself is the law, inscribed not on tables of stone, but in human hearts (cf. Jer 31:33; Ex 36:27). Cf. J. Potin, *La Fête juive de la Pentecôte* I (Paris, 1971).

4 Cf. also 2 Tim 1:9: 'This grace had already been granted to us, in Christ Jesus, before the beginning of time'.

5 Although St Paul calls only the Church 'the body of Christ', the whole universe is nevertheless destined to be united under a single head (Eph 1:10).

6 St Cyril of Alexandria, *In Joh.* IX (*PG* 74, 261), was already struck by the apparent synonymity. In our times exegetes sometimes use the one for the other.

7 No strictly Pauline letter speaks of Christ dwelling in the Church. This image is found only in one letter, where there would seem to be some lack of agreement with Pauline language: 'that Christ may live in your hearts through faith' (Eph 3:17). Further, this presence is the effect of

faith, which does not make Christ dwell in the believer as the Spirit does, but incorporates the believer into Christ.

8 In *The Resurrection* (London/New York, 1960), ch. VI, pp. 125ff., I studied at greater length the difference between the presence of Christ and that of the Spirit.

9 St Irenaeus, *Adv. haer.* IV, 18, 5 (*SC* 100, 613).

10 The first meaning of the word *diathēkē*, which is usually translated 'covenant', is 'institution', 'edict', a covenant instituted by God, with its edicts.

11 Verse 17 gives the explanation of this meaning.

12 Vatican II, *LG* 32. Cf. *PO* 3: 'The difference that the Lord has established between the sacred ministries and the rest of the people of God includes in itself union (*conjunctio*)'.

13 St Thomas, *Comm. in Rom.* 8, 1, 1; *STh* Ia IIae, q. 106, a. 1.

14 St Peter Damian, *Opusc.* XI, *Dominus vobiscum* 5 and 6 (*PL* 145, 235).

15 St Thomas, *STh* Ia, q. 20, a. 2 ad 1: '*Amans fit extra se in amatum translatus*'.

16 The usual translations 'called to be holy', 'called to be an apostle' are inaccurate. The call does not merely destine a person for sanctity, for the apostolate, it sanctifies and it makes Paul an apostle.

17 The word used by Paul (*huiothesia*) signifies in legal language the adoption of a son; in the Apostle's work, we must understand it in its etymological sense: the believer is constituted a son. ' "Sonship", in the Pauline sense, is always "natural" in so far as it is not limited to a legal decree by God, but it creates us in the spiritual order by glorifying us in reality': L. Cerfaux, *The Christian in the Theology of St Paul* (London, 1967), p. 325.

18 The Old Testament attaches little importance to the idea of sonship; it is rarely mentioned, and with an extenuated meaning, whereas it is emphasized in the New.

19 In the West, theology has scarcely been aware of the newness of this gift. A similar grace, an identical presence of the Spirit, was affirmed in the Old and the New Testaments. This opinion was derived from a juridical theology of the redemption, in which the Spirit plays no part in the work of redemption, wherein Christ, at the cost of his death, acquires for mankind the right to pardon and grace. Consequently, grace is thought of as a reality distributed by God in the same way before Christ's death as after it. But Christ did not only obtain rights for mankind; in his passover he has become salvation in person. The grace of the New Testament is given not only in virtue of the merits of death, but in an identifying union with Christ dead and risen again in the Spirit.

20 I. de la Potterie, *La Vérité dans S. Jean* (Rome, 1977), I, pp. 355f., comments: ' "He will be in you"...with the verb in the future...it is a question of the time of the resurrection... It is in the time after Easter, the era of the Church, that the promise of Jesus is directly applied to the

interior presence of the Paraclete'.

21   St Cyril of Alexandria, *Comm. in Joh.* V, 2 (*PG* 73, 757) makes this comment on the text: John was less than the least in the kingdom, for he did not possess the Spirit *in person*, although he submitted more than anyone else to his *action*. 'The holy prophets were richly enlightened by the Holy Spirit... But in the faithful there is not only this enlightenment, but the Spirit himself – we are not afraid to say so – dwells abidingly in us. That is why we are called temples of God, a statement never made about the prophets.'

22   The statement about the specific nature of the grace of the New Testament is not without its impact on pastoral theology. If the gift of the Spirit was the same in both Testaments, Christ's gospel would contain nothing essentially new, the role of the Church would consist in making non-Christians aware of a gift already possessed by all upright persons and enabling them to pass from an anonymous Christianity to a conscious Christianity. This seems inconsistent with New Testament theology, above all with that of Paul and John.

23   St Augustine, *De Trin.* 4, 9 (*CCL* 50, 177). Among the many patristic texts, cf. St Cyril of Alexandria, *In Joh.* XI, 11 (*PG* 74, 561): 'Having all received one and the same Spirit, we are in some way intimately related to one another and to God... There is only one indivisible Spirit, who assembles in himself spirits distinct one from another by reason of their individual existence; he makes them seem, as it were, to have one single existence in him'. Vatican II, *LG* 49 says emphatically, 'All, indeed, who are in Christ and who have his Spirit form one Church and *cleave together in him*'. In *LG* 13, the Council quotes St John Chrysostom, *In Joh.* 65, 1 (*PG* 59, 361): 'All the faithful scattered throughout the world are in communion with each other in the Holy Spirit so that "he who dwells in Rome knows those in most distant parts to be his brothers" '.

24   St Teresa of the Child Jesus, *Her Last Conversations* (Washington, DC, 1977), p. 131. The saint had an extraordinary intuition of the communion of saints. One of her sisters testifies: 'I was far from understanding this wonderful communion of saints which so delighted her': *Derniers entretiens* (Paris, 1971), p. 615.

25   The complete text of 2 Cor 4:10–12 merits quotation. – St Ignatius of Antioch, *Eph.* 8, 1 (*SC* 10, 77): 'I am your expiatory victim'; *Polyc.* 2, 3 (*SC* 10, 173): 'In everything I am a ransom for you'. St Thomas, *STh* IIIa, q. 48, a. 2 ad 1: 'When two people are united in love, one can make satisfaction for the other'; *Contra Gent.* 3, 158: 'Therefore it is possible to make satisfaction to God through another, as through oneself...because the love of two people makes them but one. The love of the one who suffers for a friend makes satisfaction more pleasing to God than if he suffered for himself'.

26   St John Chrysostom, *De perf. car.* (*PG* 56, 281).

27   St Thomas, *STh* IIa IIae, q. 17, a. 3.

28   The word 'I' *exists* and can be spoken, but it defies analysis.

29   St John Chrysostom, *op. cit.* (note 26): 'Love teaches you to rejoice in
     the good of others as in your own'. The explanation of the communion
     of saints is often sited on this psychological level.

30   A woman who had lost her husband once said to me: 'I have become a
     living wound through which my life is ebbing away'. Two months later
     she followed him.

31   From the Middle Ages onwards, *communio sanctorum* began to be
     understood as 'community of holy things' (*sancta*). In early times it
     designated a 'community of holy people' (*sancti*). The community of
     things is a consequence of the community of people. On earth there are
     'holy things' to be shared (the sacraments, the numerous benefits of life
     in the Church...). But on the eschatological level, there are no longer
     'things' to be shared; in the Trinity there is no 'having'. Everything is
     of the order of persons and relationships: a communion of persons.

32   In patristic literature, this aspect of the communion of saints is strongly
     emphasized. Cf. P. Bernard, 'Communion des Saints', *DTC* 3, 1, cols
     435–437.

33   St Teresa of the Child Jesus, *Last Conversations*, *op. cit.* (note 24), p. 91.

34   *Idem, ibid.*, p. 83 – 'If God answers my desires, my heaven will be spent
     on earth until the end of the world': *ibid.*, p. 102. To her 'brother', a
     seminarian, she writes these admirable words full of tenderness: 'Soon,
     little brother, I shall be with you': *Collected Letters of Saint Thérèse of
     Lisieux* (London, 1949), p. 310.

35   Acts 1:8: 'You will be my witnesses to the *eschaton* (ends) of the earth'.

36   See above, note 16.

37   We should not translate this as 'set apart to preach the gospel'. The
     Gospel cannot be reduced to an announcement, it is the mystery of
     salvation itself spreading throughout the world. Paul is caught up in the
     spread of this mystery.

38   The number twelve, deliberately chosen by Jesus (Mk 3:13f.), is
     symbolical. *The* twelve disciples of Jesus (Mt 10:1; 11:1) are the symbol
     of the coming of the new Israel.

39   L. Cerfaux, *op. cit.* (note 17), p. 270: 'They (the Old Testament
     prophets) were impelled by the Spirit of God, but this was not yet the
     Holy Spirit of the New Testament, who was a new and superior
     manifestation connected with the appearance of the Lord of glory, the
     Christ. God's mysteries were revealed [only] to the New Testament
     prophets. This thesis is consistent with the whole of Paul's theology.
     The Holy Spirit is essentially the revelation of the plan of God's
     wisdom, which was to inaugurate the new age. As such, it could not be
     manifested in the Old Testament. The Spirit of the Old Testament,
     which St Justin, Paul's faithful disciple, firmly distinguished from the
     Spirit of Christ by naming it the prophetic spirit, is still only an
     imperfect manifestation of the Holy Spirit of the New Testament'.

40   The Gospel is not only the announcement of the Good News of the

resurrection of Christ, it is this mystery itself, the mystery of salvation, spreading throughout the world (cf. e.g. Rom 1:16). It is 'accomplished' in the world by the power of the Spirit which is displayed in the apostolate. Thus Paul can write: 'Through the power of the Spirit I have "accomplished" the Good News from Jerusalem to Illyria' (cf. Rom 15:19). He ' "accomplishes" (delivers) the Word of God, the mystery hidden for centuries and generations…Christ among you, hope of glory' (cf. Col 1:25–27). Similarly, we could say that the Eucharist 'accomplishes' in the world the resurrection of Jesus (see above, p. 96).

41 H. de Lubac, *Catholicism* (London, 1950), p. 113: 'To sum up, revelation and redemption are bound up together'. In *Vatican II, la Révélation divine* (*Unam Sanctam* 70a; Paris, 1968), pp. 191f. he writes: 'Considered in its essential phase, the history of salvation goes hand in hand with that of revelation'.

42 Theological work, accomplished within the faith of the Church, also forms part of the Easter glorification of Jesus, where God submits intellects to the lordship of Christ (2 Cor 10:4f.).

43 Vatican II, *LG* 12: 'The holy people of God shares also in Christ's prophetic office'.

44 Y. Congar, *I Believe in the Holy Spirit* (London/New York, 1983), II, p. 29: 'A very common practice among the Fathers of the Church, which continued until the period of the Council of Trent and even later, was to describe the effectiveness of the Spirit in the Church by the words *revelatio* (*revelare*), *inspiratio* (*inspirare*), *illuminare*, *suggestio* (*suggerere*) and related terms'.

45 St Augustine, *Sermo* 85, 1 (*PL* 38, 520); *In Joh.* tract. 30, 1 (*CCL* 36, 289): 'Let us listen to the Gospel as to Christ among us'.

46 St Jerome, *Tract. in Ps. 145*, Anecd. Mareds. III, II, p. 301.

47 St Irenaeus, *Adv. Haer.* III, 1, 1 (*SC* 211, 11): 'At first they preached this Gospel; then, by God's will, they transmitted it to us in the Scriptures, that it might be the foundation and pillar of our faith'.

48 Jewish tradition admits such diversity. Cf. A. Zaoui in *Catholiques, Juifs, Orthodoxes, Protestants lisent le Bible* I (Paris, 1970), pp. 80f.: 'It (tradition) thinks too that inspiration "does not cease with the books of the Bible, but is extended to the rabbis who continue to make the interpretation of Scripture come alive" '.

49 Can the command, repeated several times in the Old Testament, to massacre enemy nations be placed on the same level of inspiration as the precept of the New Testament to love one's enemies? These Old Testament texts have to be seen in the context of a history which still had to develop.

50 St Jerome, *In Mich.* 1, 10 (*CCL* 76, 430): 'When explaining Scripture we always need the coming of the Holy Spirit'. Vatican II, *DV* 12: 'Holy Scripture must be read and interpreted according to the same Spirit by whom it was written'.

51 Origen, *Letter to St Gregory* (*PG* 11, 92). According to the context, these divine realities are the Scriptures. Vatican II, *DV* 25: 'Prayer should accompany the reading of Sacred Scripture, so that God and man may talk together'.

52 Freedom in the Pauline sense of the word includes being able to act without hindrance.

53 Cf. Rom 6:3: 'Baptised in Christ', where the preposition 'in' (*eis*, 'into') describes a movement of incorporation. Similarly Gal 3:27: 'You have all been baptised in (*eis*) Christ, you have all clothed yourselves in Christ'.

54 According to St Thomas Aquinas (*STh* IIIa, q. 65, a. 3 ad 2 and 4), confirmation and order delegate to the ministry.

55 Methodius of Olympus, *Banquet* III, 9 (*SC* 95, 111–113).

56 A. Vergote, 'L'Esprit, puissance de salut et de santé spirituelle' in *L'Expérience de l'Esprit* (*Le point théologique* 18; Paris, 1976), p. 213.

57 The question of fixing the age more precisely devolves not on theology but on pastoral prudence.

58 Narsai (d. 502), *Hom.* 17, *On the Expounding of the Mysteries*. Cf. A. Hamman, *Lettres chrétiennes* 7, p. 236.

59 Theodore of Mopsuestia, *Hom. cat.* 16, *Second on the Mass* 20; ed. R. Tonneau and R. Devreesse (Vatican City, 1949), p. 563. *Ibid.*, p. 575: 'We approach Christ our Lord risen from the dead with sweetness and great joy, and according to our ability we happily embrace him because we see that he is risen from the dead, and because we hope to share his resurrection'.

60 In *L'Eucharistie, sacrement pascal* (Paris, 1981) I dealt with this question of the Spirit not abolishing the bread and wine, but transforming them, creating them anew, assuming them into the mystery of Christ and making them the sacrament of his presence.

61 Latin patristic theology is also aware that the Eucharistic transformation is the work of the Spirit. Cf. St Augustine, *De Trin.* III, 4, 10 (*CCL* 50, 136): 'Consecration which makes of the fruits (of the earth) such a great sacrament comes (to man) only through the invisible action of the Spirit of God'. Greek theology in its turn recognizes the role of Christ's words: 'Bread is sanctified by word and prayer...to become the body of God, the Word': St Gregory of Nyssa, *Orat. cat.* 37 (*PG* 45, 96f.). St John Chrysostom, *De prodit. Judae*, hom. 1 and 2, 6 (*PG* 49, 380, 389) believes that the gifts are transformed by the words: 'This is my body'.

62 St Gregory Nazianzen, *Homily for Easter* (*PG* 36, 653f.): 'Doctrine is nourishment even for a person who gives it to others'.

63 Eph 5:32 is speaking of every marriage; similarly, Jesus says that every marriage is indissoluble.

64 They describe the actual person from an external point of view.

65 In the theology of marriage people often reason as if Eph 5:32 stated an *identity* between *Christian* marriage and the union of Christ with his Church, whereas the text is speaking only of the *analogy* of *every*

marriage with this ideal. The indissolubility of marriage, for example, is not of the same nature as the indestructible union between Christ and the Church. The simple fact that the death of one of the partners can end the marriage is proof of this. St Paul knows of another case in which marriage, though indissoluble, no longer exists: he says that a partner who has become a Christian is no longer 'bound', if the other partner (who is still a pagan) 'separates' (cf. 1 Cor 7:15). (The Church has interpreted the Christian partner's 'freedom' as including the possibility of remarriage.) However, he does not recognize any power of annulling an existing marriage (cf. 1 Cor 7:10–12), he does not claim any revelation or apostolic privilege for annulling a marriage (v. 12). He *states* that it does not exist. That is why we say that marriage is indissoluble and at the same time vulnerable. Could the Church not *state* other cases of irreversible break? Neither Scripture nor theology seems opposed to this.

66   St Paul states that a Christian is subject to the law of the Spirit and his love, that he is, by this fact, freed from the Mosaic law and from the jurisdiction of *every law external to his person*. Moreover, the laws written in the physiology of man and woman are also external to the person. Opposed to this thesis is the fact, recognized by St Paul, that a Christian, by reason of his earthly condition, is still subject to numerous laws external to his person; the Apostle himself gives his communities orders that he wants followed (cf. 1 Cor). The synthesis of these two apparently opposed situations can be formulated thus: a Christian is free; the absolute law is that of the Spirit and love; a Christian is not *enslaved* by a law external to his person. Laws external to the person, to which he remains subject, are secondary in relation to the primary law, that of love. This principle, applied with discernment, resolves many moral problems in married life.

67   Council of Trent, Dz-Sch 1695.
68   Cf. E. Cothenet, 'La guérison comme signe du Royaume et l'onction des malades (Jc 5, 13–16)', *Esprit et vie* 84 (1974), pp. 561–570.
69   St Ignatius of Antioch, *Eph.* 20, 2 (*SC* 10, 91).
70   'The new law which is the Holy Spirit in person': St Thomas, *Comm. in Rom. 8*, lect. 1.
71   Cf. e.g. Rom 1:7: 'saints by calling'.
72   St John Chrysostom, *In Ph. 2:12*, hom. 11, 3 (*PG* 62, 267).
73   O. Cullmann in *Paul apôtre de notre temps* (Rome, 1979), p. 570: 'Each one must make his decision within the community of the Church in order to be sure that errors and subjective wishes do not creep in'.
74   See above, note 3.
75   Cf. 1 Jn 3:23f.; 4:2, 13f. 'One could say...that the fundamental activity of the Spirit of truth...*is to awaken and develop in Christians faith in Jesus*': I. de la Potterie, *op. cit.* (note 20), I, p. 309.
76   St Irenaeus, *Adv. haer.* III, 24, 1 (*SC* 211, 473).
77   P. Evdokimov, *L'Esprit dans la tradition orthodoxe* (Paris, 1969), p. 19:

'True knowledge is always loving and love is always intelligent'.

78   St Irenaeus, *Adv. haer.* III, 24, 1 (*SC* 211, 473): 'We preserve this faith with care, for ceaselessly, under the action of God's Spirit, like something of great worth enclosed in a valuable jar, it is rejuvenated and causes even the jar containing it to be rejuvenated'. Teilhard de Chardin, quoted by H. de Lubac, *The Church: Paradox and Mystery* (Shannon, 1969), p. 92: 'Revelation *creates* a man's spirit in the measure that it illuminates that spirit'.

79   St Paul distinguishes *nous*, human understanding, from *pneuma*, spirit enlightened by the Spirit.

80   'Come, desire, thou that has become thyself in me!': St Simeon the New Theologian, *Invocation of the Holy Spirit* (*SC* 156, 151).

81   Cf. Acts 2:42. L. Duchesne, *Christian Worship: Its Origin and Evolution*, 3rd Eng. ed. (London, 1910), p. 446: 'The ideal of the Christian life was that of a constant communion with God, maintained by as frequent prayer as possible. A Christian who did not pray every day, and even frequently, would not have been considered a Christian at all'.

82   Cf. Council of Orange, Dz-Sch 373.

83   Here Luke understands the 'good things' which, according to Mt 7:11, Jesus promises to those who pray, as the Holy Spirit.

84   St Thomas, *Comp. theol.* II, 2.

85   Such is the literal translation of Rom 8:26. It is often translated: 'We do not know how to pray as we ought'. But in Rom 8:26 it is a question of a prayer, the object of which is not clearly seen, for the Spirit prays in us with inexpressible groanings (v. 26) and yet God knows what the Spirit wants, he knows what he is asking for on our behalf (v. 27).

86   Primitive theology had this firm intuition: death for Jesus was *an act* of freedom, a submission in love, a passage from this world to the Father.

87   St Ignatius of Antioch, *Rom.* 2, 2 (*SC* 10, 128) devised this formula: 'To die outside the world for God'.

88   'God who didst instruct the hearts of the faithful by the light of the Holy Spirit, grant us by the light of this same Spirit to know what is truly wise and always to rejoice in his consolation': liturgical prayer.

89   'The Son of God in his resurrection experienced mercy in a radical way, that is to say, the love of the Father which is *more powerful than death*': John Paul II, *Dives in Misericordia* (CTS, London, 1980), pp. 46–47.

90   St Teresa of the Child Jesus, *Last Conversations*, *op. cit.* (note 24), p. 100. 'Just as a mother is proud of her children, so also we shall be proud of each other, having not the least bit of jealousy': *ibid.*, p. 88; 'God wills that the saints communicate grace to each other through prayer with great love': p. 99.

91   St Gregory of Nyssa, *Hom. in Cant.* 15 (*PG* 44, 1116f.): 'Far from remaining separated, all will become one single thing, finding themselves united to the Beloved who is unique, so that, bound together by the bonds of peace, according to the words of the Apostle,

in the unity of the Holy Spirit, all will become one body and one Spirit, thanks to the unique hope in which they were called. *And this bond of unity is what is meant by glory'*.

92   'The primeval serpent' (Rev 12:9) which 'stopped in front of the woman as she was having the child' (the Messiah) (v. 4) recalls Gen 3:15.

93   Cf. Tertullian, *De resurr.* 9, 3 (*CCL* 2, 932): 'He (God) loves the flesh (corporeal reality) which is, in so many respects, his neighbour'.

Chapter 5:   The Spirit of the Father and the Son

1   This distinction by dissociation is sometimes used in polemics by Orthodox theologians against the formula *qui ex Patre Filioque procedit*, 'who proceeds from the Father and the Son'. They think that texts which speak of a sending of the Spirit by Christ (Jn 15:26; 16:7) concern the sanctifying activities of the Spirit but say nothing of an essential relationship of the Spirit with the Son.

2   As I have already said: a theology regulated by the laws of the Spirit accepts one single separating distinction, that between holiness and sin, i.e. communion and refusal of communion. Cf. my book *L'Eucharistie, sacrement pascal* (Paris, 1981), p. 182.

3   St Augustine, *Contra Faustum* 12, 32 (*PL* 42, 271): 'The mystery of God which is the Christ'; *Ep.* 187, 34 (*PL* 33, 845): 'There is no other mystery of God except Christ'.

4   Cf. E. Sjöberg, *TDNT* VI, p. 387; H. L. Strack and P. Billerbeck, *Kommentar zum Neuen Testament aus Talmud und Midrasch* II, pp. 134–138; J. Kremer, *Pfingstbericht und Pfingstgeschehen* (Freiburg, 1973), p. 78.

5   Cf. L. Cerfaux, *The Christian in the Theology of St Paul* (London, 1967), p. 241: 'The "personal" significance of the Spirit is intended'. See other trinitarian formulas in e.g. Rom 8:15–17; 2 Cor 1:21f.; Gal 4:6; Eph 2:18–22; 2 Th 2:13f.

6   *Ekeinos* (Jn 14:26; 15:26; 16:8, 13f.).

7   John repeats the article: *to Pneuma to hagion*, 'the Spirit, the holy', emphasizing the personal character of the Spirit, Cf. also Mk 3:29; 13:11.

8   M.-E. Boismard and A. Lemouille, *Synopse des quatre Evangiles* III (Paris, 1977), p. 360.

9   See the table of thirteen parallel points presented by Y. Congar, *I Believe in the Holy Spirit* (London/New York, 1983), I, pp. 55–56.

10   H. Schlier, *Grundzüge einer paulinischen Theologie* (Freiburg, 1978), p. 179.

11   St John Damascene, *De hymno trisagio* (*PG* 95, 60).

12   Creation is the joint work of the Trinity, according to a principle thus formulated by the Council of Florence (Dz-Sch 1330): '*Omnia sunt unum, ubi non obviat relationis oppositio*', (in God) all things are one,

except where there is an opposition of relationship. The work is a joint one, but each Person acts according to his own nature, to carry out the same work.

13   Since St Augustine, and following St Thomas Aquinas, the theology of the West has sought in psychology for illumination on the mystery of the Trinity. By his intellect man engenders a thought, expresses himself in words, a little like the Father who begets Wisdom, the Word. By his will, he begets nothing; he is attracted to what is good, in which he finds pleasure; in this will the mystery of the Spirit is reflected.

14   St Irenaeus, *Adv. haer.* III, 18, 3 (*SC* 211, 350f.) expressed himself in an analogous manner on the subject of Christ: 'The Son of God became son of man, as his very name indicates, for in the name of Christ (anointed) is understood the one who has anointed, the one who has been anointed, and the unction with which he has been anointed. But it is the Father who anoints, the Son who is anointed, in the Spirit who is the unction... As the Word says, through the lips of Isaiah: "The Spirit of God is upon me, because he has anointed me", which indicates simultaneously the Father who anoints and the Son who is anointed, *and the Spirit who is the unction*'.

15   The Council of Florence says (Dz-Sch 1301): 'Because the Father, in begetting the Son, has given him all he has, except to be the Father, the Son eternally has it from the Father that the Spirit proceeds from him'.

16   I. de la Potterie, *La Vérité dans Saint Jean* (Rome, 1977), I, p. 366 (author's italics).

17   St Augustine, *De Trin.* 15, 17, 29 (*CCL* 50a, 503f.): 'God the Father...from whom the Holy Spirit proceeds, as from his first principle (*principaliter*), I have added: as from his first principle, for it is proved that the Holy Spirit proceeds also from the Son. *But it is still the Father who gives the Son this privilege*, not that the Son has ever existed without it, but all that the Father has given his only Son, he has given him by begetting him'. Latin theology created the axiom: the Spirit proceeds from the Father and the Son as from a single principle. This axiom is justified in the view of a theology inspired by Scripture; but it has often been interpreted as if the difference between the Father and Son was effaced, both being *in identical manner* the single source of the Spirit. Having professed that the Spirit issues from the Father and the Son, we must immediately qualify the statement by remembering that one is Father, the other Son.

18   The Holy Spirit has been compared to the mutual, single kiss of the Father and the Son. Cf. St Bernard, *Sermo 8 in Cant.* 2 (*PL* 183, 810f.).

19   Greek theology speaks of a *perichōrēsis* (circular dance), which Latin theology calls circumincession (circular walk) or circuminsession (mutual circulation and penetration).

20   A human person is also constituted in the dynamic of love.

21   G. Madinier, *Conscience et Amour* (Paris, 1962 ed.), p. 91.

22   'God the Father, *moved by an eternal love*, proceeded to the distinction

between the hypostases': Maximus the Confessor, *Scholia on the Divine Names* 2 (*PG* 4, 221); quoted by Y. Congar, *op. cit.* (note 9), p. 140. The Father is the beginning, but at the beginning there is love.

23 St Augustine, *De Fide et Symbolo* 9, 19 reports the following opinion 'which is sympathetically received by him' (cf. *Bibliothèque augustinienne* 9, p. 57, note 5): 'Some have ventured to believe that the very communion between the Father and the Son, i.e. so to speak, the deity called by the Greeks *theotēs*, is the Holy Spirit... This deity that they wish also to understand of the mutual love and charity of the two, is called by them the Holy Spirit'.

24 St Augustine, *In Joh.* tract 99, 7 (*CCL* 36, 586). Cf. *De Trin.* 15, 19, 37 (*CCL* 50a, 513): 'The Spirit common to the Father and the Son'.

25 H. Mühlen coined this excellent formula. Cf. *Der heilige Geist als Person in der Trinität*, 2nd ed. (Münster, 1967); *Una Mystica Persona*, 2nd ed. (Paderborn, 1967; Fr. tr.: *L'Esprit dans L'Eglise*, 2 vols [Paris, 1969]).

26 This theme is amply developed in Syrian literature and liturgy, for instance: cf. E. Pataq-Siman, *L'Expérience de l'Esprit d'après la tradition syrienne d'Antioche* (*Théologie historique* 15; Paris, 1971).

27 In these verbs in the theological passive (*passivum divinum*) it is God (here the Father) who is the author of the action.

28 According to Tertullian, *De bapt.* 1, 3 (*CCL* 1, 277), Christians are little fish which do not leave the water in which they are born.

29 'O Grace (Spirit), come and ask with us, as is your custom. The world considers you as a merciful mother. Bring with you calm and peace, and spread your wings over our sinful times!': liturgical prayer quoted by E. Pataq-Siman, *op. cit.*, p. 155. The idea of the maternal role played by the Spirit is found also in the great spiritual writers. Cf. St Catherine of Siena, *Dial.* 141: 'The Holy Spirit becomes (for people who abandon themselves to Providence) a mother who feeds them from the breast of divine charity'. St John of the Cross (cf. *The Dark Night* 1, 1: *Complete Works* [London, 1947], p. 351) calls this grace 'the loving mother who regenerates the soul'.

30 See on this point M.-A. Chevallier, *Souffle de Dieu* (Paris, 1978), pp. 151–153.

31 Cf. Origen, *In Jer.* hom. 15, 4 (*GCS* III, 128); St Jerome, *In Is.* 40, 12 and *In Mich.* 7, 6 (*PL* 24, 145; 25, 1221f.).

32 According to a formula dear to the liturgy and theology of the Eastern Churches.

33 '(God) is a Father, even more he is a Mother!': John Paul II, Allocution of 10 September 1978, *DC* 1749 (1978), p. 836.

34 Even the earth, a work of the Holy Spirit, is maternal, with the universe surrounding it, an immense womb in which the life of human beings is born and develops. Several times already I have pointed out that there is a link between the Spirit in his uttermost spirituality and creation in its materiality. Matter bears in itself an essential mark of the Spirit, that of maternity.

35   Such is the thinking of St Paul (cf. 1 Cor 11:3; Eph 5:23).

36   There are ambiguities in certain *demands* for a new status for women in the Church. *Concilium* 143 (1981) provides an example: Y. Spiegel, 'God the Father in the Fatherless Society', p. 7. According to this article, the Catholic Church asserts 'the dogmatic fixation of the inferiority of woman' when it glorifies Mary through the dogma of the Assumption and sees in her the personification of the Church. Woman would thus be reduced to finding her symbol in the Church and in Mary, who are (feminine) servants, whereas man can base his claims on the Father and Christ! People forget that the Church and Mary are linked symbolically with the Spirit who also 'is Lord and gives life'; that Christ is head through the Spirit and through immolation for the Church; that there is therefore a manner of being modelled on Christ other than that of a visible ministry of government (direction). In any case, one can wonder whether the new status woman might acquire *by denying this link* would be superior with regard to the truest Christian values.

37   Of course the Church believes in the Spirit and speaks about him; but in Scripture he appears as the power of preaching and of the profession of faith. His personality and his divinity were the subject of conciliar statements only after the definition of the Christological dogmas. In the Creed of the *Apostolic Tradition* of Hippolytus (Dz-Sch 10) we find the following: 'Do you believe in God (*in Deum*) the Father almighty? Do you believe in Christ (*in Christum*) Jesus?', where the preposition expresses the movement *towards* God, *towards* Christ. 'Do you believe in the Holy Spirit (*in Spiritu Sancto*)?', where the preposition [followed by a different grammatical case] seems to express only the place or centre *in* which the act of faith is pronounced.

Conclusion

1   St Athanasius, *Fourth Letter to Serapion* (*SC* 15, 180): 'It is the prerogative of the substance of the Word and also the prerogative of the Father'.

2   Cf. the Postcommunion of the first Votive Mass of the Holy Spirit.

3   St Teresa of the Child Jesus, *Her Last Conversations* (Washington, DC, 1977), p. 206.